T0203225

TORUS 3 – Toward an Open Resource Using Services

TORUS 3 – Toward an Open Resource Using Services

Cloud Computing for Environmental Data

Edited by

Dominique Laffly

WILEY

First published 2020 in Great Britain and the United States by ISTE Ltd and John Wiley & Sons, Inc.

ISTE Ltd
27-37 St George's Road
London SW19 4EU
UK

www.iste.co.uk

John Wiley & Sons, Inc.
111 River Street
Hoboken, NJ 07030
USA

www.wiley.com

Library of Congress Control Number: 2019955390

British Library Cataloguing-in-Publication Data
A CIP record for this book is available from the British Library
ISBN 978-1-78630-601-2

Contents

Chapter 4. Atmospheric Modeling with Focus on Management of Input/Output Data and Potential of Cloud Computing Applications   73

Thi Kim Oanh NGUYEN, Nhat Ha Chi NGUYEN, Nguyen Huy LAI and Didin Agustian PERMADI

Chapter 5. Particulate Matter Concentration Mapping from Satellite Imagery   103

Thi Nhat Thanh NGUYEN, Viet Hung LUU, Van Ha PHAM, Quang Hung BUI and Thi Kim Oanh NGUYEN

Chapter 6. Comparison and Assessment of Culturable Airborne Microorganism Levels and Related Environmental Factors in Ho Chi Minh City, Vietnam

Tri Quang Hung NGUYEN, Minh Ky NGUYEN and Ngoc Thu Huong HUYNH

Chapter 7. Application of GIS and RS in Planning Environmental Protection Zones in Phu Loc District, Thua Thien Hue Province

Quoc Tuan LE, Trinh Minh Anh NGUYEN, Huy Anh NGUYEN and Truong Ngoc Han LE

Chapter 8. Forecasting the Water Quality and the Capacity of the Dong Nai River to Receive Wastewater up to 2020. 165

Quoc Tuan Le, Thi Kieu Diem Ngo and Truong Ngoc Han Le

Chapter 9. Water Resource Management 177

Imeshi Weerasinghe

Chapter 10. Assessing Impacts of Land Use Change and Climate Change on Water Resources in the La Vi Catchment, Binh Dinh Province

Kim Loi NGUYEN, Le Tan Dat NGUYEN, Hoang Tu LE, Duy Liem NGUYEN, Ngoc Quynh Tram VO, Van Phan LE, Duy Nang NGUYEN, Thi Thanh Thuy NGUYEN, Gia Diep PHAM, Dang Nguyen Dong PHUONG, Thi Hong NGUYEN, Thong Nhat TRAN, Margaret SHANAFIELD and Okke BATELAAN

Dominique LAFFLY and Yannick LE NIR

Preface

Why TORUS? Toward an Open Resource Using Services, or How to Bring Environmental Science Closer to Cloud Computing

Geography, Ecology, Urbanism, Geology and Climatology – in short, all environmental disciplines are inspired by the great paradigms of Science: they were first descriptive before evolving toward systemic and complexity. The methods followed the same evolution, from the inductive of the initial observations one approached the deductive of models of prediction based on learning. For example, the Bayesian is the preferred approach in this book (see Volume 1, Chapter 5), but random trees, neural networks, classifications and data reductions could all be developed. In the end, all the methods of artificial intelligence (IA) are ubiquitous today in the era of Big Data. We are not unaware, however, that, forged in Dartmouth in 1956 by John McCarthy, Marvin Minsky, Nathaniel Rochester and Claude Shannon, the term artificial intelligence is, after a long period of neglect at the heart of the future issues of the exploitation of massive data (just like the functional and logical languages that accompanied the theory: LISP, 1958, PROLOG, 1977 and SCALA, today – see Chapter 8).

All the environmental disciplines are confronted with this reality of massive data, with the rule of the 3+2Vs: Volume, Speed (from the French translation, "Vitesse"), Variety, Veracity, Value. Every five days – or even less – and only for the optical remote sensing data of the Sentinel 2a and 2b satellites, do we have a complete coverage of the Earth at a spatial resolution of 10 m for a dozen wavelengths. How do we integrate all this, how do we rethink the environmental disciplines where we must now consider at the pixel scale (10 m) an overall analysis of 510 million km^2 or more than 5 billion pixels of which there are 1.53 billion for land only? And more important in fact, how do we validate automatic processes and accuracy of results?

Dartmouth Summer Research Project on Artificial Intelligence, 1956
A PROPOSAL FOR THE DARTMOUTH SUMMER RESEARCH PROJECT ON ARTIFICIAL INTELLIGENCE
Marvin Minksy, MIT
1927-2016
Claude Shannon, Bell
1916-2001
John McCarthy, MIT
1927-2011
Nathaniel Rochester, IBM
1919-2001

Figure P.1. *At the beginnig of AI, Dartmouth Summer Research Project, 1956. Source: http://www.oezratty.net/wordpress/2017/semantique-intelligence-artificielle/*

Including social network data, Internet of Things (IoT) and archive data, for many topics such as *Smart Cities*, it is not surprising that environmental disciplines are interested in cloud computing.

Before understanding the technique (why this shape, why a cloud?), it would seem that to represent a node of connection of a network, we have, as of the last 50 years, drawn a *potatoid* freehand, which, drawn took the form of a cloud. Figure P.2 gives a perfect illustration on the left, while on the right we see that the cloud is now the norm (screenshot offered by a search engine in relation to the keywords: Internet and network).

What is cloud computing? Let us remember that, even before the term was dedicated to it, cloud computing was based on networks (see Chapter 4), the Internet and this is: "*since the 50s when users accessed, from their terminals, applications running on central systems*" (Wikipedia). The cloud, as we understand it today, has evolved considerably since the 2000s; it consists of the mutualization of remote computing resources to store data and use services dynamically – to understand software – dedicated via browser interfaces.

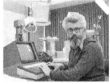

The earlier US Patent US_5485455 linked above was filed Jan 28, 1994 by Cabletron Systems Inc. and includes the following diagram:

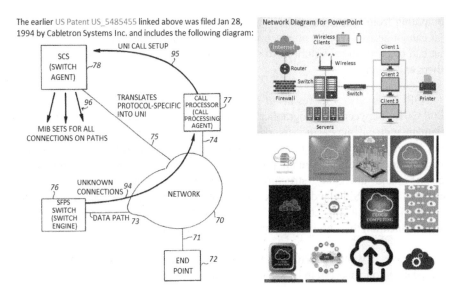

Figure P.2. *From freehand potatoid to the cloud icon. The first figure is a schematic illustration of a distributed SFPS switch. For a color version of this figure, see www.iste.co.uk/laffly/torus3.zip*

This answers the needs of the environmental sciences overwhelmed by the massive data flows: everything is stored in the cloud, everything is processed in the cloud, even the results expected by the end-users recover them according to their needs. It is no wonder that, one after the other, Google and NASA offered in December 2016 – mid-term of TORUS! – cloud-based solutions for the management and processing of satellite data: Google Earth Engine and NASA Earth Exchange.

But how do you do it? Why is it preferable – or not – for HPC (High Performance Computing) and GRIDS? How do we evaluate *"Cloud & High Scalability Computing"* versus *"Grid & High-Performance Computing"*? What are the costs? How do you transfer the applications commonly used by environmental science to the cloud? What is the added value for environmental sciences? In short, how does it work?

All these questions and more are at the heart of the TORUS program developed to learn from each other, understand each other and communicate with a common language mastered: geoscience, computer science and information science; and the geosciences between them; computer science and information sciences. TORUS is not a research program. It is an action that aims to bring together too (often) remote scientific communities, in order to bridge the gap that now separates contemporary computing from environmental disciplines for the most part. One evolving at speeds that cannot be followed by others, one that is greedy for data that others provide, one that can offer technical solutions to scientific questioning that is being developed by others and so on.

TORUS is also the result of multiple scientific collaborations initiated in 2008–2010: between the geographer and the computer scientist, between France and Vietnam with an increasing diversity of specialties involved (e.g. remote sensing and image processing, mathematics and statistics, optimization and modeling, erosion and geochemistry, temporal dynamics and social surveys) all within various scientific and university structures (universities, engineering schools, research institutes – IRD, SFRI and IAE Vietnam, central administrations: the Midi-Pyrénées region and Son La district, France–Vietnam partnership) and between research and higher education through national and international PhDs.

Naturally, I would like to say, the *Erasmus+ capacity building* program of the European Union appeared to be a solution adapted to our project:

> "*The objectives of the Capacity Building projects are: to support the modernization, accessibility and internationalization of higher education in partner countries; improve the quality, relevance and governance of higher education in partner countries; strengthen the capacity of higher education institutions in partner countries and in the EU, in terms of international cooperation and the process of permanent modernization in particular; and to help them open up to society at large and to the world of work in order to reinforce the interdisciplinary and transdisciplinary nature of higher education, to improve the employability of university graduates, to give the European higher education more visibility and attractiveness in the world, foster the reciprocal development of human resources, promote a better understanding between the peoples and cultures of the EU and partner countries.*"[1]

In 2015, TORUS – funded to the tune of 1 million euros for three years – was part of the projects selected in a pool of more than 575 applications and only 120 retentions. The partnership brings together (Figure P.3) the University of Toulouse 2 Jean Jaurès (coordinator – FR), the International School of Information Processing Sciences (EISTI – FR), the University of Ferrara in Italy, the Vrije University of Brussels, the National University from Vietnam to Hanoi, Nong Lam University in Ho Chi Minh City and two Thai institutions: Pathumthani's Asian Institute of Technology (AIT) and Walaikak University in Nakhon Si Thammarat.

---

1 http://www.agence-erasmus.fr/page/developpement-des-capacites.

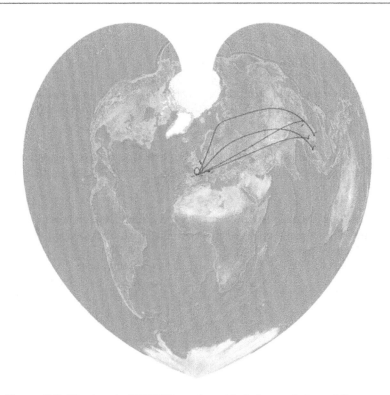

Figure P.3. *The heart of TORUS, partnership between Asia and Europe. For a color version of this figure, see www.iste.co.uk/laffly/torus3.zip*

With an equal share between Europe and Asia, 30 researchers, teachers-researchers and engineers are involved in learning from each other during these three years, which will be punctuated by eight workshops between France, Vietnam, Italy, Thailand and Belgium. Finally, after the installation of the two servers in Asia (Asian Institute of Technology – Thailand; and Vietnam National University Hanoi – Vietnam), more than 400 cores will fight in unison with TORUS to bring cloud computing closer to environmental sciences. More than 400 computer hearts beat in unison for TORUS, as well as those of Nathalie, Astrid, Eleonora, Ann, Imeshi, Thanh, Sukhuma, Janitra, Kim, Daniel, Yannick, Florent, Peio, Alex, Lucca, Stefano, Hichem, Hung(s), Thuy, Huy, Le Quoc, Kim Loi, Agustian, Hong, Sothea, Tongchai, Stephane, Simone, Marco, Mario, Trinh, Thiet, Massimiliano, Nikolaos, Minh Tu, Vincent and Dominique.

To all of you, a big thank you.

Structure of the book

This book is divided into three volumes.

Volume 1 raises the problem of voluminous data in geosciences before presenting the main methods of analysis and computer solutions mobilized to meet them.

Volume 2 presents remote sensing, geographic information systems (GIS) and spatial data infrastructures (SDI) that are central to all disciplines that deal with geographic space.

Volume 3 is a collection of thematic application cases representative of the specificities of the teams involved in TORUS and which motivated their needs in terms of cloud computing.

Dominique LAFFLY
January 2020

Introduction to Environmental Management and Services

1.1. Introduction

Environmental management is an activity involved with social management that regulates human activities based on systematic access and information coordination skills for environmental issues. Environmental management is related to people, toward sustainable development and sustainable use of resources. In environmental management, some subjects should be integrated for optimal controlling and monitoring such as (1) environmental components, (2) environmental quality, (3) environmental pollution and (4) data services for the environment.

Environmental quality is a set of properties and characteristics of the environment, either generalized or local, as they impinge on human beings and other organisms. It is a measure of the condition of an environment relative to the requirements of one or more species and/or to any human need or purpose (Johnson *et al.* 1997). Environmental quality includes the natural environment as well as the built environment, such as air and water purity or pollution, noise and the potential effects which such characteristics may have on physical and mental health (EEA). In principle, environmental quality can be measured in terms of the value the people place on these non-waste receptor services or the willingness to pay.

Many parameters of the environment (air, water, soil and biome) should be collected to assess the environmental quality and propose standards for controlling the environmental quality. We can look at water quality parameters such as pH, T,

Chapter written by Thi Kim Oanh NGUYEN, Quoc Tuan LE, Thongchai KANABKAEW, Sukhuma CHITAPORPAN and Truong Ngoc Han LE.

color, turbidity, TSS, TDS, DO, COD, BOD, bacterial parameters; air quality parameters such as SO_2, CO, NO_2, O_3, TSP, PM_{10}, $PM_{2.5}$, Pb; and soil quality parameters such as As, Cd, Pb, Cr, Cu, Zn, organic pollutants. The biome includes plants, animals and microorganisms; and can maintain and develop via ecological systems and nutrient cycles.

Human activities and natural occurrences, which release many kinds of pollutants, must be quantified and qualified through the environmental parameters. Over-release of pollutants into the environment causes the pollution which induces the environmental composition to break down and malfunction. However, nature has efficient functions to treat and overcome the stress of pollution by converting the pollutants into nutrients and energy. Therefore, understanding the functions of nature (the environment), people can monitor and control the released pollution against environmental quality parameters, and then issue the environmental standards for each activity and release.

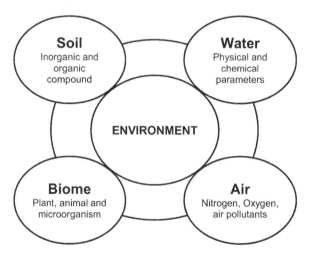

Figure 1.1. *Environmental components*

1.2. Environmental components

Global environmental components can be generally divided into four main compositions: lithosphere, atmosphere, hydrosphere and biosphere. Each sphere interacts with the others to drive the dynamic change of the Earth. The description of each sphere and its interactions are summarized in the following subsections.

1.2.1. *Lithosphere*

Lithosphere refers to the rock and rigid layers of the Earth. The crust of the Earth covering the entire planet is around 5–50 km in depth (see also Figure 1.2(a)). In particular, in terms of the environment, the lithosphere is also known as soil layers (Bleam 2017). Soil composition is determined by its parent materials, as well as the weathering of rocks and sediments. Soil composition constrains the biological availability for living organisms. Common elements found in soil are mainly oxygen, silicon and aluminum (see Figure 1.2(b)). Most minerals are formed by two or more elements during the solidification of magma or lava and/or recrystallization by weathering.

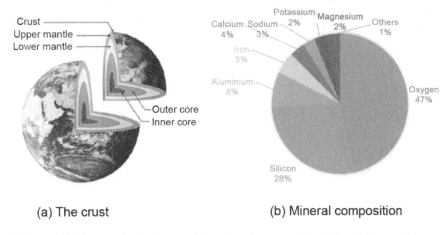

(a) The crust   (b) Mineral composition

Figure 1.2. *The crust structure and its mineral composition (adapted from: Osman 2013). For a color version of this figure, see www.iste.co.uk/laffly/torus3.zip*

1.2.2. *Atmosphere*

Atmosphere refers to the layer of air and gases surrounding the Earth. It consists of a mixture of the gases (by volume): nitrogen (78.084%), oxygen (20.9476%), water vapor (variable), carbon dioxide (0.0314%) inert gases such as argon (0.934%) and some other rare gases (Osman 2013). Atmospheric layers are divided into four layers depending on the temperature: troposphere, stratosphere, mesosphere and thermosphere. Among these layers, the troposphere is considered the most important and relevant to living organisms including humans. The layer has around 75% of the total mass of the atmosphere and most of the atmospheric elements are found here. Atmospheric composition plays an important role on the radiation budget to cool down or heat up the Earth's surface (Schlager *et al.* 2012). The composition of gases in the atmosphere is slightly altered by chemical reactions.

1.2.3. *Hydrosphere*

The hydrosphere is the water portion of the Earth's surface as it is distinguished from the solid part (in the lithosphere) and atmosphere (Glazovsky 2009). It includes the waters of oceans, seas, rivers, lakes, swamps and marshes, as well as soil moisture, underground water, water in the atmosphere and water in glaciers, ice and snow cover, as well as in all living organisms.

The distribution of water on the Earth's surface is extremely uneven. Only 3% of water on the surface is fresh; the remaining 97% resides in the ocean. Of freshwater, 69% resides in glaciers, 30% underground and less than 1% is located in lakes, rivers and swamps. Another way of looking at this is that only 1% of the water on the Earth's surface is usable by humans, and 99% of the usable quantity is situated underground (Figure 1.3).

Distribution of Earth's Water

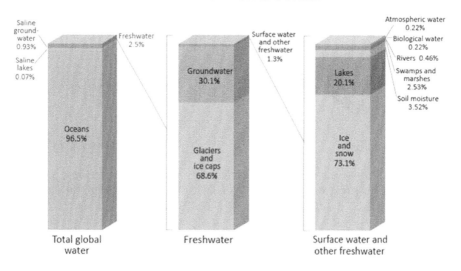

Figure 1.3. *The distribution of Earth's water (adapted from: Gleick 1993). For a color version of this figure, see www.iste.co.uk/laffly/torus3.zip*

Because Earth's water is present in three states, it can get into a variety of environments. The movement of water around the Earth's surface is the hydrologic (water) cycle (see Figure 1.4). Water changes from a liquid to a gas by evaporation by the sun to become water vapor. In surface water, only the water molecules evaporate; the salts remain in the ocean or freshwater reservoir.

The water vapor remains in the atmosphere until it undergoes condensation to become droplets. The droplets gather in to clouds that are blown about the globe by wind. As the water droplets in the clouds collide and grow, they fall from the sky as precipitation. Precipitation can be rain, hail or snow. Sometimes precipitation falls back into the ocean and sometimes it falls onto the land surface.

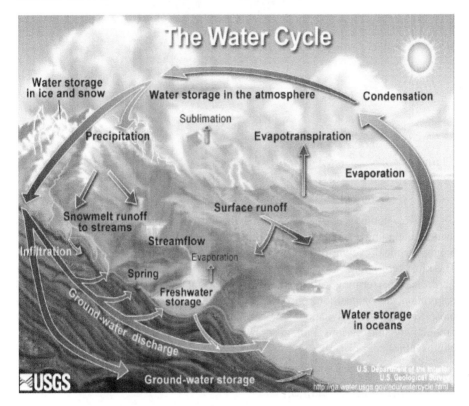

Figure 1.4. *The water cycle (source: USGS 2018). For a color version of this figure, see www.iste.co.uk/laffly/torus3.zip*

1.2.4. *Biosphere*

The biosphere is the layer of the Earth including the hydrosphere, the lowermost part of the atmosphere, and a portion of the uppermost lithosphere (see Figure 1.5). Part of the Earth's surface and atmosphere contains the entire terrestrial ecosystem and extends from the ocean. It contains all living organisms and the supporting media: soil, subsurface water, bodies of water and air. This sphere is also called the ecosphere.

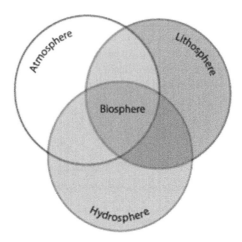

Figure 1.5. *Interactions of environmental components (adapted from: Osman 2013).
For a color version of this figure, see www.iste.co.uk/laffly/torus3.zip*

As a key component of earth systems, the biosphere interacts with and exchanges matter, including energy, with the other spheres. This helps to drive the global biogeochemical cycling of carbon, nitrogen, phosphorus, sulfur and other elements. The biosphere is the "global ecosystem", comprising the totality of biodiversity on Earth and performing all manner of biological functions: photosynthesis and respiration, decomposition, nitrogen fixation and denitrification. Interaction of the biosphere is very dynamic, undergoing strong seasonal cycles in primary productivity and various biological processes driven by the energy captured by photosynthesis.

1.3. Environmental pollution

What is pollution? Pollution occurs when pollutants contaminate the natural surroundings, which brings about changes that adversely affect our normal lifestyles. Pollutants are the key elements or components of pollution, which can be any substance or form of energy. Pollution disturbs our ecosystem and the balance in the environment. With modernization and development in our lives, pollution has reached its peak, causing changes in the environment and human disease.

1.3.1. *Air pollution*

Air pollution affects our environment and human health. Pollution occurs in different forms: gas, liquid, solid, radioactive, noise, heat/thermal and light. Every form of pollution has two sources of occurrence: the point and the non-point sources. The point sources are easy to identify, monitor and control, whereas the non-point sources are hard to control.

Effects of pollution are (1) Environment Degradation: Environment is the first casualty for an increase in pollution, whether in air, water or land. It can lead to many other problems which may be local, regional or global problems such as global warming, ozone depletion, acid rain, eutrophication or the spread of toxic chemicals. Some examples are the emission of **greenhouse gases**, particularly CO_2, that is leading to global warming, or chlorofluorocarbons (CFCs), which are a result of human activities, being released into the atmosphere, contributing to the depletion of the ozone layer. (2) Human Health: The decrease in air quality leads to several respiratory problems including asthma and lung cancer. Chest pain, congestion, throat inflammation, cardiovascular disease and respiratory disease are some of the diseases that can be caused by air pollution. Water pollution occurs due to the contamination of water and may pose skin-related problems including skin irritations and rashes. Similarly, solid waste or hazardous waste cause severe impacts on the living environments of animal species and humans.

1.3.2. Water pollution

In living activities, production and discharge create many different groups of pollutants. These substances can be collected and treated according to the regulations of each region and each country. However, the discharge of untreated waste into the environment is widespread, causing water pollution. Water contamination is caused by marine dumping, industrial waste, sewage (mainly from households) nuclear waste, oil pollution and underground storage leaks. Water pollution is also caused by natural factors such as water flowing through contaminated sites, which draws dissolved compounds into the water (iron, arsenic and some others).

Contaminated water is indicated by an increase in the concentration of inorganic and organic compounds in the water that exceeds the natural system's ability to self-treat. Water pollution primarily affects the living organisms in water and other groups of organisms that are related to the aquatic environment, including humans. The ecosystem in the water environment is altered and reduces the self-cleaning function of the field environment. Water pollution can cause eutrophication, making ecological imbalances more serious.

Water pollution affects human activity, causing infectious diseases (E. coli, Salmonella), skin diseases, intestinal diseases and parasites and neurological diseases (Hg, Cr, As). The reduction of the quality and quantity of water used for production and consumption is also a major problem which is taking place in the world, especially in developing countries.

1.3.3. *Soil pollution*

Soil pollution occurs when the toxic chemicals, pollutants or contaminants in the soil are in high enough concentrations to be a risk to plants, wildlife, humans and, of course, the soil itself.

The main cause of soil pollution is the overuse of chemicals such as pesticides and fertilizers. These chemicals affect the activity of microorganisms in the soil environment, killing beneficial organisms, reducing soil fertility. In addition, environmental pollution of the soil can be caused by the leakage of radioactive compounds, waste tanks, water permeability through polluted soil, leakage from landfills, industrial waste disposal to the land environment, open toilets and underground burial sites which are near a river.

Soil pollution can have a number of harmful effects on ecosystems and human, plant and animal health. The harmful effects of soil pollution may come from direct contact with polluted soil or from contact with other resources such as water or food which has been grown on or come in direct contact with the polluted soil.

1.3.4. *Biological pollution*

Biological pollution comes from the invasion by and development of alien species in a certain space. Biological pollution affects the development of native species, causing serious ecological imbalance. Invasive species often adapt quickly and thrive under extreme conditions of the environment.

Biological pollutants can cause a decrease in the productivity of indigenous groups of organisms or the disappearance of a living organism in the short term.

Control of bio-pollution is still facing many difficulties, especially in the case of encroachment. At present, major biological pollution control is still preventive and minimizing, such as flushing the boat and cleaning the wheel before entering the regional or national boundary.

1.4. Environmental quality management

1.4.1. *Air quality management: technical tools and data management*

Pollutants released from various sources are present and mixed in the giant reactor of the atmosphere where multiple complex chemical and physical interactions occur. Pollutants can be directly emitted from the emission sources such as dust particles (primary pollutants) or formed in the atmosphere through chemical reactions such as sulfate and nitrate particles (secondary particulate matter) or ozone. WHO (2014) reported that globally, in 2012, around 7 million people died as a result of exposure to household (indoor) and ambient (outdoor) air pollution. Regionally, low- and middle-income countries in the Western Pacific and South East Asian regions bear most of the burden, with over 5 million deaths due to exposure to both household and ambient air pollution. Air pollution is now considered as the world's largest single environmental health risk, and clean air is certainly a pressing need for sustainable development.

Air quality management (AQM) is the organized efforts to regulate the extent, duration and location of pollutant emissions to achieve ambient air quality standards, thereby minimizing the aesthetic, environmental and health risks. AQM is a dynamic process that can be illustrated as a cycle of inter-related elements to continuously improve air quality (see Figure 1.6), which comprises of the technical tools and policy actions. The technical tools of the AQM system include (1) air quality monitoring, (2) air pollution emission inventories and (3) air quality modeling. These tools generate and handle large air pollution databases which help us to understand the complex relationships between the source air pollution emissions and the multiple effects on human health, ecosystem and climate. The information provided by these technical tools can help to formulate policies to reduce the pollution emissions, thereby to (1) reduce ambient air pollutant concentrations to acceptable levels, (2) avoid adverse effects to human health and/or welfare and (3) avoid deleterious effects on animal and/or plant life and materials. The integrated AQM could also provide co-benefits in the reduction of climate radiative forcing through co-control measures of air pollution and greenhouse gases, as well as through the reduction of short-lived climate pollutants such as black carbon and tropospheric ozone (UNEP and WMO 2011).

Air pollution monitoring involves measurements of air quality by using traditional equipment (sampling and subsequent analysis) or using more advanced methods for in-situ monitoring with the aid of remote sensing (satellite) or on-line sensor systems. The monitoring results are used to compare against the ambient air quality standards (AAQSs) to assess the compliance. The monitoring equipment gives air pollution levels at a location during the measurement period; hence, a network is required to cover multiple sites to provide information on the status of air pollution in a geographical area. Monitoring should also be done over a long period to provide the pollution trend. The monitoring activity thus generates a large dataset: for example, in a small city with five monitoring stations, each measures six criteria pollutants (CO, PM2.5, PM10, O_3, NO_2, SO_2) on an hourly basis; then, every year, a huge amount of data points are generated, which need good data management strategies for handling and processing.

Emission inventory (EI) is a systematic effort to obtain systematic information on the amount and types of air pollutants and greenhouse gases from emission sources in a geographic area during a specific period of time (USEPA 2007). EI is one of the fundamental components of the AQM process. EI provides input data for air quality model applications which helps to understand the roles of local and long-range transport pollutions in the ambient air quality in a city or a region. The information on spatial distributions of the emissions is useful for siting in air quality monitoring design. The EI database for modeling purposes should include the temporal (normally hourly) emissions of every interested species on every grid (normally 1x1 km for urban scale modeling) of the domain (a few hundred km in size); hence, it is a large dataset to be handled and analyzed. A much larger emission input dataset is required for regional or global scale air quality modeling.

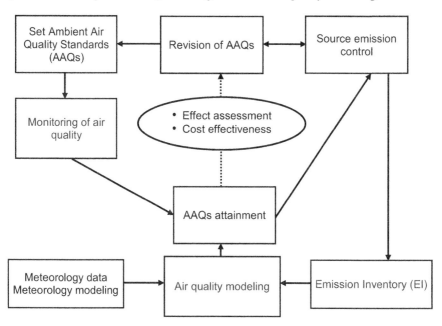

Figure 1.6. *Air quality management framework (adapted from Kim Oanh and Polprasert 2014). For a color version of this figure, see www.iste.co.uk/laffly/torus3.zip*

Air quality dispersion models use a system of mathematical equations to provide the causal links between emission and ambient concentrations of pollutants. These equations describe the processes of pollutant diffusion/transport, transformation and deposition in relation to meteorology. This is an important tool for AQM which, together with EI and monitoring, provides information to develop and analyze AQM strategies. In particular, air quality modeling provides information on the causal link between emission (current, future scenarios) and ambient concentrations and the potential effects. Such information is required for the policy-making process in formulating and analyzing emission reduction strategies.

1.4.2. *Water quality management*

Water quality management is an essential action to control and monitor the water resources for human consumption and release. Plans can be conducted to ensure the water resources for industrial, agricultural and domestic activities are available. They include contingency plans, source water protection, the treatment process, the distribution system and continuous monitoring.

Executing the plans requires agreement from stakeholders. Plans for water management depend on both national and international sectors. Plans strictly follow the national strategy for reducing poverty, economic development and balancing the benefit of stakeholders.

Figure 1.7. *Framework for water quality (Huang 2007)*

1.4.3. *Biosphere reservation and management*

1.4.3.1. *Forest in biosphere*

Biosphere is the stratum of the Earth's surface, covering a few kilometres, distance into the atmosphere to the furthest depths of the ocean (Ellatifi 2018). The biosphere is well known as a complex ecosystem composed of living organisms and the abiotic bodies that take energy and nutrients. Forests are the largest, and rich in ecosystems of the biosphere. Types of forest are classified differently depending on their species and environments. Using seasonality and latitudes, the forests are divided into three main different groups in the biosphere: tropical rainforests, boreal forests and temperate forests, including Mediterranean forests.

Recently, deforestation has gained attention and global interest since human activities significantly affect forest area reduction in the biosphere (Figure 1.8), particularly in Africa, Asia and South America. FAO (2016) also reported that the forest-covering area decreased worldwide between 1990–2010, while the agricultural area is increasing (Figure 1.9).

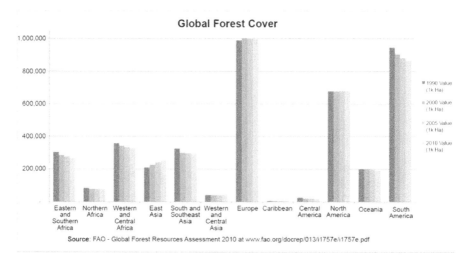

Figure 1.8. *The global change of forest cover area during 1990–2010. Source: FAO (2016). For a color version of this figure, see www.iste.co.uk/laffly/torus3.zip*

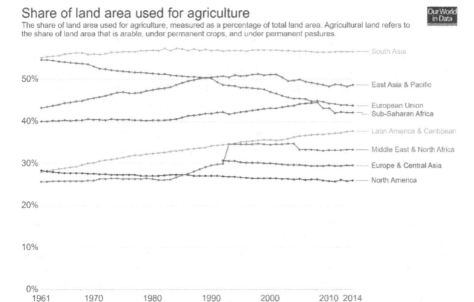

Figure 1.9. *The global area used for agriculture 1960–2014. Source: FAO (2016). For a color version of this figure, see www.iste.co.uk/laffly/torus3.zip*

1.4.3.2. Humans and biosphere reservation

1.4.3.2.1. Land use change

The factors that often affect the forest area reduction are rapid deforestation from land development for agriculture and residential areas, forest fires, etc. Since 1990, the South East Asia countries the Philippines, Thailand and Vietnam faced rapid deforestation. The forest transformation data, deforestation and reforestation, showing a lower remaining forest area (30±8%) of those three countries were lower than the other five countries where forest loss continues to decrease (68±6%, Cambodia, Indonesia, Laos, Malaysia and Myanmar) (Imai *et al.* 2018). The economic is also the important driving force to the forest transformation (FT). Lai *et al.* (2016) reported the increase in greenhouse gas emissions from land use changes and relations with the economic development between 1990 and 2010. Land use change declined in grasslands (−6.85%) and increased largely in urban areas (+43.73%), farmlands (+0.84) and forests (+0.67%).

1.4.3.2.2. Deforestation and reforestation

Deforestation and forest degradation in tropical forests are responsible for 7–14% of anthropogenic carbon emissions (Harris *et al.* 2012) and pose one of the greatest threats to global biodiversity. Therefore, reducing tropical deforestation and even reversing the trend to achieve net forest gain are top priorities of global environmental policy. Harris *et al.* (2012) applied satellite observations to collect gross forest cover loss and produce a map of forest carbon stocks, to estimate gross carbon emissions across tropical regions between 2000 and 2005 as 0.81 pentagram of carbon per year, with a 90% prediction interval of 0.57–1.22 pentagrams of carbon per year.

1.4.3.2.3. Forest fires

Biomass of a tree refers to the weight or mass of its living plant tissue and is generally expressed in the units of metric tons (t) (Walker *et al.* 2011). Biomass can be divided into two main parts: live biomass can be separated into aboveground (i.e. leaves, branches and stems) and belowground (roots). The common method to estimate the aboveground live dry biomass (AGB) of a tree is the weight of the living aboveground plant after the removal of the water content. Typically, the living tree contains water content of approximately 50% of the wet weight biomass. Forests are growing and absorb carbon dioxide from the atmosphere throughout the photosynthesis process. The carbon is stored in the biomass of their stems, branches, leaves and roots, while they release oxygen back to the atmosphere.

The methodology for the measurement and examination of aboveground biomass is variable: (a) a standard method using an allometric equation for the estimation of the tree or plot biomass (Brown 1997), (b) dry weight biomass measurement of harvested trees and (c) satellite image processing.

1.5. Data services for the environment

Any environmental data management planning process or system needs to include substantial coordination and agreement among the relevant federal agencies and international partners in order to ensure proper data stewardship. Different agencies have different missions with respect to collecting, archiving and providing access to different types of data, and these missions sometimes overlap or leave gaps in responsibility for critical data sets; for instance, the transition from research to operations has been a longstanding challenge.

Ground data and satellite data can be used for environmental services. Ground data include parameters from monitoring stations. Satellite data cover map, GIS and RS data. The combination of ground and satellite data generates plenty of tools for environmental management. The development of technologies for collecting ground and satellite data motivates us to optimize the tools for environmental management toward sustainable development and resource management.

1.6. References

Bleam, W.F. (2017). *Soil and Environmental Chemistry*. Academic Press, London.

Brown, S. (1997). Estimating Biomass and Biomass Change of Tropical Forests: A Primer. Forestry Paper 134, Forest Resources Assessment Publication, FAO, Rome.

Ellatifi, M. (2018). Forests in the Biosphere. In *Forests and Forest Plants, Volume III, Encyclopedia of Life Support Systems*, Owens, J.N., and Lund, H.G. (eds). EOLSS Publishers. Available at: https://pdfs.semanticscholar.org/9f61/65eb93c186f689078398b 955d6aa3fefd6f1.pdf.

European Environment Agency (n.d.). Environmental Quality Glossary. Environmental Terminology and Discovery Service, Copenhagen, Denmark.

Food and Agriculture Organization (FAO). (2016). Global forest cover area during 1990–2010. [Online]. Available at: http://data.worldbank.org/data-catalog/world-development-indicators.

Glazovsky, N. (2009). Environmental structure and function: Earth system. In *Earth System: History and Natural Variability, Volume IV*. [Online]. Available at: https://www.eolss.net/ Sample-Chapters/C12/E1-01-08-07.pdf

Gleick, P.H. (1993). World Fresh Water Resources. In *Water in Crisis: A Guide to the World's Fresh Water Resources*. Oxford University Press, New York.

Harris, N.L., Brown, S., Hagen, S.C., Saatchi, S.S., Petrova, S., Salas, W., Hansen, M.C., Potapov, P.V. and Lotsch, A. (2012). Baseline map of carbon emissions from deforestation in tropical regions. *Science*, 336(6088), 1573–1576.

Huang, G.H. (2007). IPWM: An interval parameter water quality management model. *Journal of Engineering Optimization*, 26(2), 79–103.

Imai, N., Furukawa, T., Tsujino, R., Kitamura, S., Yumoto, T. and Vadrevu, K.P. (2018). Factors affecting forest area change in Southeast Asia during 1980–2010. [Online]. Available at: https://www.ncbi.nlm.nih.gov/pmc/articles/PMC5953454/pdf/pone.0197391. pdf.

Johnson, D.L., Ambrose, S.H., Bassett, T.J., Bowen, M.L., Crummey, D.E., Isaacson, J.S., Johnson, D.N., Lamb, P., Saul, M. and Winter-Nelson, A.E. (1997). Meanings of environmental terms. *Journal of Environmental Quality*, 26, 581–589.

Kim Oanh, N.T. and Polprasert, C. (2014). Chapter 1: Overview of AIRPET activities and findings. In *Improving Air Quality in Asian Developing Countries: Compilation of Research Findings*, Kim Oanh, N.T. (ed.). NARENCA, Hanoi.

Lai, L., Huang, X., Yang, H., Chuai, X., Zhang, M., Zhong, T., Chen, Z., Chen, Y., Wang, X. and Thompson, J.R. (2016). Carbon emissions from land-use change and management in China between 1990 and 2010. *Science Advances*, 2016(2). [Online]. Available at: https://www.ncbi.nlm.nih.gov/pmc/articles/PMC5099982/pdf/1601063.pdf.

Osman, K.T. (2013) Soil as a Part of the Lithosphere. In *Soils: Principles, Properties and Management*, Osman, K.T. (ed.). Springer, Dordrecht.

Schlager, H., Grewe, V. and Roiger, A. (2012). Chemical composition of the atmosphere. In *Atmospheric Physics: Background – Methods – Trends*, Schumann, U. (ed.). Springer, Dordrecht.

UNEP and WMO (2011). Integrated Assessment of Black Carbon and Tropospheric Ozone. United Nations Environment Programme, World Meteorological Organization, Kenya.

USEPA (2007) Emission inventory improvement program (EEIP) Volume 1–10. [Online]. Available at: http://www.epa.gov/ttn/chief/eiip/index.html.

USGS (2018). Summary of the water cycle [Online]. Available at: https://water.usgs.gov/edu/watercyclesummary.html.

Walker, W., Faccini, A., Nepstad, M., Horning, N., Knight, D., Braun, E. and Bausch, A. (2011). Field Guide for Forest Biomass and Carbon Estimation. Version 1.0. Woods Hole Research Center, Falmouth.

WHO (2014). Seven million premature deaths annually linked to air pollution. [Online]. Available at: http://www.who.int/mediacentre/news/releases/2014/air-pollution/en/.

Environmental Case Studies

2

Air Quality Monitoring with Focus on Wireless Sensor Application and Data Management

Air pollution monitoring generates large databases that need to be properly managed and timely disseminated. Cloud computing can provide large online data storage at remote server outside the sampling area and access to the data via the Internet; hence, it is being increasingly applied to manage air pollution monitoring data. This chapter provides a review of air quality monitoring techniques ranging from traditional to advanced. A focus is on the emerging technology of small low-cost wireless sensors and the current status of their applications for air quality monitoring. Types and measurement principles of currently available sensors for the monitoring of particulate matters (PMs) and gases are highlighted with their advantages and shortcomings. The case studies of sensor calibrations and applications with online data publicizing, conducted by the Air Quality Research group at the Asian Institute of Technology, are detailed. These calibration experiments showed that some sensors performed better than others in the field applications. PM sensors would not produce reliable readings at high relative humidity (RH) commonly found in the tropical areas, while the available CO sensors have poor detection limits to measure the sub-ppm levels in the ambient air. The fact of being low cost makes it affordable to deploy many sensors in multiple sites to provide sufficient data points to characterize spatial patterns of air pollution. Although currently available low-cost sensors cannot yet fully substitute the existing reference instruments or networks, these sensors have been used in several applications when satisfying the data quality objectives. To ensure data quality, the user community should properly calibrate the sensors against the reference equipment. There is a need to develop harmonized standards and guidelines for sensor performance evaluations and common metrics of data quality to be used in such evaluations. The data science techniques and the open access data policies are expected to further facilitate the development, applications and continuous improvement of sensor performance.

Chapter written by Tan Loi HUYNH, Sathita FAKPRAPAI and Thi Kim Oanh NGUYEN.

2.1. Introduction

Air quality, expressed by the concentrations of pollutants in the air, highly varies in time and space. The variation in air quality is caused by the changes in (1) emission rates, for example episodic emissions, periodic emission cycles (daily, weekly and yearly) or long-term change in source locations and strengths; (2) large-scale meteorology, for example weather cycles and synoptic weather patterns; (3) local topography and urban effects that modulate the large-scale meteorology; (4) variations in the rates of chemical transformations and deposition; and (5) random fluctuations owing to atmospheric turbulence (Munn 1981). It is therefore a challenging task to obtain representative information on air quality in a geographical domain, during a specific time period.

The air quality management (AQM) system uses several technical tools to provide information on the air quality. Key technical tools include (1) air quality monitoring, (2) air pollution emission inventory and (3) air quality modeling. These tools generate large air pollution datasets which help to provide insights into the complex relationships between the emission sources of air pollution and ambient air levels, and, consequently, the induced effects on human health, ecosystems and climate. The information extracted from these datasets is useful for understanding the air quality situation in an area in order that effective policies can be formulated and implemented to reduce source emissions, thereby minimizing the adverse effects (Kim Oanh et al. 2012).

This chapter provides insights into air pollution monitoring techniques, traditional and advanced monitoring, with an emphasis on the emerging technology of small low-cost wireless sensors. The satellite air quality monitoring techniques are discussed in other chapters of this book and hence will not be detailed here. The state of the art of applications of cloud computing (CC) to handle and publicize the air quality information is highlighted. Details of the other technical tools are provided in chapters about Emission Inventory and Air Quality Modeling.

2.2. Development of air pollution monitoring techniques

Air quality monitoring involves measurements of air pollutant concentrations by using traditional standard equipment (sampling and subsequent analysis), advanced methods for in-situ monitoring with the aid of remote sensing (e.g. satellite) and online sensor systems, or a combination of several of these techniques. Monitoring data are used to assess the associated risks of air pollution exposure to human health and ecosystems. Regulatory monitoring, conducted by governmental agencies, is done for criteria pollutants following the requirements set by the national ambient air quality standards (NAAQS), in terms of measurement method, averaging time period and monitoring frequency. The main purpose of regulatory monitoring is to determine whether air quality in an area is complying with the NAAQS, so that regulatory actions can be taken to reduce pollution in case of non-compliance. Monitoring data should be disseminated to ensure a timely flow of the air quality information to relevant stakeholders, for example to the public to avoid excessive exposure during pollution episodes or to authorities to enforce control measures.

Monitoring equipment (monitor) only gives the air pollutant level at the location where the monitor locates and only for the time period over which the measurement is done. Therefore, spatially, a network consists of multiple monitoring sites that are required to provide information on the status of air pollution in a given geographical domain, such as a city, province, country or region. Temporally, monitoring should produce data at fine resolution (e.g. hourly) and continuously over a long period to provide the information on the trend of air pollution, to assess, for example, the efficacy of certain interventions on air quality. The monitoring activity thus generates large air quality datasets. To illustrate, a small city has three monitoring stations; each provides hourly levels of the criteria pollutants (CO, $PM_{2.5}$, PM_{10}, O_3, NO_2, SO_2) plus meteorology (wind speed, wind direction, temperature, atmospheric pressure, solar radiation, rain and humidity) would generate a huge amount of the hourly data points over a year. In a country with hundreds to thousands of monitoring stations, data management is a big challenge to ensure the data quality, archive and retrieval, and publicizing. Good data management strategies are therefore required to handle, process and share the air quality information; hence, cloud computing (CC) could play an important role.

2.2.1. Conventional air pollution monitoring

Traditionally, air pollution is monitored by conventional air pollution monitoring systems with stationary monitors. These monitors are highly reliable, accurate and able to measure a wide range of air pollutants by following two principal approaches: (1) manual monitoring and (2) automatic continuous monitoring.

2.2.1.1. Manual air quality sampling and analysis

Manual fixed monitors have been among the first pieces of equipment used in air quality monitoring. Manual air quality monitoring has two separate tasks: (1) sampling or sample collection and (2) subsequent laboratory analysis of samples. The active sampling method uses an air-moving device, such as a pump or an evacuated container; hence, the sampled air volume is readily known. The sampling period in this case is normally short, for example between less than 1 hour and 24 hours. Depending on the target pollutants and purpose of sampling, the sampling devices are designed to collect bulk/whole air samples or selective samples for specific compounds. The bulk air samples are collected in a sampling bag, syringe or canister, which takes the actual air mixture at the site in the sample. The selective air sampling retains the pollutants of interest on selected sampling media, such as using a filter to collect PM or an activated carbon sorbent trap to retain volatile organic compounds (VOCs).

Conversely, passive air sampling does not use any air-moving device. Instead, the pollutants are collected based on physical principles such as the diffusion of gases in the diffusive samplers, or settling of particles on a surrogate collecting surface. Passive sampling normally collects a sample over a longer period, for example two to three weeks; hence, it provides the time-weighted-average over the entire sampling period. In the passive sampling, the volume of air passed through the collector is not readily known; hence, it should be calculated using the meteorological variables (Klánová *et al.* 2008; Fan 2011; Choi *et al.* 2012). A comparison between active and passive sampling methods for air monitoring is given in Table 2.1.

Monitoring methods	Advantages	Disadvantages
Active	– Numerous validated methods exist – Large sampling volumes improve sensitivity – Sampling trains with multiple samplers in series reduce sample losses – Isokinetic (flow weighted) sampling can be used to minimize sampling errors	– Higher cost – Needs for frequent calibration of flow meters and pumps – Needs for skillful personnel to operate – Bulky equipment and sampling trains are cumbersome and often fragile – Often requires a reliable power source to operate in the field
Passive	– Lower cost – More compact size – Do not require a power source – Ease of use – Minimal training for operation of samplers – Large number of samples can be collected	– Theoretical sampling rate must be validated for field conditions – Temperature, humidity and air velocity extremes adversely affect collection efficiency – Sensitivity to wind direction or sampler orientation

Table 2.1. *Advantages and disadvantages of active and passive monitoring methods (source: compiled by Loi (2016))*

The analysis task subsequently quantifies the amount of the pollutants trapped in a sample. For example, the amount of fine PM ($PM_{2.5}$) collected on a filter is normally quantified using the gravimetric method (e.g. using a microbalance), while the amount of specific toxic organic compounds, such as polycyclic aromatic hydrocarbons or organic pesticides trapped in a sorbent (charcoal, resin), is determined using gas chromatography. The manual active monitoring technique guarantees the data accuracy and quality because most of the standard reference methods are based on this technique (Yi *et al.* 2015). However, both sampling and analysis tasks are time consuming and the method relies on bulky equipment and skillful human resources. An example of a PM_{10} sampler is shown in Figure 2.1. This sampler is designed with a special inlet to collect only PM_{10} (particles with aerodynamic diameters not more than 10 µm) on the filter for subsequent gravimetric and other chemical analyses.

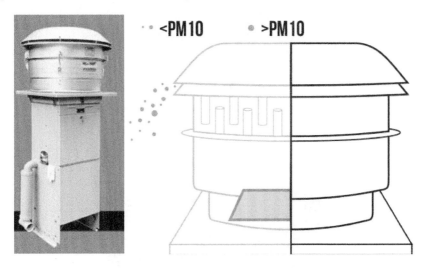

Figure 2.1. *High-Vol PM_{10} sampler with an inserted PM_{10} inlet (Pfeiffer 2005). For a color version of this figure, see www.iste.co.uk/laffly/torus3.zip*

2.2.1.2. Continuous automatic monitoring instruments

Continuous monitors have been used to measure SO_2, NO_2, CO, O_3 and PM since the early 1970s in the USA to check the compliance with the US NAAQS (Watson *et al.* 1998). These instruments generate consecutive hourly average pollution levels and are used in the automatic air monitoring stations worldwide. Such an automatic monitor uses a sampling pump that collects and sends an amount of air to an analyzer which then provides online readings.

Automatic monitors measure the mass surrogate of PM using optical methods, such as light scattering and light obscuration, or measure the beta ray absorption of PM collected on a filter and convert to PM mass concentrations. A PM monitor uses the beta ray absorption principle and is called the beta attenuation monitor (BAM), as shown in Figure 2.2. This is the most widely used automatic PM monitoring system. Firstly, the interested size range of PM in the air sample is separated by a selective inlet (to retain PM_{10} or $PM_{2.5}$ as the target pollutant). The PM of the target size range is collected on a filter tape over a period of time, for example 1 hour. Subsequently, the filter slot with the collected PM is exposed to beta rays emitted from a source and attenuated when they pass through the PM layer on the filter slot. The comparison between beta attenuation through the PM stained filter and a blank filter is converted to PM mass concentrations (Watson *et al.* 1998).

Figure 2.2. *Beta attenuation monitor for PM (Gobeli* et al. *2008)*

Tapered element oscillating micro-balance (TEOM) is another type of automatic PM monitor used in conventional air pollution monitoring stations. The mass of PM is determined by "gravimetric" method that is based on the changing oscillation frequency of a tapered quartz tube (Watson *et al.* 1998).

For gaseous pollutants, a wide range of automatic analyzers are available which measure target gaseous pollutants based on their physico-chemical properties, for example: chemiluminescence for oxides of nitrogen ($NOx = NO + NO_2$) and ozone (O_3), non-dispersive infrared absorption (NDIR) and gas filter correlation (GFC) techniques for carbon monoxide (Murena and Favale 2007), NDIR for carbon dioxide (Kaneyasu et al. 2000), non-dispersive ultraviolet (UV) absorption for O_3, or UV fluorescent radiation technology for sulfur dioxide (SO_2).

However, these traditional instruments for PM and gases are large, heavy and expensive (Yi et al. 2015). The high cost of the equipment, in particular, limits the number of monitoring stations deployed in an area. In this situation, the selection of representative sites to measure air pollution is critical, and this proves to be a very challenging task in a crowded urban area, with multiple emission sources (Kim Oanh et al. 2009). Over 60 automatic monitoring stations in Thailand, for example, are divided into two broad categories: (1) road side (2–5 m from the traffic lane) and (2) general sites, further classified into residential, commercial, institutional and industrial sites and so on (PCD 2018). The sparsely distributed governmental monitoring networks in many Asian countries can only provide a low spatial resolution of air quality datasets and hence cannot reflect the highly variable air pollution levels in a domain to be used subsequently in health effect assessment studies.

2.2.2. Sensing technology for air monitoring

To resolve the limitations of conventional air monitoring instruments, sensors of small size and low cost are a promising alternative. The sensors for PM commonly use the optical method (light scattering, light obstruction, etc.), while for gaseous pollutants, several principles may be used, as summarized in Table 2.2.

The most low-cost light scattering PM sensors used for particle number concentration measurements can only observe particles in the size range of ~400–10,000 nm (Wang et al. 2010). There are no low-cost sensors available that can measure ultrafine particles (particles with diameter <100 nm). Beside, PM sensors showed a non-consistent performance at high RH in the air, for example with worsening performance at RH ~80–85% (Crilley et al. 2018). Future PM sensors should properly address the RH effects to render their applications in the tropical highly humid areas. It is noted that several standard (and high cost) PM monitoring instruments also use the optical principle but they typically maintain a constant RH in the inlet for measurements and use specific technologies to accurately monitor very fine particles, whereas none of these are commonly incorporated in the low-cost PM sensors (Budde et al. 2012).

Pollutants	Example products	Measurement principle	Measurement range
PM	Sharp Microelectronics DN7C3CA006 $PM_{2.5}$ Module	Light obscuration	25–500 $\mu g/m^3$
	Sharp GP2Y1010AU Air Quality Sensor	Light scattering	0–500 $\mu g/m^3$
	Alpha sense OPC-N2 Particle Monitor	Light scattering	Not provided
	SYhitech DSM501	Light scattering (particle counter)	0–1.4 mg/m^3
	Shinyei AES-1	Light scattering	300–300,000 pcs/ft^{3} [1]
	Shinyei PPD4NS	Light scattering	0–800,000 pcs/ft^3
CO	Alpha sense B4 Series CO Sensor	Electrochemical sensor	0–1,000 ppm
	MiCS-5525	Semiconductor	0–1,000 ppm
	MQ9	Semiconductor	0–1,000 ppm
	Hanwei MQ-7 CO Sensor	Solid-state sensor	20–2,000 ppm
NO_2	Alpha sense B4 Series NO_2 Sensor	Electrochemical sensor	0–20 ppm
	SGX SensorTech MiCS-2714 NO_2 Sensor	Solid-state sensor	0.05–10 ppm
VOCs	AH2 Photo Ionisation Detector	PID	0.01–50 ppm
	A12 Photo Ionisation Detector	PID	< 0.05–6,000 ppm
CO_2	MG-811	Semiconductor	350–10,000 ppm
	U.S.A.GE/6004/6113	NDIR	0–2,000 ppm
	Korea ELT H550	NDIR	0–10,000 ppm
	Japan FIGARO CDM4160	Solid electrolyte	400–45,000 ppm

Table 2.2. *Several types of available sensing technologies for air pollution monitoring source: Alphasense (2016); Loi (2016); Yi et al. (2015)* [1] *pcs/ft^3: particles per ft^3*

The gas sensors may be classified into five types: electrochemical sensors, catalytic sensors, metal oxide semiconductor (MOS) sensors, non-dispersive infrared absorption and miniature photoionization detector (PID) sensors (Yi *et al.* 2015). Electrochemical sensors measure gaseous concentrations by using oxidation–reduction reactions between electrochemicals inside the sensor and the target gases. The electric signal produced is related to the concentration of the target pollutant. Electrochemical sensors appear to have interferences from RH and temperature (Castell *et al.* 2017). Catalytic sensors use the principle of burning the target gases at a much lower temperature than its normal ignition temperature, with the aid of a catalyst present on the surface of the sensor. A MOS sensor consists of one or several metal oxides and measures the electrical change on the surface of the metal oxide film when the target gas adsorbs and subsequently relates it to the gas concentration (Kadri *et al.* 2013; Yi *et al.* 2015). MOS sensors have some sensitivity to environmental conditions and have interferences from other gases (Rai *et al.* 2017). The NDIR sensor uses the principle of absorption spectrometry, i.e. the target gases absorb IR at specific wavelengths (Beer–Lambert law), and the attenuation of these wavelengths is measured by the detector to determine the gas concentration (Watson *et al.* 1998; Liu *et al.* 2011). PID sensors use an ultraviolet light source to break down the target gases into ionized gas molecules (positive and negative ions) and measure the electric current produced to relate to the gas concentrations (IST 2016). PID sensors are commonly used for VOC measurements but have limitations because they do not ionize every VOC present in the air with equal efficiency. Thus, the compounds that are efficiently ionized can be more readily detected than other compounds; hence, PID signals depend on the VOC mixture being measured.

Broadly, the sensors translate the physical environment conditions, in this case the levels of air pollutants, to electrical signals (Maraiya *et al.* 2011). Sensing units are usually composed of two sub-units: sensors and analog to digital converters (ADCs). ADCs convert the analog signals of sensors – which reflect the observed conditions – to digital signals which are inputed into the processing unit. The output signals of sensors need to be calibrated against the reference standard instruments to produce a calibration curve that relates the responses of the air sensor (electronic signal) to the reference instrument data, or to the gas standard concentrations, in order to obtain the measurement data in the concentration unit. The most suitable method is to calibrate the sensors using the gas standards which are done in the laboratory (Williams *et al.* 2014). The collocation technique of a sensor node (placing the node near a reference air quality monitoring instrument) is another common calibration method but one needs to make sure that two devices are close enough to measure the same air bubble. The collocation is also necessary to validate the sensor performance.

2.3. Wireless sensor network for air monitoring

Development in wireless communications and electronics technology has made the Wireless Sensor Network (WSN) into reality (Hejlová and Vozenílek 2013), and it can be applied in environmental or socioeconomic monitoring. For the environmental monitoring, the WSN is applied for air quality, water quality and natural disasters such as landslides, forest fires or volcanic eruptions (Akyildiz *et al.* 2002; Othman and Shazali 2012). In air pollution monitoring, the WSN relies on low cost, low power and multi-functional sensors that are small in size and can communicate air pollutant information though the Internet.

A typical WSN has three layers: (1) wireless sensor network layer, (2) control layer and (3) application layer (Guo *et al.* 2012). In the first layer, the sensor nodes are deployed for measuring the environmental conditions. A sensor node has (i) Sensor(s); (ii) Microcontroller or Microprocessor (μC) and (iii) transceiver equipment (Ferdoush and Li 2014). In the second layer, the measurement data are sent to a server (control layer) through a wireless access point to the Internet. Finally, the server receives data (application layer), where they are processed and kept in a database (Guo *et al.* 2012; Brienza *et al.* 2015). In the system architecture, the gateway node of wireless sensor network, database server and web server are combined in one single-board computer (SBC) hardware platform that helps to reduce the cost and complexity of this multi-functional WSN system. A web application is developed to support users to conveniently access web interfaces of the system. Users can interact with the web application within the local area network or from the Internet, to update the sensor data or condition of each sensor node every time and everywhere (Yang *et al.* 2010). Figure 2.3 shows the fundamental architecture of the wireless sensor network for air quality monitoring.

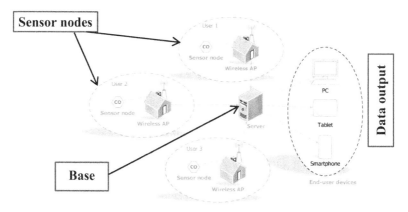

Figure 2.3. *Wireless sensor network architecture (Brienza et al. 2015). For a color version of this figure, see www.iste.co.uk/laffly/torus3.zip*

2.3.1. *Case studies of application of wireless sensors for air quality monitoring*

Many projects for sensor networks are planned around the world with several reported applications of WSN for air pollution monitoring, as detailed in Kadri *et al.* (2013), Liu *et al.* (2011), Méndez *et al.* (2011) or Wong *et al.* (2009).

USEPA conducts a wide range of sensor development, evaluation and demonstration projects with results published on their Air Sensor Toolkit website[1]. For example, the Village Green project has monitoring stations integrated into park benches in several US cities, for example Philadelphia, Washington DC, Kansas and Durham (USEPA 2015) with examples shown in Figure 2.4. The monitoring data are being used in research to improve the understanding of air quality and to increase community awareness of local air quality conditions. The creativity of this project is the combination between wireless sensor networks and renewable energy, with wind and solar energy used for supplying power to monitoring stations (Jiao *et al.* 2015). All Village Green stations measure ozone and fine particulate matter ($PM_{2.5}$) plus weather parameters such as wind speed and direction, temperature and RH. The air pollution and weather real-time measurements are automatically streamed to the Village Green Project webpage and available to the public[2].

Figure 2.4. *Monitoring stations in Philadelphia and Washington DC (USEPA 2015)*

In Asia, the Hong Kong Green Marathon sensor network was deployed along the marathon route to measure NO_2, CO, O_3 and $PM_{2.5}$ (Sun *et al.* 2016). The sensor network in Taiwan measures $PM_{2.5}$ (Chen *et al.* 2017) and displays near real-time data[3]. The air quality research group at the Asian Institute of Technology (AIT) have

---

1 https://www.epa.gov/air-sensor-toolbox.
2 https://www.epa.gov/sites/production/files/2017-05/documents/village-green-project-fact-sheet.pdf.
3 https://airmap.g0v.tw/.

also been developing sensor nodes for air quality monitoring since 2016, and the case studies are detailed below.

2.3.2. AIT case study 1

The study (Loi 2016) developed two wireless sensor nodes with the node configuration given in Figure 2.5. First, the existing sensors were screened to select those suitable, in terms of measurement range and environmental conditions, to measure open burning smoke/haze related pollutants (CO, CO_2, PM). The selected sensors included the Sharp GP2Y1010 sensors for PM, MQ9 sensors for CO, and MG811 sensors for CO_2. In addition, a DHT22 sensor was used to measure air temperature and humidity. ArduinoYUN was used as a microcontroller in the sensor node. Solar panels were installed to supply power, necessary when sensors are deployed in remote areas. The sensor nodes used 3G wireless communication for real-time data transfer to an Internet open source called "Thing-speak".

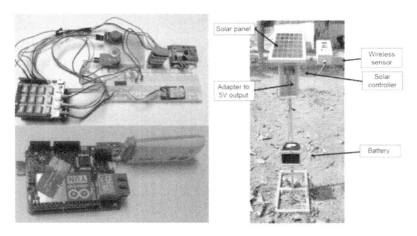

Figure 2.5. *Wireless sensor arrangement and sensor node with a solar panel (Loi 2016)*

Before deployment, the sensors were calibrated by collocating with the reference air quality monitoring equipment available in the ambient air quality stations in Bangkok. The PM sensors showed good performance at high PM concentrations, having good linear and nonlinear regressions with the data produced by the reference equipment (R^2 about 0.92). The CO sensor showed lower concentrations, largely due to its detection problem of the relatively low CO levels in the air, but still quite acceptable R^2 values (about 0.70). However, the CO_2 sensor was found not stable during the experiments, and this still needs further investigations. The results of sensor calibrations are shown in Figure 2.6.

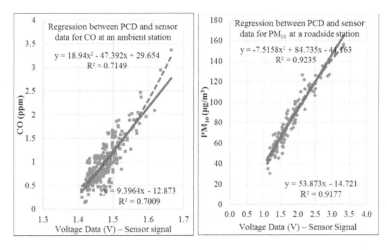

Figure 2.6. *Calibration results for CO and PM_{10} at different sites in Bangkok (Loi 2016). For a color version of this figure, see www.iste.co.uk/laffly/torus3.zip*

The calibration curves were used to convert the sensor signals into the pollutant concentrations. The validated sensors (PM and CO) were applied in a trial application to monitor smoke from maize crop residue field burning and in a demonstration of monitoring a smoke haze episode in Chiang Rai, Thailand, as depicted in Figure 2.7.

Figure 2.7. *Field deployment of sensors for haze monitoring in Chiang Rai (Loi 2016). For a color version of this figure, see www.iste.co.uk/laffly/torus3.zip*

NOTE.– inserted are wind rose, prevalent wind directions (red arrows), hotspot of biomass burning (red dots) during the monitoring period (March 23–26, 2016) and examples of the online data display for PM, CO, humidity and temperature in "Thing-speak".

2.3.3. *AIT case study 2*

In this case, Sathita (2017) evaluated the performance of additional sensors that were commercially available for the field experiments. Eight types of sensor were selected which included three types of PM sensors (SharpGP2Y1010, PMS3003 and PMS7003), two types of CO_2 sensors (MH-Z14 and MH-Z16), one type of NO_2 (WSP1110), one type of VOCs (MS1100-P11) and one type of CO sensors (MQ9). As compared to Loi (2016), two more air pollution parameters were included: VOC (volatile organic compound) group and NO_2. Note that SharpGP2Y1010 (among three PM sensor types deployed in this study) and the CO sensor were of the same brands with those used by Loi (2016). The two CO_2 sensors used in this study were different from that used by Loi (2016). Three wireless sensor nodes were built, each of them had five sensors to monitor six target pollutants of $PM_{2.5}$, PM_{10}, CO, CO_2, NO_2 and VOCs plus meteorology (Figure 2.8).

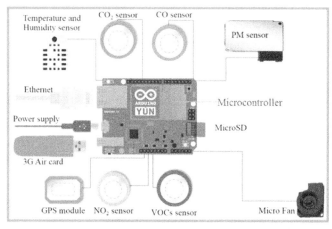

Figure 2.8. *Sensor node: components and a sensor box with shelter. For a color version of this figure, see www.iste.co.uk/laffly/torus3.zip*

First, the sensors were evaluated in the laboratory under more controlled environmental conditions for $PM_{2.5}$, PM_{10}, CO, CO_2, NO_2 and VOC measurements. The sensor nodes were placed in the controlled chamber together with the reference devices, and both were exposed to the target pollutants in a controlled chamber. In this laboratory experiment, one PM sensor type (PMS7003) and the CO_2 sensors produced signals showing good linear relationships with the reference monitoring instruments. Accordingly, the PM sensors had good linear correlations with the Met One AEROCET 531S, higher R^2 for the high $PM_{2.5}$ concentration range, $R^2 > 0.90$ for $PM_{2.5} > 100$ $\mu g/m^3$, but lower R^2 for lower concentration range (and this happens to be the normal range observed in the ambient air), $R^2 = 0.56$ for $PM_{2.5}$: 22–75 $\mu g/m^3$. CO_2 sensors also had signals linearly correlated with the measurements produced by the Quest AQ-5000 (CO_2), with an R^2 of 0.82. The VOC sensors were calibrated against the MultiRAE portable device in measuring 1,3-butadiene gas standard, and this showed a very good nonlinear relationship of the two monitoring datasets ($R^2 = 0.99$). The NO_2 sensor was calibrated against the measurements made by an API Model 200AU Chemiluminescent NOx Analyzer which also showed an acceptable linear relationship with $R^2 = 0.70$–0.76 after excluding the signals of the first 20 minutes from the 2-hour experiment period. Note that for NO_2 sensors, the recommended warming up period of the sensor is 48 hours; hence, our laboratory experiment period was too short for the proper sensor evaluation. It was necessary to rely more on collocated sampling in the field for the measurements, when the NO_2 sensors were exposed for an extended period. All the sensors were set to provide output signals every minute, except for CO and CO_2 sensors, which had an output at a 5-minute interval for better signal stabilization, as recommended by Loi (2016).

For the field calibration experiments, the sensor nodes were collocated with the reference equipment available at two selected governmental (PCD) automatic air quality monitoring stations in Bangkok for PM, NO_2 and CO monitoring. For VOC monitoring, the sensors were placed at a residential site in Bangkok and the signals were compared with the levels of benzene, toluene and xylenes measured by the adsorption technique (NIOSH 2003). The number of data points was still too small to produce calibration curves, but R^2 values were much lower (<0.31) than that obtained for 1,3-butadiene measurements in the laboratory calibration. For black carbon (BC), a monitoring site in Chiang Rai was used, and the regression between BC concentrations (measured on 24h-$PM_{2.5}$ filter samples using the OT-21 equipment) and PM sensor responses (PMS3003 and PMS7003) showed a good linear relationship with an R^2 of 0.73–0.91. However, the available monitoring dataset was rather small to produce a representative calibration curve for BC measurements.

The responses of CO sensors were related to the measurements produced by a CO analyzer Model 48i at the PCD stations and showed varying results. The sensor (MQ9) produced reasonable results with linear $R^2 = 0.61$ but only for a relatively high range of CO levels (>0.7–0.9 ppm); hence, lower CO concentrations in the ambient air may not be properly measured by the sensor. Both NO_2 sensors showed good performance in the field monitoring with signals in a good linear relationship with the measurements produced by the NOx analyzer Model 42i, i.e. linear $R^2 = 0.70$–0.84. PM sensors showed quite low linear relationships with the BAM 1020 measurement results, for $PM_{2.5}$ with $R^2 = 0.35$–0.39 at RH<95%, while at higher RH, the R^2 dropped to 0.06–0.19; hence, the sensor performance is still questionable.

The selected wireless sensors were set up and operated for the trial field monitoring. The real-time data publicizing system was set and run for the testing period via Wi-Fi or 3G network to Internet of Things (IOT) media (Figure 2.9).

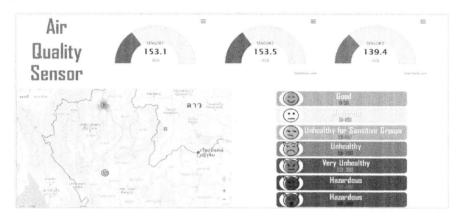

Figure 2.9. *Use of sensor nodes for trial monitoring and publicizing data (Sathita 2017). For a color version of this figure, see www.iste.co.uk/laffly/torus3.zip*

Overall, the results of our case studies showed that the accuracy and the consistency of the sensors are the key issues when deployed for the actual monitoring of air quality. The RH was found to have significant effects on the performance of the PM sensors; hence, the use of these sensors for monitoring in humid tropical climates during the high RH period is still a challenge. The warm-up time had an effect on NO_2 sensor performance, while the low levels of CO commonly existing in the ambient air may not be accurately monitored by the tested sensors. Two CO sensors of the same type had different responses when collocated; thus, there is a need to calibrate each sensor before deployment in the field to ensure the data quality.

2.3.4. *Influencing factors of low-cost sensor performance in air pollution monitoring*

The low-cost small sensors are being developed in several applications for ambient air monitoring to reduce limitations in the spatial and temporal coverage of conventional air monitoring. The key advantages of these sensors are their low cost, small, lightweight size and minimum energy consumption, hence they can be distributed densely in an area. They also require minimal user knowledge and can therefore gain broad community participation and awareness. They provide near-real-time measurement data that can be readily publicized online.

Thus, the use of wireless low-cost sensors widens the spatial and temporal distributions of the monitoring data which is important for the health effect assessment and overall air quality management. The fine spatial resolution provided by these sensors can help to reveal hotspots of high concentrations so that air quality management actions can be taken. The low-cost sensors thus create exciting new potential atmospheric applications.

However, there are a number of important limitations that should be overcome before they can substitute the traditional monitors. Key drawbacks of these wireless sensors in air monitoring include their low accuracy, being less reliable and having poor detection range compared to conventional equipment. The signals are affected by the environmental conditions (humidity, wind, temperature, rain, insects, etc.). For example, ozone interference is frequently reported as an interference with signals produced by NO_2 sensors (Lewis and Edwards 2016; Jerrett *et al.* 2017).

Smaller and/or cheaper sensing devices tend to be less sensitive, less precise and less chemically specific to the compounds of interest than the standard reference equipment. There is the need for calibration of the sensors to ensure the data quality but there is still a lack of data quality assurance and standard metrics for the sensors' performance (Laki 2014; Williams *et al.* 2014; Yi *et al.* 2015). If the sensors might be used in similar ways to the existing standard reference equipment, i.e. with regular calibration, data storage, QA/QC procedures, etc., then the cost would be exacerbated.

A sensor node design has many influencing factors which can affect its performance (Akyildiz *et al.* 2002; Akyildiz and Vuran 2010) including, for example, the fault tolerance (ability to sustain sensor network functionalities without any interruption), scalability of the sensor network, production cost of the sensors, hardware constraints, power consumption (battery lifetime) and atmospheric conditions (sunlight, temperature and humidity).

2.4. Summary: toward application of cloud computing for air quality monitoring data management

Currently available low-cost sensors cannot yet fully substitute the existing reference instruments or networks. To ensure data quality, the user community should properly calibrate the sensors against the standard equipment. The calibration experiments conducted at AIT showed that some sensors performed better than others in the field applications. PM sensors would not produce reliable readings at the high RH commonly found in tropical areas during certain months of the year. The currently available CO sensors have poor detection limits to measure the sub-ppm levels commonly found in ambient air. The low-cost sensors can be used in several applications when meeting the data quality objectives. Being low cost makes it affordable to deploy many sensors in multiple sites to provide sufficient data points to characterize spatial patterns of air pollution. For example, if calibration results prove that several sensors perform similarly in measuring a given pollutant, then a network of these calibrated sensors can be used to detect areas of high pollutant levels or "hotspots" in a domain. To detect the air pollution trends over time, the sensors should first be shown to perform stably over inter-annual time periods. There is a need to develop harmonized standards and guidelines for sensor performance evaluations and common metrics of data quality to be used in such evaluations.

Air pollution monitoring generates large databases that need to be properly managed and timely disseminated. Access to low-cost sensors facilitates the generation of a huge amount of monitoring data points over space and time, to characterize pollution levels and to use in health effect studies. Cloud computing can provide large online data storage at remote servers outside the sampling area and access to the data via the Internet from anywhere and anytime, hence it is increasingly being applied to manage air pollution monitoring data. Data science techniques and open access data policies would further facilitate the development, applications and continuous improvement of sensors, according to the performance targets.

2.5. References

Akyildiz, I.F. and Vuran, M.C. (2010). *Wireless Sensor Networks*, vol. 4. John Wiley & Sons, West Sussex, UK.

Akyildiz, I.F., Su, W., Sankarasubramaniam, Y., and Cayirci, E. (2002). Wireless sensor networks: A survey. *Computer Networks*, 38(4), 393–422. Available at: https://doi.org/10.1016/S1389-1286(01)00302-4.

Alphasense (2016). Alphasense air sensors for air quality networks. Retrieved 22 August 2016. Available at: http://www.alphasense.com/index.php/products/pid-air/.

Brienza, S., Galli, A., Anastasi, G., and Bruschi, P. (2015). A low-cost sensing system for cooperative air quality monitoring in urban areas. *Sensors*, 15(6), 12242–12259. Available at: https://doi.org/10.3390/s150612242.

Budde, M., Busse, M., and Beigl, M. (2012). Investigating the use of commodity dust sensors for the embedded measurement of particulate matter. *Networked Sensing Systems (INSS), 2012 Ninth International Conference on IEEE*, 1–4.

Castell, N., Dauge, F.R., Schneider, P., Vogt, M., Lerner, U., Fishbain, B., Broday, D., and Bartonova, A. (2017). Can commercial low-cost sensor platforms contribute to air quality monitoring and exposure estimates? *Environment International*, 99, 293–302.

Chen, L.J., Ho, Y.H., Lee, H.C., Wu, H.C., Liu, H.M., Hsieh, H.H., Huang, Y.T., and Lung, S.C.C. (2017). An open framework for participatory PM2.5 monitoring in smart cities. *IEEE Access*, 5, 14441–14454.

Choi, S.D., Kwon, H.O., Lee, Y.S., Park, E.J., and Oh, J.Y. (2012). Improving the spatial resolution of atmospheric polycyclic aromatic hydrocarbons using passive air samplers in a multi-industrial city. *Journal of Hazardous Materials*, 241, 252–258.

Crilley, L.R., Shaw, M., Pound, R., Kramer, L.J., Price, R., Young, S., Lewis, A.C., and Pope, F.D. (2018). Evaluation of a low-cost optical particle counter (Alphasense OPC-N2) for ambient air monitoring. *Atmospheric Measurement Techniques*, 11, 709–720.

Fan, Z.H.T. (2011). Passive air sampling: advantages, limitations, and challenges, presented at ISEE 22nd Annual Conference, Seoul, Korea, 28 August–1 September 2010: Assessment Methodology for Newly Emerging Exposures in Environmental Epidemiology. *Epidemiology*, 22(1), S132.

Ferdoush, S. and Li, X. (2014). Wireless sensor network system design using Raspberry Pi and Arduino for environmental monitoring applications. *Procedia Computer Science*, 34, 103–110. Available at: https://doi.org/10.1016/j.procs.2014.07.059.

Gobeli, D., Schloesser, H., and Pottberg, T. (2008). Met one instruments BAM-1020 beta attenuation mass monitor US-EPA $PM_{2.5}$ federal equivalent method field test results. *Air & Waste Management Association (A&WMA) Conference*, Kansas City, USA.

Guo, Z., Huang, J., Wang, B., Zhou, S., Cui, J.H., and Willett, P. (2012). A practical joint network-channel coding scheme for reliable communication in wireless networks. *IEEE Transactions on Wireless Communications*, 11(6), 2084–2094.

Hejlová, V. and Voženílek, V. (2013). Wireless sensor network components for air pollution monitoring in the urban environment: Criteria and analysis for their selection. *Wireless Sensor Network*, 5(12), 229–240. Available at: https://doi.org/10.4236/wsn.2013.512027.

IST (2016). Photoionization Detectors. Retrieved 22 August 2018, Available at: www.intlsensor.com/pdf/catalyticbead.pdf.

Jerrett, M., Donaire-Gonzalez, D., Popoola, O., Jones, R., Cohen, R.C., Almanza, E., de Nazelle, A., Mead, I., Carrasco-Turigas, G., Cole-Hunter, T., Triguero-Mas, M., Seto, E., and Nieuwenhuijsen, M. (2017). Validating novel air pollution sensors to improve exposure estimates for epidemiological analyses and citizen science. *Environmental Research*, 158, 286–294.

Jiao, W., Hagler, G.S.W., Williams, R.W., Sharpe, R.N., Weinstock, L., and Rice, J. (2015). Field assessment of the village green project: An autonomous community air quality monitoring system. *Environmental Science and Technology*, 49(10), 6085–6092. Available at: https://doi.org/10.1021/acs.est.5b01245.

Kadri, A., Yaacoub, E., Mushtaha, M., and Abu-Dayya, A. (2013). Wireless sensor network for real-time air pollution monitoring. *1st International Conference on Communications, Signal Processing, and their Applications (ICCSPA)*, 1–5. Available at: https://doi.org/10.1109/ICCSPA.2013.6487323.

Kaneyasu, K., Otsuka, K., Setoguchi, Y., Sonoda, S., Nakahara, T., Aso, I., and Nakagaichi, N. (2000). A carbon dioxide gas sensor based on solid electrolyte for air quality control. *Sensors and Actuators B: Chemical*, 66(1–3), 56–58.

Kim Oanh, N.T., Pongkiatkul, P., Upadhyay, N., and Hopke, P.P. (2009). Designing ambient particulate matter monitoring program for source apportionment study by receptor modeling. *Atmospheric Environment*, 43(21), 3334–3344.

Kim Oanh, N.T., Pongkiatkul, P., Cruz, M.T., Dung, N.T., Phillip, L., Zhuang, G., and Lestari, P. (2012). Monitoring and source apportionment for particulate matter pollution in six Asian cities. In *Integrated Air Quality Management: Asian Case Studies*. Taylor and Francis Group, CRC Press, USA.

Klánová, J., Èupr, P., Kohoutek, J., and Harner, T. (2007). Assessing the influence of meteorological parameters on the performance of polyurethane foam-based passive air samplers. *Environmental Science & Technology*, 42(2), 550–555.

Laki, T. (2014). Air quality sensor performance evaluation center (AQ-SPEC). Retrieved 9 September 2015. Available at: http://www.baaqmd.gov/~/media /files/communications-and-outreach/community-outreach/events/laki-tisopulos-capcoa-air -sensors-worksh%0Aop.pdf?la=en%0A.

Lewis, A. and Edwards, P. (2016). Validate personal air-pollution sensors. *Nature News*, 535(7610), 29.

Liu, J.H., Chen, Y.F., Lin, T.S., Lai, D.W., Wen, T.H., Sun, C.H., Juang, J.Y., and Jiang, J.A. (2011). Developed urban air quality monitoring system based on wireless sensor networks. *2011 Fifth International Conference on Sensing Technology*, 549–554. Available at: https://doi.org/10.1109/ICSensT.2011.6137040.

Loi, H.T. (2016). Performance Assessment of Selected Wireless Sensors for Biomass Smoke Air Quality Monitoring. Asian Institute of Technology, Thailand.

Maraiya, K., Kant, K., and Gupta, N. (2011). Application based study on wireless sensor network. *International Journal of Computer Applications*, 21(8), 9–15. Available at: https://doi.org/10.5120/2534-3459.

Méndez, D., Perez, A.J., Labrador, M.A., and Marron, J.J. (2011). P-Sense: A participatory sensing system for air pollution monitoring and control. *2011 IEEE International Conference on Pervasive Computing and Communications Workshops (PERCOM Workshops)*, 344–347. Available at: https://doi.org/10.1109/PERCOMW.2011.5766902.

Munn, R.E. (1981). *The Design of Air Quality Monitoring Networks*. Macmillan, Canada.

Murena, F. and Favale, G. (2007). Continuous monitoring of carbon monoxide in a deep street canyon. *Atmospheric Environment*, 41(12), 2620–2629.

NIOSH (2003). Hydrocarbons, Aromatic: Method 1501, Issue 3, 15 March 2003. Available at: https://www.cdc.gov/niosh/docs/2003-154/pdfs/1501.pdf.

Othman, M.F. and Shazali, K. (2012). Wireless sensor network applications: A study in environment monitoring system. *Procedia Engineering*, 41, 1204–1210.

PCD (2019). Thailand's air quality and situation reports. Retrieved 31 January 2019. Available at: http://air4thai.pcd.go.th/webV2/download.php.

Pfeiffer, R. (2005). Sampling for PM_{10} and $PM_{2.5}$ particulates. *Sampling for PM_{10} and $PM_{2.5}$ Particulates*, 227–245. University of Nebraska, USA.

Rai, A.C., Kumar, P., Pilla, F., Skouloudis, A.N., Di Sabatino, S., Ratti, C., Yasar, A., and Rickerby, D. (2017). End-user perspective of low-cost sensors for outdoor air pollution monitoring. *Science of the Total Environment*, 2017 Dec 31, 607–608:691–705. doi: 10.1016/j.scitotenv.2017.06.266.

Sathita, F. (2017). Evaluation of Low-Cost Air Quality Sensors for Monitoring Biomass Burning – Induced Air Pollution. Asian Institute of Technology, Thailand.

Sun, L., Wong, K., Wei, P., Ye, S., Huang, H., Yang, F., Westerdahl, D., Louie, P.K.K., Luk, C.W.Y., and Ning, Z. (2016). Development and application of a next generation air sensor network for the Hong Kong marathon 2015 air quality monitoring. *Sensors*, 16(2), 211.

USEPA. (2015). Village Green Project. Retrieved 15 September 2015, Available at: http://www2.epa.gov/air-research/village-green-project.

Wang, C., Yin, L., Zhang, L., Xiang, D., and Gao, R. (2010). Metal oxide gas sensors: sensitivity and influencing factors. *Sensors*, 10, 2088.

Watson, J., Chow, J., Moosmuller, H., Green, M., Frank, N., and Pitchford, M. (1998). Guidance for using Continuous Monitors in PM2.5 Monitoring Networks. US EPA, Office of Air Quality Planning and Standards, Research Triangle Park, NC 27711. EPA-454/R-98-012, May.

Williams, R., Long, R., Beaver, M., Kaufman, A., Zeiger, F., Heimbinder, M., Hang, I., Yap, R., Acharya, B., Ginwald, B., Kupcho, K., Robinson, S., Zaouak, O., Aubert, B., Hannigan, M., Piedrahita, R., Masson, N., Moran, B., Rook, M., Heppner, P., Cogar, C., Nikzad, N., and Griswold, W. (2014), Sensor evaluation report EPA/600/R-14/143. Available at: https://cfpub.epa.gov/si/si_public_record_report.cfm?dirEntryId=277270 &simpleSearch=1&searchAll=sensor+evaluation+report.

Wong, K.-J., Chua, C.-C., and Li, Q. (2009). Environmental monitoring using wireless vehicular sensor networks. *5th International Conference on Wireless Communications, Networking and Mobile Computing*, 1–4. Available at: https://doi.org/10.1109/WICOM.2009.5303846.

Yang, J., Zhang, C., Li, X., Huang, Y., Fu, S., and Acevedo, M.F. (2010). Integration of wireless sensor networks in environmental monitoring cyber infrastructure. *Wireless Networks*, 16(4), 1091–1108, Springer/ACM.

Yi, W., Lo, K., Mak, T., Leung, K., Leung, Y., and Meng, M. (2015). A survey of wireless sensor network based air pollution monitoring systems. *Sensors*, 15(12). https://doi.org/10.3390/s151229859.

3

Emission Inventories for Air Pollutants and Greenhouse Gases with Emphasis on Data Management in the Cloud

Development of an emission inventory (EI) is building up a complex and comprehensive dataset to provide useful information for air quality management (AQM) and assessment of greenhouse gas mitigation options. Accurate EI database is required to prioritize the emission reduction measures. This chapter highlights necessary steps of EI process and emphasizes the QA/QC required to minimize the uncertainty of EI estimates. A grid network for spatial allocations and temporal variations is required for identifying the hotspots and trends of the emissions in the domain. High resolution of gridded EI datasets would provide more detailed information of air pollution of a region during a specific time thus providing large datasets. When EI results are used to prepare the input data for 3D air quality modeling, hourly emissions of each species on every grid are required for the modeling period (a few months to several years) which can lead to a big challenge when tackling the overflow of data. Data computing and management through cloud system could potentially help to facilitate the storage and flows of an intensive amount of EI information. This chapter also illustrates with examples of EI databases developed by the authors for various domains, ranging from the whole Southeast Asia region to national and urban scales.

Chapter written by Thi Kim Oanh NGUYEN, Nguyen Huy LAI, Didin Agustian PERMADI, Nhat Ha Chi NGUYEN, Kok SOTHEA, Sukhuma CHITAPORPAN, Thongchai KANABKAEW, Jantira RATTANARAT and Surasak SICHUM.

3.1. Introduction

Emission inventory (EI) is a comprehensive list of emissions from various sources of air pollutants and/or greenhouse gases (GHGs) in a defined area during a specific time (USEPA 2007). The emission sources covered in an EI include both artificial (e.g. fuel combustion, industrial manufacturing and biomass open burning among others; Shrestha *et al.* 2013) and natural (e.g. biogenic and geogenic emissions) sources. For an EI of GHGs, the emissions related to land-use and land-cover changes are also included (IPCC 2006). EI can be developed for a specific pollutant such as sulfur dioxide (SO_2) or black carbon (BC), a group of atmospheric substances or multi-pollutants depending on the intended uses of the dataset. Some of the key air pollutants that are important in air quality management (AQM) include particulate matter (PM), carbon monoxide (CO), SO_2, oxides of nitrogen (NO_x) and non-methane volatile organic compounds (NMVOCs). The key species of GHGs covered in an EI include carbon dioxide (CO_2), methane (CH_4), nitrous oxide (N_2O) and F-gases. Recently, a group of pollutants known as the short-lived climate pollutants (SLCPs) is of interest from the toxic effects and climate forcing points of view.

The EI is an important activity in AQM. Based on EI results, key pollutants of concern and their key sources could be identified; thereby, the source emission control efforts can be prioritized to reduce air pollution in the domain. An accurate EI database, thus, is a prerequisite for effective AQM. For public information, the EI results presented in a simplified graphic format showing the pollution loads from different sources can be publicized to raise awareness of people, hence enhancing the participatory approach to the emission reduction. For air quality modeling, the emission input data generated by an accurate EI is a foremost requirement.

To ensure a high quality of an EI database, appropriate quality assurance and quality control procedure (QA/QC) should be applied which is viewed as an integral part in the EI process. The core elements of data quality objectives are to ensure transparency, consistency, comparability, completeness and accuracy (IPCC 2006). Estimation of emission amounts is commonly done by multiplying emission factors (EFs) and activity data (AD) of each considered source. Obtaining the representative EF for a specific emission source in a given geographical area would primarily require experimental studies involving the direct measurements which, in turn, would require large resources. In the lack of measurement data for a source, the EFs are normally obtained from the literature, thus entailing large uncertainty. Other source of uncertainty is the one inherited from the AD which rapidly changes in the developing countries. EI development therefore needs tremendous and continuous efforts to improve, and it is done periodically to ensure the representative EI database (USEPA 2007).

In principle, the EI database should be easily assessed and understood by many kinds of audiences and readers. The data providers could provide simplified graphics or maps for the public to track the trend of air pollution emissions in their locations. Because there are numerous sources present in a geographical EI domain which ranges from the urban to continental/global scale, the detailed EI datasets for a given time period would be huge. Therefore, the EI databases should be handled properly, and this data management can be supported by cloud computing (CC). Particularly, CC can be used to store and publicize the data, and manage the intensive data flow. This chapter therefore also highlights the potentiality of CC in EI data management.

3.2. Methodology for development of EI database

3.2.1. *Framework of EI development*

The overall framework of EI is presented in Figure 3.1. The EI Design phase is the first important task in preparing an EI, and it includes the following steps:

– identification of EI manager and EI compiler;

– identification of the key issues;

– selection of air pollutants and then further selection of sources along with respective data sources needed;

– selection of airshed (inventory domain), for example, based on administrative boundaries;

– selection of temporal resolution, for example hourly, daily or annual, which depends on the purpose of EI;

– design reporting document of EI.

Two main inputs for the EI calculation are EF and AD, and they have to be compiled in the next steps for the target sources. The AD includes, for example, the fuel consumption rate per year in industry and power plant (for point source category), number of vehicles and the average traveling distance per year (for on-road mobile source category), or fuel consumption rate for domestic cooking or amount of biomass subjected to open burning (for area source category). Relevant EFs, emission amount per unit of AD, for each source type within a category should be compiled from existing EI manuals or other published sources if locally developed EFs are not available. Emission calculation is done with QA/QC procedures employed to ensure the accuracy of the EI database (detailed in Shrestha *et al.* 2013).

The EI results can be verified by comparison with emission estimates prepared by other bodies and by comparison with estimates derived from fully independent assessments, for example atmospheric concentration measurements. There are several tools for verification of the EI results, including among others: (1) back-estimates to cross check the results with the previous EIs, (2) inverse modeling, opposite to dispersion modeling, to calculate back the EI that fits with the observation data and (3) satellite data may be used for the species that have relatively short life time in the atmosphere so that the observed levels can reflect the sources of emissions. The emission results of each species are normally presented with the uncertainty level or in the form of the best estimate along with a high and a low estimate.

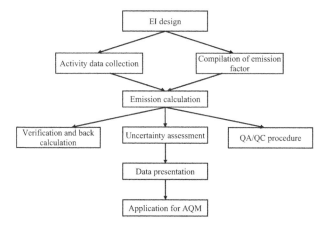

Figure 3.1. *Framework of emission inventory (source: adapted from MoE NZ 2001 and UNEP-APCAP 2018)*

The EI results are then presented to relevant stakeholders and used for AQM, for example for the formation of regulations and mitigation measures by policy makers, to general public to raise awareness, and as the input to dispersion modeling.

3.2.2. Calculation of EI

The common formula for emission calculation is by multiplying AD and EF, and for the sources that have control devices, the emission control efficiency (η) is also included as shown in equation [3.1]. The AD types required are varied by source; for example, fuel consumption rate is required for the EI of thermal power plants, manufacturing industry, residential and commercial combustion, while the amount of biomass subjected to burning is used in the EI of biomass open burning, the vehicle kilometer traveled (VKT) and the number of engine start-ups required for EI of traffic, etc. The collection of the actual emission control efficiencies (η) is also one of the challenges, as the values are varied according to the device's configuration, operation and maintenance:

$$Em_{i,j} = AD_{i,j} \times EF_{i,j} \times \frac{\left(100 - \eta_{i,j}\right)}{100} \qquad [3.1]$$

where $Em_{i,j}$ is the emission load of pollutant i of source j (mass unit/year); $AD_{i,j}$ is the activity data of pollutant i from source j; $EF_{i,j}$ is the emission factor of pollutant i from source j; and $\eta_{i,j}$ is the emission control efficiency (in percent) of pollutant i from source j.

3.2.3. Sources of data

3.2.3.1. Emission factors

In order to have a good emission estimate, the EFs should be measured for each key local source to generate EFs, taking into account the different fuel usage, operation of control devices, etc. This is a resource consuming task; hence, it is normally conducted comprehensively only in some countries such as United States of America (USA) (i.e. AP-42). For other places where no locally measured EFs are available, the compiled values by different published sources may be used (Table 3.1). However, most of the EFs from these databases are based on the measurements made in developed countries; hence, uncertainties may arise when applied for emission estimates in low- and middle-income countries.

No.	Source of information	References
1	Atmospheric Brown Cloud: Emission Inventory Manual (ABCEIM)	Shrestha *et al.* (2013)
2	EMEP/EEA Emission Inventory Guidebook 2016	EMEP/EEA (2016)
3	USEPA Emission Factor & AP-42	USEPA (2005)
4	IPCC Guidebook	IPCC (2006)
5	GAP: Global Air Pollution Forum Emission Manual	SEI (2004)

Table 3.1. *Summary of several EF compilations*

3.2.3.2. Activity data

AD should be collected at local sources by survey or from the national statistical books for the emission calculation. In many cases, these data are not available for many sources in the EI domain of interest. Several organizations have collected, synthesized and publicized the AD at the country level on the websites (Table 3.2) that can be extracted for use.

No.	Activity data	Source of information	Website
1	Fuel consumption data	International Energy Agency	http://www.iea.org/statistics/
2	International biomass fuel consumption data	United Nations Energy Statistics Yearbooks	https://unstats.un.org/Unsd/energy/yearbook/default.htm
3	Large point source (in Asia)	Regional Air Pollution Information and Simulation Model (RAINS-ASIA)	http://www.iiasa.ac.at/~heyes/docs/rains.asia.html/
4	Vehicle statistics	International Road Federation (IRF) World Road Statistics	http://www.irfnet.org
5	Ship movements	Lloyd's Maritime Information Service	http://www.lr.org
6	Data on manufacturing and process industries	United States Geological Survey	https://www.usgs.gov/
		Mineral Yearbooks	http://minerals.usgs.gov/minerals/pubs/country/asia.html/
		Steel Statistical Yearbook	http://www.worldsteel.org/pictures/publicationfiles/
		United Nations Industrial Commodity Statistics Yearbooks	
		Food and Agriculture Organization (FAO)	http://faostat.fao.org/faostat/

7	Country-specific yield per hectare	Food and Agriculture Organization (FAO)	http://faostat.fao.org/site/567/DesktopDefault.aspx
8	Forest fire area	World Fire Web	http://ptah.gvm.sai.jrc.it/wfw/
		Along Track Scanning Radiometer (ATSR)	http://dup.esrin.esa.int/ionia/wfa/index.asp
		Moderate Resolution Imaging Spectroradiometer (MODIS)	http://modis-fire.umd.edu/MCD45A1.asp & http://www.geoinfo.ait.ac.th/mod14/
9	Solid waste generation per capita	United Nations Human Settlements Program	http://www.unhabitat.org

Table 3.2. *Available sources of activity data for emission inventory*

3.2.3.3. *QA/QC measures*

Quality assurance/quality control (QA/QC) procedure is an important part of EI to minimize the errors of EF and AD, estimation methods and finally in EI databases. Several QA/QC procedures are presented in IPCC (2006) and USEPA (2007) that provide various QA/QC elements to be applied, such as reality checks, peer review, sample calculations, computerized checks, sensitivity analysis, statistical checks, independent audit and emission estimation validation.

3.2.3.4. *Structure of EI database*

Depending on the purposes of the EI, the key sources and key pollutants may vary. Major anthropogenic sources include transportation, thermal power plants, manufacturing and processing industries, residential combustion, biomass open burning, etc. Major natural sources include biogenic emissions, forest fires, volcano eruptions, oceanic sources and so on.

The EI species can include the criteria gaseous pollutants (CO, SO_2, NO_x and NMVOC), specific VOCs (benzene, toluene, etc.) and other gases such as ammonia (NH_3) and hydrogen sulfide (H_2S), aerosol species: PM with the aerodynamic diameter less than 10 μm (PM_{10}) and 2.5 μm ($PM_{2.5}$), BC and organic carbon (OC), and GHGs. Temporally, the EI is normally developed for a period of one year (annual), but when the EI results are used for air pollution dispersion modeling purpose, an hourly emission database is required. Spatially, the EI can be conducted based on administrative boundaries (country, city/province, ward, etc.) for AQM purpose and by grid for dispersion modeling purposes.

3.2.3.5. *Existing global and regional EI databases*

Global and regional EI databases have been developed by international research projects and organizations, in order to get the input emission data for modeling applications. The regional and global EI databases have been normally developed using the top-down approach, using available AD from international and national statistical books. The EI databases are first developed based on historical data or projected estimation and, subsequently, are tested by simulating global or regional models to verify the developed EI databases and analyze the uncertainties before publishing. Table 3.3 presents the available global and regional EI databases (with online sources) conducted by organizations worldwide. Basically, these existing EI databases overlap each other by one or more emission sources, or by assessing and using previous EI to project or re-grid to form new datasets (i.e. emissions related to agricultural activities for Asian Russia and Central Asia of REAS2.1 were based on EDGAR 4.2). The common emission sources covered in these databases are usually key anthropogenic sources and biogenic sources, or individual sources such as biomass open burning or oceanic sources.

Dataset	Scale	Year	Major parameters	References
EDGAR v4.3.2 (Anthropogenic)[a]	Global ($0.1°$ × $0.1°$)	1970–2012	SO_2, NO_x, CO, NMVOC, PM_{10}, $PM_{2.5\_bio}$, $PM_{2.5\_fossil}$, BC, OC and NH_3	Crippa *et al.* (2018)
EDGAR v4.3.2 (Anthropogenic)[b]	Global ($0.1°$ × $0.1°$)	1970–2012	GHGs (CH_4, CO_2, N_2O)	Janssens-Maenhout *et al.* (2017a)
EDGAR v4.3.2_FT2016 (Anthropogenic)[c]	Country level	1990–2016	Fossil CO_2 and GHGs (CH_4, CO_2, N_2O)	Janssens-Maenhout *et al.* (2017a,b); Olivier *et al.* (2017)
EDGAR v4.tox2 (Anthropogenic)[d]	Global ($0.1°$ × $0.1°$)	1970–2012	Mercury	Muntean *et al.* (2018)
CGRER (Anthropogenic)[e]	Asia ($0.5°$ × $0.5°$)	2000–2006	SO_2, NO_x, CO, VOC, PM_{10}, $PM_{2.5}$, BC and OC	Street *et al.* (2000); Zhang *et al.* (2009)

Dataset	Scale	Year	Major parameters	References
REAS (Anthropogenic)[f]	Asia (0.5° × 0.5°)	2000–2008	SO_2, NO_x, CO, NMVOC, PM_{10}, $PM_{2.5}$, BC, OC, NH_3, CH_4, N_2O and CO_2	Ohara et al. (2007); Kurokawa et al. (2013)
	Northeast Asia (0.5° × 0.5°)	2005	Polycyclic aromatic hydrocarbons (USEPA priority PAH species, from fluoranthene to benzo[g,h,i]perylene	Inomata et al. (2012)
MACCity-anthro[g] (Anthropogenic)	Global (0.5° × 0.5°)	1960–2020	CO, NH_3, NO_x, SO_2, BC and OC	Granier et al. (2011)
MACCity-bb[g] (Biomass burning)	Global (0.5° × 0.5°)	1960–2020	CH_4, NMVOC, CO_2, CO, NH_3, NO_x, SO_2, BC and OC	Granier et al. (2011)
CAMS-REG-GHG (Anthropogenic)	Europe (0.0625° × 0.0625°)	2003–2009	CH_4, CO, NH_3, NMVOC, NO_x, PM_{10}, $PM_{2.5}$ and SO_2	Kuenen et al. (2014)
CAMS-GLOB-ANT (Anthropogenic)	Global (0.5° × 0.5°)	2018	CH_4, NMVOC, CO, NH_3, NO_x, SO_2, BC and OC	Elguindi et al. (n.y)
CAMS-GLOB-BIO (Biogenic)	Global (0.5° × 0.5°)	2016–2017	BVOC (isoprene, monoterpenes, methanol, acetone, sesquiterpenes)	Sindelarova et al. (2014)
CAMS-GLOB-SHIP (Shipping)	Global (0.25° × 0.5°)	2016–2018	CO_2, NO_x, SO_x, CO and $PM_{2.5}$	Jalkanen et al. (2016)
ECLIPSE-GAINS-V5a (Anthropogenic)[h]	Global (0.5° × 0.5°)	1990–2050	CO, NO_x, SO_2, NMVOC, NH_3, CH_4, BC, OC, $PM_{2.5}$, PM_{10} and OM	Kilmont et al. (2013)
RETRO (Anthropogenic, biogenic, oceanic, and biomass burning)[i]	Global (0.5° × 0.5°)	1960–2000	CO, NO_x, CH_2O, CH_4, BC, OC and SO_2	Schultz et al. (2007a, 2007b); Schultz et al. (2008)
Junker-Liousse (Anthropogenic)[j]	Global (1° × 1°)	1860–2003	BC, POC	Junker and Liousse (2008)

Dataset	Scale	Year	Major parameters	References
Andres-CO2-v2016 (Anthropogenic)[k]	Global ($1° \times 1°$)	1950–2011	CO_2	Andres et al. (1996)
GFASv1.3 (Biomass burning)[l]	Global ($0.1° \times 0.1°$)	2003–2016	CO_2, CO, VOC, NO_x, N_2O, $PM_{2.5}$, TPM, TC, OC, BC, SO_2, NH_3, H_2	Kaiser et al. (2012)
GFED4 (Biomass burning)[m]	Global ($0.25° \times 0.25°$)	1997–2015	C, CO_2, CO, CH_4, NMVOC, H_2, NO_x, N_2O, $PM_{2.5}$, TPM, TC, OC, BC, SO_2	Giglio et al. (2013); van der Werf et al. (2010)
IS4FIRES (Biomass burning)[n]	Global ($0.5° \times 0.5°$)	2000–2011	$PM_{2.5}$, PM_{10}	Sofiev et al. (2009)
DECSO-NOx (Anthropogenic)[o]	East Asia, Middle East, South Africa and India ($0.25° \times 0.25°$)	2007–2014	NO_x	Mijing et al. (2013)
PKU (Anthropogenic)[p]	Global ($0.1° \times 0.1°$)	2002–2013	OC	Huang et al. (2015)
GICC (Biomass burning)[q]	Global ($1° \times 1°$)	1900–2005	CO, NO_x, BC, OC	Mieville et al. (2010)
GUESS-ES (Biomass burning and biogenic)[r]	Global ($1° \times 1°$)	1970–2009	CO_2, CO, CH_4, NMVOC, TPM, $PM_{2.5}$, NO_x, N_2O, NH_3, SO_2, BC, OC	Knorr et al. (2012)
AMMABB (Biomass burning)[q]	Africa ($0.5° \times 0.5°$)	2001–2006	CO_2, CO, NO_x, SO_2, BC, OC	Liousse et al. (2010)
MEGAN-MACC (Biogenic)[s]	Global ($0.5° \times 0.5°$)	1980–2010	BVOC	Sindelarova et al. (2014)
APIFLAME (Biomass burning)[t]	Euro-Mediterranean ($0.001° \times 0.001°$)	2012–2014	CO, CO_2, VOC, NH_3, SO_2, NOx, BC, $PM_{2.5}$, TPM	Turquety et al. (2014)
EMEP (Anthropogenic)[u]	Europe ($0.5° \times 0.5°$)	1980–2020	SO_2, NO_x, VOC, PM, GHG	Vestreng et al. (2007)

Dataset	Scale	Year	Major parameters	References
IASB-TD-OMI (Biomass burning and biogenic)[v]	Global (0.5° × 0.5°)	2005–2014	HCHO	Stavrakou *et al.* (2015)
L14-Africa (Anthropogenic)[w]	Africa (0.25° × 0.25°)	2005–2030	CO, NO$_x$, SO$_2$, NMVOC, BC, OC	Liousse *et al.* (2014)

[a]http://edgar.jrc.ec.europa.eu/.

[b]http://edgar.jrc.ec.europa.eu/overview.php?v=432&SECURE=123.

[c]http://edgar.jrc.ec.europa.eu/overview.php?v=432_AP.

[d]http://edgar.jrc.ec.europa.eu/overview.php?v=4tox2.

[e]https://cgrer.uiowa.edu/projects/emmison-data.

[f]https://www.nies.go.jp/REAS/.

[g]http://www.pole-ether.fr/eccad.

[h]http://www.iiasa.ac.at/web/home/research/researchPrograms/air/ECLIPSEv5.html.

[i]http://accent.aero.jussieu.fr/RETRO_metadata.php.

[j]http://accent.aero.jussieu.fr/Junker_metadata.php.

[k]http://cdiac.ess-dive.lbl.gov/trends/emis/overview_2010.html.

[l]ftp://ftp.mpic.de/GFAS/v1p3.

[m]https://daac.ornl.gov/VEGETATION/guides/fire_emissions_v4.html.

[n]http://www.geiacenter.org.

[o]http://www.globemission.eu.

[p]http://inventory.pku.edu.cn/.

[q]http://accent.aero.jussieu.fr/GICC_metadata.php.

[r]http://stormbringer.nateko.lu.se/public/guess030124/.

[q]http://accent.aero.jussieu.fr/AMMABB_metadata.php.

[s]http://gmes-atmosphere.eu/about/project_structure/input_data/d_emis/.

[t]http://www.pole-ether.fr/eccad.

[u]http://www.emep-emissions.at/emission-data-webdab.

[v]http://emissions.aeronomie.be/index.php/omi-based.

[w]http://www.aeris-data.fr/redirect/L14-Africa.

Table 3.3. *Existing global and regional emission inventory databases*

3.2.3.6. *State of the art of cloud computing for EI compilation*

EI compilation requires mathematical operation which involves large datasets. Comprehensive input databases are normally stored in a place and are further processed to get the output of calculated emissions. Further, the results need to be visualized and summarized, and whenever necessary, the EI compiler is often required to report to the authorized organization. The EI process should be updated regularly, and in this case, the size of the database is getting larger. Previously, EI compilers use dedicated EXCEL tools (IPCC, GAP, ABCEIM) or database program (dBASE) to compile EI and at the same time to process and visualize the outputs. Many EI compilers of the regional/global initiatives mentioned in Table 3.3 publicize the EI output in the relevant project websites, but process the EI development separately in the individual system. Recently, with the emerging CC technology and the advantages of automation and scalability (Bijwe *et al.* 2015), some EI compilers have started using the technology.

Multi-resolution Emission Inventory (MEIC) is a technology-based bottom-up air pollutant and GHG inventories for anthropogenic sources in China, which is developed and maintained on the basis of CC platform by Tsinghua University, and it allows users to conveniently access all customized emission products online (http://www.meicmodel.org/). A streamlined EI (SLEIS) data management application has been developed by a private company, Windsors, which is known as an interface program to compile EI in cloud system (http://www.windsorsolutions.com/products/SLEIS). The city of Alberquerque is reported to use a cloud-based version of SLEIS, and the system is hosted on an Amazon server. CC has been successfully employed to run USEPA Motor Vehicle Emission Simulator (MOVES) model that provides abundant computing resources on demand (Faler *et al.* 2012). A cloud-based Greenhouse Gas Air Pollution Interaction and Synergies (GAINS) model was developed to facilitate larger reusability and warehousing system of the global GAINS emission data (Nguyen *et al.* 2011). Further development of Database-as-a-service (DBaaS) in cloud would be potential and useful for EI compilation in the future.

3.3. Case studies

3.3.1. *Southeast Asia (SEA)*

The emission database for the SEA region was compiled from the EI developed for major anthropogenic sources in Indonesia, Thailand and Cambodia in 2007, and the online sources of CGRER and EDGAR v4.3.2 for other countries in the modeling domain (Permadi *et al.* 2018). The major anthropogenic sources covered by the EI for the three selected countries included power generation, manufacturing industry, on-road transport, aviation, residential and commercial cooking, fugitive emissions (from fuel), agro-residue open burning, forest fire, solid waste open burning, agriculture-related activities, and solvent and product use (Table 3.4). The EFs were compiled from the published sources, including those measured in SEA as detailed in Permadi et al. (2018).

Sectors	Types of activity data	Activity data		
		Indonesia	Thailand	Cambodia
Power generation	*Fuel consumptions (Mt/year)*			
	Coal	23.4	20.5	–
	Natural gas	3.2	29.8	–
	Fuel oil	9.4	0.75	0.62
	Biomass	6.3	–	–
Manufacturing industry	*Fuel consumptions (Mt/year)*			
	Coal	5.4	12.3	–
	Gasoline	0.34	0.013	–
	Fuel oil	18	2.4	0.52
	Biomass	–	20.7	–
On-road transport	Number of registered vehicle (million/year)	48	26	1.9
Aviation	Landing and take-offs (LTO) (×1000/year)	344	555	39
Residential and commercial cooking	*Fuel consumption (Mt/year)*			
	Coal	0.028	–	–
	Wood	100.5	7.6	0.4
	Kerosene	7.3	0.13	0.0003
	LPG	1	1.15	0.005
	Charcoal	20.4	3.9	0.042
	Other biomass	–	0.14	–
Fugitive emissions (from fuel)	Coke production (Kt/year)	182	–	–
	Gas production (Tg/year)	8,654	31.24	–
	Oil production (Tg/year)	29	6.2	–
	Gasoline distributed (Mt/year)	13.7	5.4	–
Agro-residue open burning	Total dry crop residue openly burned (Mt/year)	43.5	18.2	4.3
Forest fire	Total forest area burned, including peatland fire (ha/year)	545,881	1,851,850	98,761
Solid waste open burning	Total dry solid waste burned (Mt/year)	1.26	0.28	0.175
Agriculture-related activities	Total number of livestock population (head, ×10^6)	1,359	328	22.3

	Fertilizer consumption (Mt/year)	6.8	3.6	–
Solvent and product use	Paint (Kt/year of paint)	606	–	–
	Degrease (t/year of solvent consumed)	103	–	–
	Chemicals (Kt/year of products)	1,269	–	–
	Other product use (i.e., ink, domestic solvent, glue and adhesives) (Kt of products)	161	–	–

Table 3.4. *Summary of activity data from the considered emission sources in three countries in 2007 (Permadi et al. 2018)*

The results of national emission estimated for Indonesia, Thailand and Cambodia for the base case of 2007 are presented in Table 5.5 for 12 species (SO_2, NO_x, CO, NMVOC, NH_3, CH_4, PM_{10}, $PM_{2.5}$, BC, OC, CO_2 and N_2O). Sector-wise, the emissions of PM and the carbonaceous species, i.e. PM_{10}, $PM_{2.5}$, BC and OC, were mainly contributed by the residential and commercial combustion in Indonesia (43–80%) and Cambodia (55–78%), while biomass open burning (including forest fire and crop residue) was the main sources for these pollutants in Thailand (31–74%). In Indonesia, the SO_2 emission was mainly from the transport sector (36%) and the power generation (33%). However, the manufacturing industry was the main contributor of SO_2 in Thailand and Cambodia, i.e. 66% and 33% respectively. NO_x emission was dominated by the oil and gas operation in Indonesia (44%), power generation in Thailand (34%) and forest fires in Cambodia (60%). NH_3, an important precursor for $PM_{2.5}$, was mostly contributed by manure management and fertilizer practices in all three countries, i.e. 63% for Indonesia, 75% for Thailand and 78% for Cambodia.

Table 3.7 also presents the emissions from other SEA countries and from the Southern part of China included in the modeling domain which, in fact, showed significant contributions to the emission in the domain. In the SEA region, it is seen that Indonesia and Thailand were collectively the largest contributors of all pollutants, covering 25–62% of 2007 in SEA domain and 15–41% of the modeling domain (including Southern China).

Species	Indonesia	Thailand	Cambodia	Other SEA countries	SEA countries	Southern part of China	Total modeling domain
SO_2	997	827	41	2,695	4,560	6,204	10,781
NO_x	3,282	701	97	2623	6703	4166	10,910
CO	24,169	9095	2877	19,054	55,195	33,377	89,252
NMVOC	3840	1120	331	5644	10,935	4441	15,613
NH_3	1258	469	110	1543	3380	2247	5613

CH₄	3950	1053	713	13,833	19,549	14,640	34,218
PM₁₀	2046	782	115	1763	4706	3644	8458
PM₂.₅	1644	607	65	1466	3782	2653	6519
BC	226	47	7	159	439	362	821
OC	674	240	40	604	1558	643	2245
CO₂	508,022	260,988	28,296	856,225	1,653,531	1,406,860	3,092,654
N₂O	180	84	60	271	595	346	941

Table 3.5. *El results for base year in the Southeast Asia and the modeling domain in 2007 (Permadi et al. 2018)*

The emission data were prepared for each district in Indonesia, and each province in Thailand and Cambodia on annual average which were further derived to monthly and hourly data using relevant proxies used for modeling purpose. The extracted emission data for the rest of the modeling domain were also gridded and converted from annual basis to monthly and hourly emissions as detailed in Permadi *et al.* (2018). Overall, the emission database consisted of hourly emissions of 33 species for every grid (169 × 133) and 12 months of the year; hence, it is a large dataset to be further processed by the modeling system.

Spatially, it is clearly shown that pollutant emissions were densely concentrated in the city areas in all countries. Figure 3.2 shows the spatial distributions of the annual average emissions of BC and CO at $0.25° × 0.25°$ over the modeling domain.

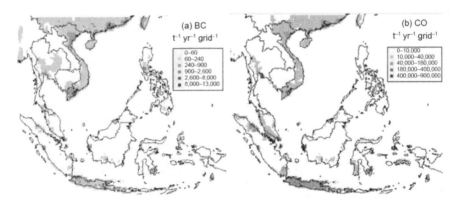

Figure 3.2. *Gridded (0.25°×0.25°) annual emissions for selected pollutants (BC and CO) over modeling domain (Permadi et al. 2018). For a color version of this figure, see www.iste.co.uk/laffly/torus3.zip*

3.3.2. *Vietnam inland domain*

The EI for the entire Vietnam inland domain, covering 63 provinces/cities, was conducted for the base year of 2010 (Huy 2015; Huy and Kim Oanh 2017). The study domain of inland Vietnam has a total area of 331,210 km^2. Six major anthropogenic sources were covered, including the on-road vehicle, biomass open burning (forest fires and agricultural residues), residential combustion, gasoline filling stations, industrial activities and power generation sector, and the natural biogenic source.

The AD were collected by an actual survey conducted for the gasoline filling stations and also from various published reports for different emission sources as summarized in Table 3.6. The EFs for traffic fleets were compiled from previous vehicle emission modeling studies for Vietnam (Kim Oanh *et al.* 2012; Van 2014; Trang *et al.* 2015), while for other sources, the EFs were taken from the compilation in ABCEIM (Shrestha *et al.* 2013).

No.	Requested data/emission sources	Data collected and data sources
1	General information of Vietnam Demographic data	General Statistical Office (GSO)
2	*Emission inventory*	
	Transportation	Emission factors (EFs), Vehicle Kilometer Traveled (Kim Oanh *et al.* 2012; Van 2014; Trang *et al.* 2015), number of vehicles (Vietnam Register Report)
	Biomass open burning	EI prepared by Dong (2013)
	Residential cooking	EFs, activity data (Shrestha *et al.* 2013), fuel consumption per capita, fuel type) (JICA 2010; Phuc 2012; Nhung 2013)
	Gasoline station	Number of gasoline stations (surveyed using Google Earth) Available gasoline sale/consumption/demand data (surveyed and compiled from Internet sources)
	Industrial source	Fuel consumption of industrial sector (surveyed and compiled from Internet sources) National industrial productivity from Ministry of Industry and Trade (MOIT) Downscaled data from Emission Database for Global Atmospheric Research (EDGAR)
	Thermal power plants	Activity data (compiled by Internet sources and personal communication with Vietnam Electricity (EVN))
3	Biogenic source	Global Biosphere Emissions and Interactions System (GLOBEIS)

Table 3.6. *Major EI sources and data collection (Huy 2015)*

The total 2010 annual emissions of SO_2, NO_x, CO, NMVOC, CH_4, NH_3, PM_{10}, $PM_{2.5}$, BC and OC in Gg/year are presented in Table 3.7.

Source	SO_2	NO_x	CO	NMVOC	CH_4	NH_3	PM_{10}	$PM_{2.5}$	BC	OC
Anthropogenic sources (Gg/year)										
On-road mobile source	8.3	366	3542	767	15.8	16	62	46.3[a]	11	12
Biomass open burning	7	73	5350	223	134	118	285	259	17	97
Gasoline station	-	-	-	8.14	-	-	-	-	-	-
Industry	387	179	350	49.3	6.63	12.4	246	71	2.54	4.61
Thermal power plants	142	141	11.3	2.29	0.60	0.49	19.3	8.01	0.02	0.10
Residential cooking	71.4	68	5552	206	324	21.9	380	288	62	182
Total anthropogenic sources										
	616	827	14,805	1256	481	169	992	626	93	296
Biogenic source (Gg/month)										
August	-	6.6[b]	94[c]	364	-	-	-	-	-	-
December	-	4.82[b]	51[c]	198	-	-	-	-	-	-
Total biogenic source (Gg/year)										
	-	68.5	870	3372	-	-	-	-	-	-
Total emission (Gg/year)	616	896	15,675	4628	481	169	992	626	93	296

[a]Based on $PM_{2.5}/PM_{10}$ ratio of 0.70 (Kim Oanh *et al.* 2013);

[b]NO emission (GLOBEIS model);

[c]CO emission (GLOBEIS model)

Table 3.7. *Annual emissions from different sources in Vietnam (Gg/year), 2010 (Huy 2015)*

The emission shares of the sources are presented in Figure 3.3. It is clearly seen that CO emission was mainly contributed by three sources: on-road vehicle (22%), biomass open burning (33%) and residential cooking (35%). For NMVOC, the biogenic emission (73%) was nearly three times higher than the total from the major anthropogenic sources (27%). On-road mobile source was the main contributor to NO_x (40%), while the industrial sector was the largest contributor to SO_2 (61%). Two important sources of PM were residential cooking and biomass open burning: residential cooking shared 36% of PM_{10} and 41% of $PM_{2.5}$ emissions, whereas biomass open burning accounted for 27% of PM_{10} and 37% of $PM_{2.5}$.

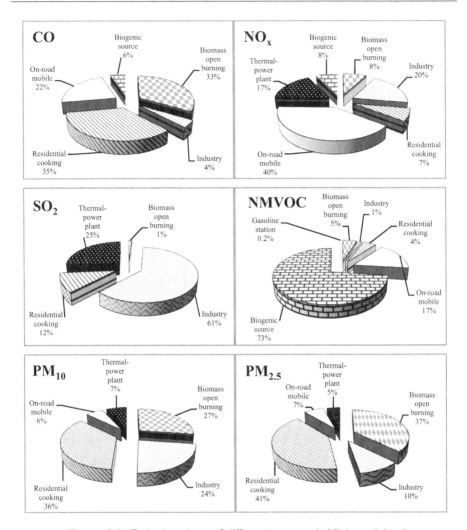

Figure 3.3. *Emission share of different sources in Vietnam inland domain in 2010 (Huy 2015). For a color version of this figure, see www.iste.co.uk/laffly/torus3.zip*

The emissions of the 10 species were prepared for each province of the inland Vietnam. Further, for the modeling purpose, the emissions were gridded (12 km), and gridded hourly emissions were calculated for considered species which resulted in a large dataset to handle. Examples of the spatial distributions of $PM_{2.5}$ and SO_2 emissions from industrial activities in inland Vietnam (Huy and Kim Oanh 2017) are presented in Figure 3.4.

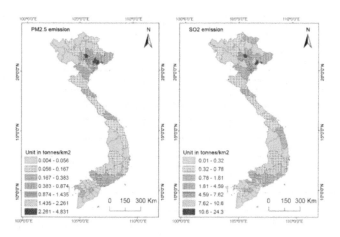

Figure 3.4. *Spatial distributions of PM$_{2.5}$ and SO$_2$ emissions (tonnes/km^2) from industrial activities in inland Vietnam, 2010 (Huy and Kim Oanh 2017)*

3.3.3. Bangkok Metropolitan Region, Thailand

The EI domain covered the Bangkok city and eight provinces, namely, Nonthaburi, Pathum Thani, Samut Prakan, Samut Sakhon, Nakhon Pathom, Chachoengsao, Nakhon Nayok and Chon Buri, with the total area of 70 × 100 km² (Figure 3.5) and hereby named as the Bangkok Metropolitan Region (BMR) domain for short. The EI results for the domain by several AIT studies from key sources were updated to 2016, and the results for key pollutants of NO$_x$, CO, NMVOC, SO$_2$, NH$_3$ and PM$_{10}$ are presented in Table 3.8.

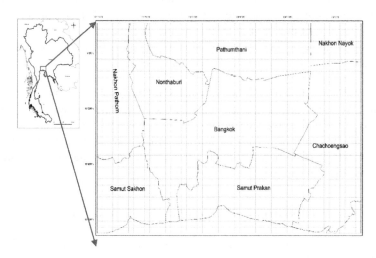

Figure 3.5. *Location and provincial boundaries of the BMR EI domain (Ha Chi 2018)*

No.	Emission Source	NO_x	CO	NMVOC	SO_2	NH_3	PM_{10}
1	Aviation	17.6	17.6	8.85	1.19	–	0.18
2	Biogenic	0.34	0.83	116	–	–	–
3	Biomass open burning	3.74	227	8.93	0.75	5.40	13.1
4	Cremation	0.01	0.01	0.001	0.03	–	0.001
5	Farm machine	0.12	0.07	0.03	–	–	0.02
6	Gasoline station	–	–	6.88	–	–	–
7	Industry	53.3	134	14.7	90.7	–	12.4
8	Livestock	–	–	–	–	10.9	–
9	Oil tank	–	–	0.98	–	–	–
10	On-road mobile sources	256	377	44.4	0.74	1.21	27.3
11	Power plant	26.3	23.4	3.38	2.53	1.02	0.87
12	Residential	5.12	1.22	0.20	0.43	2.94	0.29
13	Soil	1.22	–	–	–	0.24	–
Total Emission		**364**	**782**	**204**	**96**	**22**	**54**

Table 3.8. *EI updated to 2016 for the BMR domain, Gg/year (Ha Chi 2018)*

In the domain, the on-road mobile source was the main contributor of PM_{10} (50% of the total), NO_x (70%) and CO (48%), while the natural biogenic emission had the highest share for NMVOC (with 57%). About 94% of the total SO_2 emission was from industry, while 50% of NH_3 was from livestock activities. Note that some important sources of coarse particles – for example soil, road and construction dust – were not included in this EI; hence, it may underestimate the PM_{10} emissions. The PM emitted from vehicle exhausts and biomass open burning, on other side, would predominantly be in the fine particle size range ($PM_{2.5}$).

The emissions of the considered species of biogenic emission were directly calculated for every cell (2×2 km) of the 50 x 35 grid net in the EI domain. The emissions of the anthropogenic sources were first prepared for each province in the domain and then further segregated into 2×2 km. The gridded hourly emissions were then calculated to be used in the air quality modeling; hence, it resulted in a large dataset to manage.

3.3.4. Forest fire emissions from Nakhon Si Thammarat, Thailand

Emissions from forest fires cause a serious air pollution problem in many tropical countries. The forest fires frequently cause air pollution episodes in nearby local communities that particularly cause adverse health impacts, especially for children and the elderly people (WHO 2016).

Nakhon Si Thammarat (NST), located in the Southern Thailand, is rich in swamp forest (Figure 3.6) which occupies a total area of 560 km^2. The swamp forest in the province has been declared as the National Preservation Forest (The Project of Preservation and Development for Kuan Kreng Peat Swamp Forest); hence, the area is named as the "Kuan Kreng Swamp Forest". Almost every year around May to August, the swamp forest experiences drought conditions and, subsequently, forest fires occur intensively during this period. Photos in Figure 3.6 show the typical vegetation cover of the swamp forest.

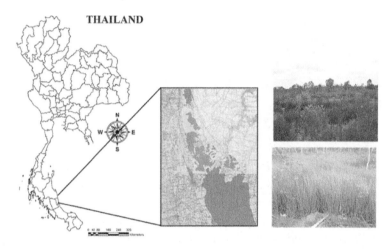

Figure 3.6. *Study area and typical vegetation cover of swamp forest. For a color version of this figure, see www.iste.co.uk/laffly/torus3.zip*

The EI was conducted for nine (9) species: CO, NO_2, SO_2, CO_2, NH_3, CH_4, NMVOC, BC and OC for a 10-year period from 2003 to 2012. Satellite hotspot data were collected to represent biomass burning in the area. Hotspots were overlaid with the land-use map of NST, and the only hotspots appeared in the forest area were attributed to forest fires. Figure 3.7 shows the number of hotspots overlaid on the forest area in 2012 in comparison with the forest fires obtained from the ground observation made by the Office of National Preservation Forest. Satellite and ground data indicated a good agreement for the fire observations in the area.

The activity data are the amount of burned biomass calculated from satellite hotspot detection (number of hotspots × effective burned area per fire pixel × burning efficiency × dry matter density). The values used for the listed parameters were taken from ABC EIM (Shrestha *et al.* 2013), except for the dry matter density that was taken from locally measured data for the Kuan Kreng Swamp Forest by Chaiyarak and Wanthongchai (2014). The EFs of each pollutant species were also taken from the compiled data in the ABC EIM (Shrestha *et al.* 2013).

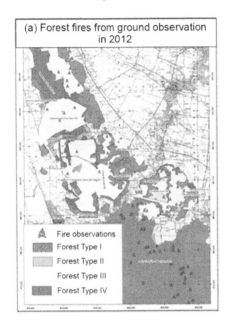

Figure 3.7. *Satellite hot spots (a) and ground observation of forest fires (b). For a color version of this figure, see www.iste.co.uk/laffly/torus3.zip*

The 10-year EI results show higher emissions in 2005, 2010 and 2012 (Table 3.9). These years also had high numbers of hotspots of 59, 82 and 68 respectively. Kirtphaiboon *et al.* (2014) found that rainfall variability in Thailand is related to ENSO. For example, years 2009 and 2010 were classified as strong and weak El Niño respectively with low intensity of rainfall (Kirtphaiboon *et al.* 2014). The strong El Niño and droughts in 2009 could induce fires in the swamp forest also in the subsequent year of 2010. During the intensive burning periods in the mentioned years, smoggy blanket was observed to cover the nearby area and communities for a few days to weeks. A sharp increase of air pollution levels in the rural areas during fire episodes could be easily felt and seen by naked eyes which would cause substantial adverse health effects, yet to be quantified. The year 2011 had no forest fire hotspots detected by satellite that may be due to short fire periods that could not be detected by MODIS (TERRA and AQUA) which overpasses the area twice a day (10:30 and 13:30 respectively).

The EI results can be used further for modeling study to capture how the pollutant plume is dispersed and spreads the pollution to the surrounding areas. The EI data should then be segregated into a grid net and with refined temporal distributions (hourly) and hence could result in a large dataset to be potentially managed by CC.

Year	Emission estimates (Mg/year)								
	CO	SO$_2$	NO$_2$	CO$_2$	NH$_3$	CH$_4$	NMVOC	BC	OC
2003	256.2	0.9	2.8	2077.6	3.1	25.4	8.5	0.7	5.2
2004	530.7	1.8	5.7	4303.7	6.4	52.6	17.7	1.4	10.9
2005	1079.7	3.7	11.6	8755.7	13.1	106.9	36.0	2.9	22.1
2006	109.8	0.4	1.2	890.4	1.3	10.9	3.7	0.3	2.2
2007	164.7	0.6	1.8	1335.6	2.0	16.3	5.5	0.4	3.4
2008	91.5	0.3	1.0	742.0	1.1	9.1	3.1	0.2	1.9
2009	54.9	0.2	0.6	445.5	0.7	5.4	1.8	0.1	1.1
2010	1500.6	5.1	16.2	12169.0	18.2	148.6	50.0	4.1	30.7
2011[a]	n.a.	n.a.	n.a.	n.a.	n.a.	n.a.	n.a.	n.a.	n.a.
2012	1244.4	4.2	13.4	10091.4	15.1	123.3	41.5	3.4	25.5

[a]In 2011, EI data were not available since no satellite hotspot data were detected in this year.

Table 3.9. *Emission from the Kuan Kreng forest fires during 2003–2012*

3.3.5. *Phnom Penh (PNH), Cambodia*

An EI for the Phnom Penh (PNH) city of Cambodia was developed under the joint cooperation between the air quality research group of AIT, the Royal University of Phnom Penh (RUPP) and the Ministry of Environment of Cambodia (MOE) for the base year of 2013 with the financial support from the ASEAN-GTZ project on "Clean air for smaller cities". The study domain covers an area of 28 km^2 of the core city center (Chamkar Mon, Daun Penh, Prampir Markara and Toul Kork districts) (Figure 3.8). The EI covered key anthropogenic emission sources of on-road and non-road mobile sources, residential cooking, power plant, industrial diesel generator (industrial manufacturing process and boiler were not considered), commercial back-up generator and medical waste incinerator. Six emission species were included in the inventory, including PM$_{10}$, NO$_x$, SO$_2$, CO, NMVOCs and CO$_2$. The bottom-up approach using the actual survey was mainly used for the AD collection. The relevant EFs for the considered sources were extracted from the compiled EF in ABC EIM (Shrestha *et al.* 2013).

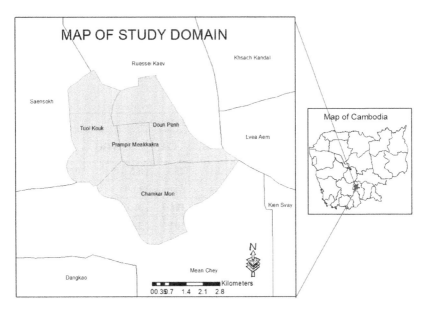

Figure 3.8. *Map of the EI domain of PNH*

The total annual emissions from the considered emission sources are presented in Table 3.10. The total emissions from the domain in 2013 (Kt/year) were 7.2 NO_x, 88 CO, 20 NMVOC, 0.6 PM_{10}, 2,613 CO_2 and 7 SO_2. Note that for all pollutants and CO_2, the emissions were mostly contributed by the on-road mobile source (55–98%), except for SO_2 that was dominated by the point source (99%). The EI results will be segregated into grids with fine resolution (about 2 km) and into hourly emissions for the dispersion modeling purpose which will be a large dataset to handle.

Source	NO_x	CO	NMVOC	PM_{10}	CO_2	SO_2
Power Plant	1,586	94	31	140	485,471	6,910
Industrial generator	80.0	17.3	6.5	5.7	2,977	5.3
Commercial sector generator	9.5	2.1	0.8	0.7	354.4	0.6
Residential cooking	14.6	3,054	175	109	57,762	6.4
On-road mobile source	5,087	84,078	19,612	310	1,938,699	11.2
Non-road mobile source (railway and airport)	420	379	37.9	4.0	127,445	26.6
Incinerator	1.2	0.1	0.4	8.7	506	0.3
Total	7198	87,625	19,864	578	2,613,214	6960

Table 3.10. *Emission inventory for PNH, 2013 (GIZ 2015)*

3.4. Summary and conclusion

Emission inventory is a comprehensive list of air pollutants emitted by different anthropogenic and natural sources from a geographical domain during a specific period of time. Development of good EI databases requires accurate AD and representative values of EFs for considered sources. A standard QA/QC procedure should be applied to minimize the uncertainty in EI results. An accurate EI database is a prerequisite for effective AQM, particularly to identify the major sources of key pollutants to prioritize the emission control efforts. EI results are further used to prepare the emission input data for 3D air pollution dispersion modeling which should be segregated into hourly values of the interested species and in every grid of the model domain. This would result in a large dataset to handle, and therefore there is a good potential to apply CC in this research area.

The case studies of EI development in various Southeast Asia domains, from the Southeast Asia region to city scale, or for specific source of forest fires illustrated the EI development process and the size of the EI databases, and highlighted the potentiality of CC applications.

3.5. References

Andres, R.J., Marland, G., Fung, I., Matthews, E. (1996). A 1° × 1° distribution of carbon dioxide emissions from fossil fuel consumption and cement manufacture. *Global Biogeochem. Cycles*. 10, 419–429.

Bijwe, S.D. and Ramteke, P.L. (2015). Database in cloud computing: Database as a service (DBaas) with its challenges. *IJCSMC*, 4(2), 73–79.

Chaiyarak, S. and Wanthongchai, K. (2014). Fire behaviour at Kuan Kreng peat forest, Nakhorn Sri Thammarat province. *5th International Conference on Sustainable Energy and Environment (SEE 2014): Science, Technology and Innovation for ASEAN Green Growth*, Bangkok.

Crippa, M., Guizzardi, D., Muntean, M., Schaaf, E., Dentener, F., van Aadenne, J.A., Moni, S., Doering, U., Olivier, J.G.J., Pagliari, V., and Janssens-Maenhout, G. (2018). Gridded emissions of air pollutants for the period 1970–2012 within EDGAR v4.3.2. *Earth Syst. Sci. Data. Discuss*. https://doi.org/10.5194/essd-2018-31.

Dong, N.P. (2013). Development of spatial and temporal emission inventory for biomass open burning in Vietnam. Master Thesis, Asian Institute of Technology, Bangkok.

Elguindi, N., Granier, C., Darras, S., and Liousse, C. (n.y.). Global anthropogenic projected emission. In preparation.

EMEP/EEA (2016). EMEP/CORINAIR Emission Inventory Guidebook 2016 [Online]. Available: https://www.eea.europa.eu/publications/emep-eea-guidebook-2016. [Accessed 31 May 2018].

Faler, W., Michaels, H., and Aikman, W. (2012). Using cloud computing to do large numbers of MOVES run. International Emission Inventory Conference "Emission Inventories – Meeting the Challenges Posed by Emerging Global, National, Regional and Local Air Quality" [Online]. Available: https://www3.epa.gov/ttnchie1/conference/ei20/session8/wfaler.pdf. [Accessed 31 May 2018].

Giglio, L., Randerson, J.T., and van der Werf, G.R. (2013). Analysis of daily, monthly, and annual burned area using the fourth-generation global fire emissions database (GFED4). *J. Geophys. Res. Biogeosci.* 118, 317–328.

GIZ (2015). Phnom Penh atmospheric emission inventory. Clean air for smaller cities in the ASEAN region. Report, The Deutsche Gesellschaft für Internationale Zusammenarbeit GmbH, Phnom Penh.

Granier, C., Bessagnet, B., Bond, T., D'Angiola, A., van der Gon, H.D., Frost, G.J., Heil, A., Kaiser, J.W., Kinne, S., Klimont, Z., Kloster, S., Lamarque, J.-F., Liousse, C., Masui, T., Meleux, F., Mieville, A., Ohara, T., Raut, J.-C., Riahi, K., Schultz, M.G., Smith, S.J., Thompson, A., van Aardenne, J., van der Werf, G.R., and van Vuuren, D.P. (2011). Evolution of anthropogenic and biomass burning emissions of air pollutants at global and regional scales during the 1980-2010 period. *Clim Change*, 109, 163–190.

Ha Chi, N.N. (2018). Assessment of particulate matter, surface ozone air quality and associated health burdens in the Bangkok Metropolitan Region using a photochemical grid model. Master Thesis, Asian Institute of Technology, Bangkok.

Huang, Y., Shen, H., Chen, Y., Zhong, Q., Chen, H., Wang, R., Shen, G., Liu, J., Li, B., and Tao, S. (2015). Global organic carbon emissions from primary sources from 1960 to 2009. *Atmos. Environ.*, 122, 505–512.

Huy, L.N. (2015). Evaluation of performance of photochemical smog modelling system for air quality management in Vietnam. Master Thesis, Asian Institute of Technology, Bangkok.

Huy, L.N., Kim Oanh, N.T. (2017). Assessment of national emissions of air pollutants and climate forcers from thermal power plants and industrial activities in Vietnam. *Atmos. Pollut. Res.*, 8(3), 503–513.

Inomata, Y., Kajino, M., Sato, K., Ohara, T., Kurokawa, J.-I., Ueda, H., Tang, N., Hayakawa, K., Ohizumi, T., and Akimoto, H. (2012). Emission and atmospheric transport of particulate PAHs in Northeast Asia. *Environ. Sci. Technol.*, 46(9), 4941–4949.

IPCC. (2006). IPCC guidelines for national greenhouse gases inventories. Report, Intergovernmental Panel on Climate Change.

Jalkanen, J.-P., Johansson, L., and Kukkonen, J. (2016). A comprehensive inventory of ship traffic exhaust emissions in the European sea areas in 2011. *Atmos. Chem. Phys.*, 16, 71–84.

Janssens-Maenhout, G., Crippa, M., Guizzardi, D., Muntean, M., Schaaf, E., Dentener, F., Bergamaschi, P., Pagliari, V., Olivier, J.G.J., Peters, J.A.H.W., Aardenne, J.A., Monni, S., Doering, U., and Petrescu, A.M.R. (2017a). EDGAR v4.3.2 Global atlas of the three major greenhouse gas emissions for the period 1970–2012. *Earth Syst. Sci. Data. Discuss.*, https://doi.org/10.5194/essd-2017-79.

Janssens-Maenhout, G., Crippa, M., Guizzardi, D., Muntean, M., Schaaf, E., Olivier, J.G.J, Peters, J.A.H.W., and Schure, K.M. (2017b). Fossil CO_2 and GHG emissions of all world countries. Report, Publications Office of the European Union, Luxembourg.

JICA. (2010). Supported collection of information and data basic framework for establishing a national plan for air pollution control in Vietnam. Report, Japan International Cooperation Agency, Hanoi.

Junker, C. and Liousse, C. (2008). A global emission inventory of carbonaceous aerosol from historic records of fossil fuel and biofuel consumption for the period 1860–1997. *Atmos. Chem. Phys.*, 8, 1195–1207.

Kaiser, J.W., Heil, A., Andreae, M.O., Benedetti, A., Chubarova, N., Jones, L., Morcrette, J.-J., Razinger, M., Schultz, M.G., Suttie, M., and van der Werf, G.R. (2012). Biomass burning emissions estimated with a global fire assimilation system based on observed fire radiative power. *Biogeosciences.*, 9, 527–554.

Kim Oanh, N.T., Permadi, D.A., Phuc, N.H., and Zhuang, Y. (2013). Chapter 1: Air quality status and management practices in Asian developing countries. In *Integrated Air Quality Management: Asian Case Studies*, Kim Oanh, N.T. (ed.). CRC Press, Florida.

Kim Oanh, N.T., Thuy Phuong, M.T., and Permadi, D.A. (2012). Analysis of motorcycle fleet in Hanoi for estimation of air pollution emission and climate mitigation co-benefit of technology implementation. *Atmos. Environ.*, 59, 438–448.

Kim Oanh, N.T., Permadi, D.A., Kingkaew, S., Chatchupong, T., and Pongprueksa, P. (2014). Study of ground-level Ozone in Bangkok Metropolitan Region (BMR) by advance mathematical modeling for air quality management. Report, Asian Institute of Technology, Bangkok.

Kirtphaiboon, S., Wongwises, P., Limsakul, A., Sooktawee, S., and Humphries, U. (2014). Rainfall variability over Thailand related to the El Nino-Southern Oscillation (ENSO). *J. Sustain. Energy Environ.*, 5, 37–42

Klimont, Z., Smith, S.J., and Cofala, J. (2013). The last decade of global anthropogenic sulphur dioxide: 2000-2011 emissions. *Environ. Res. Lett.*, 8(1), 1–6.

KMITL (2015). Emission inventory of industrial source in Thailand in 2013. Personal communication, King Mongkut's Institute of Technology Ladkrabang, Bangkok.

Knorr, W., Lehsten, V., and Arneth, A. (2012). Determinants and predictability of global wildfire emissions. *Atmos. Chem. Phys.*, 12, 6845–6861.

Kuenen, J.J.P., Visschedijk, A.J.H., Jozwicka, M, and Denier van der Gon, H.A.C. (2014). TNO-MACC_II emission inventory; a multi-year (2003-2009) consistent high-resolution European emission inventory for air quality modelling. *Atmos. Chem. Phys.*, 14, 10963–10976.

Kurokawa, J., Ohara, T., Morikawa, T., Hanayama, S., Janssens-Maenhout, G., Fukui, T., Kawashima, K., and Akimoto, H. (2013). Emissions of air pollutants and greenhouse gases over Asian regions during 2000-2008: Regional Emission inventory in ASia (REAS) version 2. *Atmos. Chem. Phys.*, 13, 11019–11058.

Liousse, C., Guillaume, B., Grégoire, J.M., Mallet, M., Galy, C., Pont, V., Akpo, A., Bedou, M., Castéra, P., Dungall, L., Gardrat, E., Grainier, C., Konaré, A., Malavelle, F., Mariscal, A., Mieville, A., Rosset, R., Serca, D., Solmon, F., Tummon, F., Assamoi, E., Yoboué, V., and van Velthoven, P. (2010). Updated African biomass burning emission inventories in the framework of the AMMA-IDAF program, with an evaluation of combustion aerosols. *Atmos. Chem. Phys.*, 10, 9631–9646.

Liousse C., Assamoi, E., Criqui, P., Granier, C., and Rosset, R. (2014). Explosive growth in African combustion emissions from 2005 to 2030. *Environ. Res. Lett.*, 9, 035003.

MfE NZ. (2001). Good practice guide for preparing emission inventory. Ministry of Environment New Zealand. Wellington, New Zealand [Online]. Available: http://www.mfe.govt.nz/sites/default/files/emissions-good-practice-guide.pdf [Accessed 31 May 2018].

Mieville, A., Granier, C., Liousse, C., Guilaume, B., Mouillot, F., Lamarque, J.-F., Grégoire, J.-M., and Pétron, G. (2010). Emissions of gases and particles from biomass burning during the 20th century using satellite data and an historical reconstruction. *Atmos. Environ.*, 44(11), 1469–1477.

Mijing, B., van der A, R.J., and Zhang, Q. (2013). Regional nitrogen oxides emission trends in East Asia observed from space. *Atmos. Chem. Phys.*, 13, 12003–12012.

Muntean, M., Janssens-Maenhout, G., Song, S., Giang, A., Zhong, N.E., Zhao, Y., Olivier, J.G.J., Guizzardi, D., Crippa, M., Schaaf, E., and Dentener, F. (2018). Evaluating EDGARv4.tox2 speciated mercury emissions ex-post scenarios and their impacts on modelled global and regional wet deposition patterns. *Atmos. Environ.*, 184, 56–68.

Nguyen, T.B., Wagner, F., and Schoepp, W. (2012). *Cloud intelligent services for calculating emissions and costs of air pollutants and greenhouse gases*. Springer, Verlag Berlin Heidelberg.

Nhung, C.P. (2013). Emission inventory for residential cooking activity in Hanoi Capital Region for assessment of potential co-benefits under various fuel-stove scenarios. Master Thesis, Asian Institute of Technology, Bangkok.

Ohara, T., Akimoto, H., Kurokawa, J., Horii, N., Yamaji, K., Yan, X., and Hayasaka, T. (2007). An Asian emission inventory of anthropogenic emission sources for the period 1980–2020. *Atmos. Chem. Phys.*, 7, 4419–4444.

Olivier, J.G.J., Schure, K.M., and Peters, J.A.H.W. (2017). Trends in global CO_2 and total greenhouse gas emissions. Report, PBL, The Hague.

Permadi, D.A., Kim Oanh, N.T., Kanabkaew, T., and Sothea, K. (2014). Chapter 15: Emission inventory for air quality modelling. In *Improving Air Quality in Asian Developing Countries: Compilation of Research Findings*, Kim Oanh, N.T. (ed.). NARENCA, Hanoi.

Permadi, D. A., Kim Oanh, N. T., and Vautard, R. (2018). Integrated emission inventory and modelling to assess distribution of particulate matter mass and black carbon composition in Southeast Asia. *Atmos. Chem. Phys.*, 18, 2725–2747.

Phuc, N.H. (2012). Assessment of air quality, health and climate co-benefit potential for residential cooking: A case study of a commune in Vietnam. Master Thesis, Asian Institute of Technology, Bangkok.

Rucksunchart, P. (2017). Analysing particulate matter air quality in Bangkok Metropolitan region using a 3-dimensional modelling tool. Master Thesis, Asian Institute of Technology, Bangkok.

Schultz, M.G., Backman, L., Balkanski, Y., Bjoerndalsaeter, S., Brand, R., Burrows, J.P., Dalsoeren, S., de Vasconcelos, M., Grodtmann, B., Hauglustaine, D.A., Heil, A., Hoelzemann, J.J., Isaksen, I.S.A., Kaurola, J., Knorr, W., Ladstaetter-Weißenmayer, A., Mota, B., Oom, D., Pacyna, J., Panasiuk, D., Pereira, J.M.C., Pulles, T., Pyle, J., Rast, S., Richter, A., Savage, N., Schnadt, C., Schulz, M., Spessa, A., Staehelin, J., Sundet, J.K., Szopa, S., Thonicke, K., van het Bolscher, M., van Noije, T., van Velthoven, P., Vik, A.F., and Wittrock, F. (2007a). REanalysis of the TROpospheric chemical composition over the past 40 years (RETRO) — A long-term global modeling study of tropospheric chemistry. Report, Jülich/Hamburg.

Schultz, M.G., Rast, S., van het Bolscher, M., Pulles, T., Brand, R., Pereira, J., Mota, B., Spessa, A., Dalsoren, S., van Nojie, T., and Szopa, S. (2007b). Emission data sets and methodologies for estimating emissions – Working Package 1.

Schultz, M.G., Heil, A., Hoelzemann, J.J., Spessa, A., Thonicke, K., Goldammer, J.G., Held, A.C., Pereira, J.M.C., and van het Bolscher, M. (2008). Global wildland fire emissions from 1960 to 2000. *Global Biogeochem. Cy.*, 22, GB2002.

SEI (2004). GAP: Global Air Pollution Forum Emission Manual [Online]. Available: https://www.sei.org/projects-and-tools/tools/gap-global-air-pollution-forum-emission-manual/ [Accessed 31 May 2018].

Shrestha, R.M., Kim Oanh, N.T., Shrestha, R.P., Rupakheti, M., Rajeshwari, S., Permadi, D.A., Kanabkaew, T., and Iyngararasan, M. (2013). Atmospheric Brown Clouds (ABC) Emission Inventory Manual. Report, United Nations Environment Programme, Nairobi.

Sindelarova, K., Granier, C., Bouarar, I., Guenther, A., Tilms, S., Stavrakou, T., Muller, J.-F., Kuhn, U., Stefani, P., and Knorr, W. (2014). Global data set of biogenic VOC emissions calculated by the MEGAN model over the last 30 years. *Atmos. Chem. Phys.*, 14, 9317–9341.

Sofiev, M., Vankevich, R., Lotjonen, M., Prank, M., Petukhov, V., Ermakova, T., Koskinen, J., and Kukkonen, J. (2009). An operational system for the assimilation of the satellite information on wild-land fires for the needs of air quality modelling and forecasting. *Atmos. Chem. Phys.*, 9, 6833–6847.

Stavrakou, T., Müller, J.-F., Bauwens, M., De Smedt, I., van Roozendael, M., de Mazière, M., Vigouroux, C., Hendrick, F., George, M., Clearbaux, C., Coheur, P.-F., and Guenther, A. (2015). How consistent are top-down hydrocarbon emissions based on formaldehyde observations from GOME-2 and OMI? *Atmos. Chem. Phys.*, 15, 12007–12067.

Streets, D.G., Bond, T.C., Carmichael, G.R., Fernandes, S.D., Fu, Q., He, D., Klimont, Z., Nelson, S.M., Tsai, N.Y., Wang, M.Q., Woo, J.-H., and Yarber, K.F. (2000). An inventory of gaseous and primary aerosol emissions in Asia in the year 2000. *J. Geophys. Res. Atmos.*, 108, D21.

Trang, T.T., Van, H.H., and Kim Oanh, N.T. (2015). Traffic emission inventory for estimation of air quality and climate co-benefits of faster vehicle technology intrusion in Hanoi, Vietnam. *Carbon Manag.*, 6, 117–128.

Turquety, S., Menut, L., Bessagnet, B., Anav, A., Viovy, N., Maignan, F., and Wooster, M. (2014). APIFLAME v1.0: High-resolution fire emission model and application to the Euro-Mediterranean region. *Geosci. Model Dev.*, 7, 587–612.

UNEP-APCAP (2018). Part 1 Training – Capacity Building Programme for National Air Quality Managers. Workshop Training, Asian Institute of Technology, Bangkok.

USEPA (2005). Emission Factors & AP-42, Technology Transfer Network clearinghouse for Inventories & Emissions Factors [Online]. Available: http://www.epa.gov/ttn/chief/ap42/ [Accessed 31 May 2018].

USEPA (2007). Emission Inventory Improvement Program (EEIP) Volume 1-10 [Online]. Available: http://www.epa.gov/ttn/chief/eiip/index.html [Accessed 31 May 2018].

Van, H.H. (2014). Development of emission inventory for vehicle fleet in Ho Chi Minh City to estimate environment and climate co-benefit of faster technology intrusion. Master Thesis, Asian Institute of Technology, Bangkok.

van der Werf, G.R., Randerson, J.T., Giglio, L., Collatz, G.J., Mu, M., Kasibhatla, P.S., Morton, D.C., DeFries, R.S., Jin, Y., and van Leeuwen, T.T. (2010). Global fire emissions and the contribution of deforestation, savanna, forest, agricultural, and peat fires (1997–2009). *Atmos. Chem. Phys.*, 10, 11707–11735.

Vestreng, V., Myhre, G., Fagerli, H., Reis, S., and Tarrasón, L. (2007). Twenty-five years of continuous sulphur dioxide emission reduction in Europe. *Atmos. Chem. Phys.*, 7, 3663–3681.

WHO (2016). Ambient air pollution: A global assessment of exposure and burden of disease. Report, World Health Organization.

Zhang, Q., Streets, D.G., Carmichael, G.R., He, K.B., Huo, H., Kannari, A., Klimont, Z., Park, I.S., Reddy, S., Fu, J.S., Chen, D., Duan, L., Lei, Y., Wang, L.T., and Yao, Z.L. (2009). Asian emissions in 2006 for the NASA INTEX-B mission. *Atmos. Chem. Phys.*, 9, 5131–5153.

4

Atmospheric Modeling with Focus on Management of Input/Output Data and Potential of Cloud Computing Applications

Atmospheric modeling has been widely used to understand the physical and chemical processes in the atmosphere that involve the climate, weather and air quality research. Several air quality dispersion models exist which are applied worldwide, including CAMx, CMAQ, GEOS-Chem and CHIMERE, among others. These air quality models are used to establish quantitative relationships between the emissions and the ambient air concentrations driven by meteorological variables commonly produced by meteorological models. This chapter provides an introduction to the atmospheric modeling with emphasis on the conceptual modeling structure. Specific features of several commonly applied air quality models are provided together with their online information. Further, this chapter describes the model application practices and highlights the issue of big input and output datasets involved where applications of cloud computing would hold potential. Several dispersion modeling case studies covering different domain scales in Southeast Asia (urban, national and regional) conducted by the air quality research group at the Asian Institute of Technology (Thailand) are provided to facilitate the comprehension of modeling application process and the involved big input and output datasets for processing and handling in the modeling system.

Chapter written by Thi Kim Oanh NGUYEN, Nhat Ha Chi NGUYEN, Nguyen Huy LAI and Didin Agustian PERMADI.

4.1. Introduction

4.1.1. *Atmospheric modeling*

The compositions of the Earth's atmosphere have been vastly changing more rapidly in recent decades due to the increased emissions from human-made activities. As a result, there is a significant increase in the levels of toxic constituents that are harmful to human health, ecosystems and the Earth's climate system. Several atmospheric issues such as global warming, ozone layer depletion and air pollution have been intensively studied in the last few decades (Ramanathan and Feng 2008, and references therein).

The atmospheric processes are of a wide range of scale and far too complex to be reproduced physically in the laboratory (Schneider *et al.* 1989). To some extent, instead of building a physical analog of the whole atmospheric system, these processes can be simulated mathematically using some computer model systems known as the atmospheric modeling systems. Such a modeling system uses a system of mathematical equations to describe physical and chemical processes in the atmosphere, and this modeling approach is applied for climate, weather forecast and air quality studies. Although these models are not able to reproduce the full complexity of reality, they can reveal the logical consequences of assumptions about how the atmospheric system changes. Atmospheric models include at least four major categories: (1) atmospheric general circulation model (AGCM) for simulating the global climate, (2) regional climate model (RCM) to simulate the climate in different regions, (3) mesoscale meteorological model for simulating the details of regional and local meteorological phenomena and (4) chemistry transport model (CTM) to simulate changes in chemistry in the atmosphere that are applied in air quality studies (Dawson *et al.* 2008).

AGCM simulates the global climate with a grid resolution at about one degree (~100 km), while RCM simulates the regional scale climate and can use the input supplied by AGCM. Air quality models (or CTM) are equipped with various chemistry mechanisms which use complex chemical reactions of species involved to simulate, for example, the formation of ground-level ozone (O_3), secondary particulate matters (PM) and acidic compounds in the atmosphere. These models can treat multiple air quality issues and simulate the consequences of past and future emission scenarios to examine the effectiveness of abatement strategies (Daly and Zannetti 2007). Meteorological models provide important input data of meteorological variables/fields to CTM. These meteorological fields affect the dispersion, chemical reaction rates and formation of secondary air pollutants in the atmosphere. Atmospheric models have different details of processes simulated, and they can run with different grid resolutions and time scales, which in turn require specific input and output data management. In this chapter, we focus on mesoscale meteorological models and the air quality models which are commonly used worldwide to provide scientific information to develop and analyze air quality management (AQM) strategies.

Specifically, this chapter describes the common model types that are available and their typical features. Several case studies of the model applications conducted by the air quality research group at the Asian Institute of Technology (AIT) are provided for with illustrations. The detailed input and output data for PM and O_3 air quality modeling in various domain scales are described in the case studies.

4.1.2. Roles of modeling in air quality management

High levels of air pollution are observed in many developing countries that cause harmful effects on human health and ecosystems (Kim Oanh *et al.* 2013a and references therein). The high emission strength, mainly from human-made activities, and insufficient management capacities are among the important factors leading to the serious pollution situations. Effective AQM requires an in-depth understanding of the causal relationship between the emissions and meteorology on one side, and the resulting air pollution concentrations, deposition and consequent effects on the other side. Air pollution modeling is a technical tool used in the AQM to establish such a quantitative relationship. Particularly, air quality models reveal the deterministic relationship between emissions and concentrations/depositions that can be used to analyze past and future emission scenarios in order to assess the efficacy of various abatement strategies (Daly and Zannetti 2007). Three-dimensional (3D) air quality models are normally driven by 3D mesoscale meteorological models or, in other words, the meteorological models provide required meteorological input data to run the air quality models. Applications of air quality models for AQM have attracted attention among researchers around the world. Especially in Asian developing countries where the air quality is worsening, the applications of air quality models become increasingly popular.

Air quality models can be used for historical simulations (hindcast) and provide comprehensive spatial coverage for air pollution data that are especially useful for the places where the monitoring data coverage is insufficient. The models can be used to simulate the present and future air quality (nowcast and forecast) using the corresponding emissions and meteorological input data. The hindcast simulation can be applied for the investigation of past air pollution episodes, assessment of associated health, environmental and climate effects. The nowcast and forecast, in addition to the aforementioned applications, also provide the current and future air quality information to assess the associated health and ecosystem impacts. Interactions between air quality and climate change can also be investigated using the modeling approach, and this helps to analyze the potential co-benefits (to air quality and climate) resulting from different interventions (Permadi *et al.* 2018 and references therein).

4.1.3. *Existing modeling systems*

4.1.3.1. *Air quality dispersion model*

The air quality dispersion model has been evolving from the simple Gaussian plume models to the complex one-atmosphere models that are commonly used at present. The simple Gaussian plume model was initially applied for estimating the maximum ground-level impact of the plumes and the distance of maximum impact from the source, especially for non-reactive pollutants (Bosanquet 1936). However, the air pollution problem is a complex phenomenon that involves chemical reactions, dispersion and deposition processes at various scales, hence cannot be handled by this type of simple model. More atmospheric processes need to be simulated, especially for the secondary pollutants which are formed in the atmosphere, such as ground-level O_3 and secondary inorganic (such as sulfate and nitrate particles) and organic particles. The model domains need to be enlarged to simulate the large-scale phenomena at regional and global scales. Long-range transport models were then developed following the Lagrangian approach, mainly based in Europe (Rohde 1972). At the urban scale, the first-generation Eulerian photochemical smog models were developed in the United States (Reynolds 1973). These became a basis for the development of new one-atmosphere models, which simulate the changes of pollutant concentrations in the atmosphere at multiple scales. These CTM models have been equipped with chemistry mechanisms with complex reactions and species involved, such as the carbon bond (CB-IV, CB-V), Regional Acid Deposition Model (RADM) and State-wide Air Pollution Research Centre (SAPRC) mechanism (Stockwell *et al.* 1990; Carter 2000). The inclusion of these complex chemistry mechanisms added requirements to higher computational resources and the need for big data management.

Presently, the advanced CTMs are most commonly used. They are believed to be the most powerful to involve the least restrictive assumptions, and to be the most computationally intensive. The CTM development has been mainly initiated in the United States, but similar efforts have been conducted in other regions lately. A summary of commonly applied photochemical smog models is presented in Table 4.1. In the United States, the 3D variable-grid Urban Air shed Model (UAM-V) was developed and maintained by the System Applications International (SAI), which was formerly the most widely applied photochemical air quality model. Later on, more advance models have been developed, such as the Models-3/Community Multi-scale Air Quality (CMAQ) and the Comprehensive Air Quality Model with extensions (CAMx), which are well maintained and updated by the community. The above-mentioned models belong to the Eulerian photochemical dispersion model category that allows a "one-atmosphere" assessment of gaseous and particulate air pollution at different scales ranging from sub-urban to continental. These models simulate the emissions, dispersion, chemical reactions and removal of pollutants in the troposphere on a system of nested 3D grids.

Model		Full name	Model type	Chemistry mechanisms	Grid size and features	Website
US-based models	CAMx	Comprehensive Air Quality Model with Extensions	Eulerian, multiscale, two-way nested, multilayer	CB-IV, RADM2, SAPRC, CB-V	4–36 km	http://www.camx.com/home.aspx
US-based models	MODEL-3/ CMAQ	Models-3/Community Multi-Scale Air Quality	Eulerian, multiscale, two-way nested, multilayer	CB-IV, RADM2, SAPRC, CB-V	4–36 km	https://www.cmascenter.org/cmaq/
US-based models	GEOS-Chem		3D chemical transport model (CTM)	FlexChem; GEOS-Chem Chemical Mechanism	Global and regional scale, 0.25°–5°	http://acmg.seas.harvard.edu/geos/
US-based models	WRF-Chem	Weather Research and Forecasting (WRF) model coupled with Chemistry	Eulerian, multiscale, two-way nested, multilayer	CB-IV, CB-V, RADM2, SAPRC99	1–100 km	https://ruc.noaa.gov/wrf/wrf-chem/
European-based models	CHIMERE		Eulerian, multiscale, one-way nested, multilayer	MELCHIOR	2–100 km	www.lmd.polytechnique.fr/chimere/

Model	Full name	Model type	Chemistry mechanisms	Grid size and features	Website
MATCH	Multiple-Scale Atmospheric Transport and Chemistry Model	Eulerian, multiscale, one-way nested, multilayer	EMEP (Simpson 1993)	2–100 km	https://www.smhi.se/en/research/research-departments/air-quality/match-transport-and-chemistry-model-1.6831
EURAD	European Air Pollution Dispersion	Eulerian, multilayer, nested grid, one-way nested	RADM2, RACM	Variable grid (about 80 km)	http://www.uni-koeln.de/math-nat-fak/geomet/eurad/index_e.html?/math-nat-fak/geomet/eurad/modell/eurad_descr_e.html
SPRINTARS **Japanese-based model**	Spectral Radiation-Transport Model for Aerosol Species	Eulerian with aerosol module	Gas phase – aerosol interaction (Takemura et al. 2000)	30–100 km	https://sprintars.riam.kyushu-u.ac.jp/indexe.html

Table 4.1. Commonly applied air quality dispersion models (modified from Kim Oanh and Permadi 2009)

Several CTMs have also been developed in Europe and applied worldwide. CHIMERE is a 3D multi-scale Eulerian model, which is applied for real-time forecasts and long-term simulations (http://www.lmd.polytechnique.fr/chimere/). It consists of a European-scale model with a horizontal resolution of 0.5° × 0.5° and different regional models (Schmidt et al. 2001). The Multiscale Atmospheric Transport and Chemistry Model (MATCH), another European model, is a 3D one-way nesting Eulerian model that can be configured for different geographical areas with different resolutions. The model is driven by meteorological input data taken from operational numerical weather prediction models, such as the High-Resolution Limited Area Model (HIRLAM) or the European Centre for Medium-Range Weather Forecasts (ECMWF), or objective analyses such as Mesoscale Analysis (MESAN) or from combinations of these. The Spectral Radiation-Transport Model for Aerosol Species (SPRINTARS) is a global CTM developed in Japan which is mainly used to simulate aerosol concentrations over different scales (Table 4.1).

Beside the models listed in Table 4.1, other models have been developed by various projects, such as MOZART (Model for OZone and Related chemical Tracers), LOTOS (Long-Term Ozone Simulation) or REM3 (Regional Eulerian Model with three different chemistry schemes), which also gained applications in several studies. These and other models being further developed may gain popular applications in the future.

4.1.3.2. Mesoscale meteorological model

Several mesoscale meteorological models exist. Among the first to be mentioned are the Systems Applications International Meteorological Model (SAIMM), which used a terrain-following vertical coordinate system with variable vertical grid spacing and the 4D data assimilation (SAI 1995), the Fifth-Generation Pennsylvania State University/National Centre for Atmospheric Research (PSU/NCAR) Mesoscale Meteorological Model (MM5) (http://www.mmm.ucar.edu/mm5/) and the ECMWF model. More recently, the community support for MM5 has been diverted to a new model, namely the Weather Research Forecast (WRF) meteorological model (http://www.wrf-model.org/).

Key input data for those mesoscale meteorological models can be derived from local meteorological observations (e.g. SAIMM) or from National Centres for Environmental Prediction (NCEP) final (FNL) (global NCEP FNL) and reanalysis data (e.g. MM5 and WRF). The most recent models used lateral boundaries and initial meteorological conditions taken from the NCEP FNL global analyses that are available at 1° × 1° grid resolution for every six hours (http://rda.ucar.edu/datasets /ds083.2/). Each model is normally equipped with a module to process the geographical input data (i.e. land use, vegetation index, soil type, albedo, etc.) which can be obtained from the global dataset. Physics options are provided in the models to represent physical processes that occurred in the atmosphere: microphysics, land-surface scheme, Rapid Radiative Transfer Model (RRTM), planetary boundary layer (PBL) parameterization scheme and convection scheme. These schemes should be scrutinized to select the most suitable for a specific region of interest (Jankov *et al.* 2005; Osuri *et al.* 2012).

4.2. Model architecture of chemistry transport model

A more detailed description on structure, architecture and data management is provided in this section for the chemistry transport model (CTM) with the mesoscale meteorological modeling considered as a supporting tool to provide meteorological input data for CTM operations.

4.2.1. *Conceptual framework and structure*

CTMs require input data including emissions, topography and meteorology that determine the processes of formation of atmospheric pollutants and their accumulation in a domain. Two main types of CTMs exist, namely the Eulerian and Lagrangian. However, most of the currently used models belong to the Eulerian model type, which uses a fixed reference/observer with respect to the earth and calculates the pollutant concentration in each cell by using equation [4.1]:

$$\begin{array}{|c|}\hline \text{Change C with}\\ \text{time in a cell}\\\hline\end{array} = \begin{array}{|c|}\hline \text{Advection by}\\ \text{average motion}\\\hline\end{array} + \begin{array}{|c|}\hline \text{Turbulent}\\ \text{diffusion}\\\hline\end{array} + \begin{array}{|c|}\hline \text{Molecular}\\ \text{diffusion}\\\hline\end{array} + \begin{array}{|c|}\hline \text{Source/sink}\\ \text{(E + R + D)}\\\hline\end{array} \qquad [4.1]$$

where "Change C" is the change of the average level of an air pollutant over the time period ΔT, and this is defined as the sum of several processes involving the pollutants listed on the right-hand side of equation [4.1], for example advection described by the net amount of pollutants carried in and out by the 3D wind field, turbulent diffusion caused by 3D wind fluctuations, molecular diffusion and emission source/sink parameters (E – emission, D – deposition, R – reactions). All these processes are considered in every grid cell (differential control volume). Note that in the atmosphere, the molecular diffusion is considered negligible as it is several orders of magnitude smaller than the turbulence diffusion. The atmospheric turbulent diffusion of the pollutants through the control volume is caused by wind fluctuations in x, y and z directions respectively. More details of each term are provided in Kim Oanh and Permadi (2009).

Equation [4.1] is then expressed in a mass continuity differential equation [4.2] that relates the changes in the pollutant concentration with time due to dispersion (i.e. advection and turbulent diffusion), chemical reactions, deposition and emissions.

$$\frac{\partial f}{\partial t} + \nabla(uf) = \nabla(k\nabla f) + P - L \qquad [4.2]$$

where f is the vector containing concentrations of all species in every grid, u is the 3D wind vector, k is the eddy diffusivity, P is the formation due to chemical reactions and emissions, and L is the decay due to deposition and chemical reactions.

The CTMs attempt to solve equation [4.2], but different models have their own software architecture to solve the numerical equations. The general structures of CHIMERE and CAMx are given as examples in Figure 4.1.

Overall, each CTM consists of at least five major modules: emission, meteorology, boundary and initial condition, geographical data and chemistry mechanisms. CAMx has a core model, which is supported by the pre-processors interface that processes the output of the five major modules before getting into the core process. CMAQ, another USEPA model, has a similar structure to CAMx but with an additional emission processing module of SMOKE.

In CHIMERE, the whole system is driven by the top calling script *chimere.sh*, which reads parameters of the simulation, links all necessary files into a temporary directory where all programs are executed, compiles all necessary code, runs the three dynamic pre-processors (meteorology, emission and boundary conditions) and runs the model itself. It has the following sub-directories:

– *Chempreps*: data files for gas, aerosols and chemistry;

– *Domain*: set coordinates of the domain;

– *src/*: source code of CHIMERE;

– *Util/*: some utility programs.

One important feature in CTM is the chemistry mechanism. Many models now have several choices of chemistry mechanisms incorporated. CTM ideally requires a numerical simulation of all involved chemical reactions, but this would be practically impossible due to a huge number of reactions involved. To avoid excessive simulation time and cost, several chemistry mechanisms have been developed which commonly use condensed computationally affordable kinetic schemes. Accordingly, the chemistry mechanism can use surrogate species where a few volatile organic compounds (VOCs) are selected as the representative of the respective VOC class, or lumped molecule where the VOC from the same class are lumped together and a hypothetical species is then defined to represent the entire class. An example of the surrogate species type is the SAPRC mechanism (Byun and Ching 1999), while an example of lumped molecule type is the RADM version 2 (RADM-2) (Stockwell *et al.* 1990). The most popular mechanism is the lumped structure in which the VOC classification is based on their hydrocarbon (HC) chemical bonds and reactivity, for example CB Mechanism versions 4 and 5 (CB-IV and CB-V respectively) (Dodge 2000). CAMx, WRF/Chem and CMAQ have all the mentioned mechanisms incorporated. However, the CHIMERE model has its own chemistry mechanism, namely the MELCHIOR mechanism (Middleton *et al.* 1990), which consists of 33 species including trace gases and aerosol.

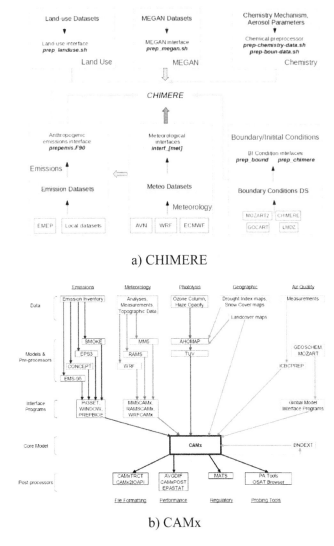

Figure 4.1. *General model structures of CTMs: (a) CHIMERE (www.lmd.polytechnique .fr/chimere/) and (b) CAMx (http://www.camx.com/home.aspx). For a color version of this figure, see www.iste.co.uk/laffly/torus3.zip*

4.2.2. *Data flow and processing*

Figure 4.2 presents the main framework on how the data flow in most of the CTMs.

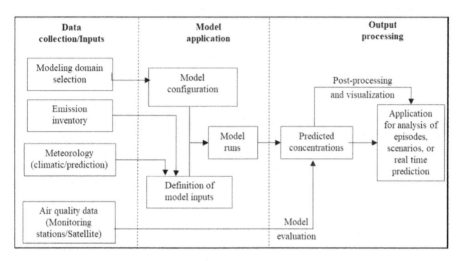

Figure 4.2. *Framework of air quality dispersion model application with data flows (adapted from Kim Oanh and Permadi 2009)*

4.2.2.1. *Input/output (I/O)*

CTMs require 3D meteorological fields, which are supplied by a meteorological model (e.g. MM5, WRF, etc., as described above), and include wind speed and direction, temperature, pressure, water vapor, cloud cover, rainfall and vertical diffusivity. Advection and diffusion processes in the atmosphere are largely affected by the meteorological fields. These meteorological fields further interact with the chemistry mechanisms to treat sources and sinks in the main module of CTMs. Thus, there is a transfer of big 3D meteorological input data, and it is normally managed using a CTM-meteorological module. For example, CMAQ uses a meteorology chemistry interface processor (MCIP), while CAMx uses a MM5-CAMx or WRF-CAMx module as an interface program to handle various meteorological parameters and to only screen the necessary ones to be used for further calculations. These interface programs work in an "offline" mode, which means that 3D meteorological parameters need to be prescribed before transferring the data to be processed by the main module of CTMs. The stand-alone simulation by the mesoscale meteorological models is used in this case. The advantage is that the meteorological data can be evaluated prior to the CTM run so that necessary improvements can be done to reduce potential bias caused by the meteorological input. However, this creates a disadvantage involving massive data transfer, which in turn would increase computational power and time for processing.

A recent CTM model of WRF/Chem can generate meteorological fields simultaneously with the simulation of the chemistry; hence, the total simulation time can be reduced. However, this "online" mode could not isolate potential bias caused by meteorological input parameters alone, but rather the results of simulation are the interaction between the meteorology and chemistry. The later application is however useful to study the interaction of air pollution and climate change, for example.

Other required input data include emission, boundary and initial conditions of air quality, land use and albedo, O_3 column and photolysis rate. Each mentioned dataset should be pre-treated by a stand-alone module, and often users need to develop their own program to prepare emission input data while others are provided in the model source code repository. Model-ready input data should be stored in the provided folders when running the main process, which will call all the data from the respective pathway.

The typical output of the CTM is 3D time-varying average concentration files for user-selected species for surface layer and all other layers of the master grid file and fine grid file (if nesting is applied). An instantaneous concentration file is also generated, for example the output of the last two hours of simulation for model restart. The *I/O* file types are model-specific, i.e. CAMx requires binary input and produces binary output, while CMAQ requires *netcdf* and binary input and produces binary output. CHIMERE uses a *homogen* data format in *netcdf* that requires a specific tool for visualization and manipulation. The common tools are CHIMPLOT for visualization and NCO/CDO for *netcdf* data processing. The Fortran program is commonly used to process the binary output from CAMx and CMAQ.

4.2.2.2. *Main process*

The main processing of CTM can only be done after all the input data are ready in the provided places (mainly located in a working folder). A "*run*" folder contains a job script that will compile the executable file and call the data prepared earlier in the working folder. Model configuration such as domain definition (vertical and horizontal), time for simulation and atmospheric mechanisms should be declared in this job script. The pathway for *I/O* should also be defined in this file.

The main process simulates the codes that are compiled, including dynamical, physical and chemical processes of the model represented by equation [4.2]. There is considerable time required to process input data, computation, as well as to write the output to the output file. However, 85–95% of the total time is required to finish the computational tasks while others are considered to be minor. Depending on the model configuration and computer architecture, one model can perform better than others. To illustrate this, here is an example: a recent version of CHIMERE requires a total simulation time of seven hours to simulate 10 days of air quality in the Southeast Asia (SEA) domain (30 km × 30 km) with a total number of grids of almost 40,000 using an HPC with 32 processors in an application at AIT, Thailand (Permadi *et al.* 2018). CHIMERE processes biogenic emissions online using the global land-cover and meteorological data; hence, more time is required. For a smaller domain, a metropolitan city in SEA, with 400 grids, CAMx required 4 hours for 30 days air quality simulation using the cluster computing with 8 processors available at AIT (Ha Chi 2018). Note that for the CAMx case, all emission data need to be *a priori* prepared and no emission calculation is incorporated in the main process.

4.3. Output data processing

4.3.1. *Output data processing*

As mentioned above, the output format of CTMs varies depending on the model. Therefore, the output data need to be processed/manipulated for various purposes such as visualization, performance evaluation or other analyses such as trend, status and emission scenarios. For example, CAMx and CMAQ generate output files with the binary format that cannot be directly extracted. Therefore, to manipulate the file, a Fortran program can be prepared to convert the file to a text file. The most common tool to visualize the binary output is the open-source tool of the Package for Analysis and Visualization of Environmental data (PAVE) or the Visualization Environment for Rich Data Interpretation (VERDI). However, the support for PAVE was stopped in 2008 and the community continues the online support for VERDI. The software is also capable of converting the binary files to the text file directly. Note that the software has size bandwidth, which means the too large files should be split into several smaller files. The data transfer is also required for this process; hence, it may take time and spaces. CHIMERE and WRF/Chem generate output files in *netcdf* format that are easier to view since there are some readily available software to visualize this file format, such as NCVIEW or NCAR Command Language (NCL). There are also some ready package tools to manipulate/process this file format, such as *netcdf* operators (NCO) or climate data operator (CDO), which can process the data directly.

By using these tools, the output data which are normally generated in a large size (hundreds of megabytes to a maximum of two gigabytes) can be handled and used for various data analyses and presentation. However, this process requires data transfer and additional spaces are required to store the intermediate and output files that can be double in size. It is worth mentioning that the whole process deals with big datasets and thus needs to be well managed. For example, if the data are to be publicized for public awareness of air quality forecast during a forest fire event, they may need to be transferred to a mobile application. Hence, the data should first be transferred to Internet of Things (IOT) format. To manage this, CC is a promising interface which can also deal with big data management. The above-mentioned post-processing tools should be prerequisitely used, for example, to enable data streaming in a cloud-compatible environment which in turn can be publicized.

4.3.2. Model performance evaluation

Model performance evaluation is normally done using both statistical and graphical methods to assess the modeled pollutant concentrations against the observed concentrations. Model performance evaluation is a must step which assesses if the model is adequately representing the real situation and analyzes the accuracy of the prepared input data (emission and meteorological fields). The air quality model performance can be statistically evaluated using a set of criteria, for example the USEPA (1991) guidelines for ground-level O_3 (Table 4.2) and that proposed by Boylan and Russell (2006) for PM (Table 4.3). Besides the ground-level observations, the satellite measurements such as the aerosol optical depth (for PM) are also useful for the model performance evaluation.

Statistical measure	Equation	Suggested criteria
Mean normalized bias (MNB)	$MNB = \dfrac{1}{n}\sum_1^n \left[\dfrac{(C_p - C_o)}{C_o} \right]$	±15%
Mean normalized error (MNE)	$MNE = \dfrac{1}{n}\sum_1^n \left[\dfrac{|C_p - C_o|}{C_o} \right]$	35%
Unpaired peak prediction accuracy (UPA)	$\dfrac{C_{p\,max} - C_{o\,max}}{C_{o\,max}}$	±20%

NOTE.– n is the number of monitoring stations or number of measurement times. C_o is the observed values. C_p is the predicted value at monitoring station i for hour t. $C_{o\,max}$ is the maximum hourly observed concentration over all hours or all monitoring stations. $C_{p\,max}$ is the maximum hourly predicted concentration over all hours or all surface grid squares.

Table 4.2. *USEPA (1991) recommended statistical measures for air quality model for O_3*

Parameters	Formula	Suggested criteria
Mean fractional bias (MFB)	$$MFB = \frac{1}{N}\sum_{i=1}^{N}\left[\frac{(M_i - O_i)}{(M_i/2 + O_i)}\right] \times 100\%$$	$\leq \pm30\%$ (goal) $\leq \pm60\%$ (criteria)
Mean fractional error (MFE)	$$MFE = \frac{1}{N}\sum_{i=1}^{N}\left[\frac{|M_i - O_i|}{(M_i/2 + O_i)}\right] \times 100\%$$	$\leq 50\%$ (goal) $\leq 75\%$ (criteria)

NOTE.– O is the observation value, M is the model prediction value and N is the number of observations.

Table 4.3. *Evaluation criteria for model performance for PM air quality simulation (Boylan and Russell 2006)*

Using a separate dedicated tool for the statistical analyses mentioned above would be resourceful in terms of data transfer and processing. For example, using simple Microsoft EXCEL or IBM SPSS® would require a huge data transfer, especially to work on two different operating systems (e.g. from Linux to Windows). It would be useful to have cloud-based statistical processing to reduce data transfer and time for analysis.

4.4. Potential applications of cloud computing in atmospheric modeling

4.4.1. *Current status of cloud computing applications in atmospheric modeling*

CC is defined as a computing environment where the computing needs of one party can be outsourced to another party and when the computing power is needed, it can be accessed via the Internet (Jadeja and Modi 2012). Thanks to the large-scale proliferation of the Internet around the world, applications can now be delivered as services over the website, and this reduces the overall cost.

Atmospheric models generally require a large amount of central processing unit (CPU) power, which increases drastically for a big geographical domain with a high resolution (Goga *et al.* 2017). A large number of computing resources are required to satisfy the computational demand through infrastructures such as clusters in grid or cloud. The traditional solution using a high-performance computing (HPC) system requires a considerable cost to build the cluster infrastructure, and its core module should be installed and operated inside the HPC. Recently, all major information technology (IT) players (Amazon, Google, Microsoft, IBM, etc.) have provided public cloud service for users to use their powerful computing resources which is known as Infrastructure as a Service (IaaS). In addition, the most common service recently is pay-as-you-go CC service tailored for atmospheric models including mesoscale meteorological and air quality models, such as WRF and WRF/Chem (http://www.sabalcore.com/vertical-markets/weather-environment/wrf/) and other air quality models (e.g. CALPUFF, AERMOD and CMAQ). These are known as Software as a Service (SaaS). Lakes Environment Co. Ltd. developed the Air Quality Management Information System (AQMIS Cloud), which provides a state-of-the-science cloud solution for emissions management and air quality modeling (https://www.weblakes.com/products/aqmis/index.html). This allows users to manage emissions from thousands of sources, run models, issue permits, forecast air quality impacts and much more, all through the Internet.

CC solution has not been widely applied in developing countries, especially regarding the air quality modeling purposes. Perhaps the public cloud-based services mentioned above do not always provide enough simplicity in the practical applications and some cost is still applied. It is generally known that air quality models are complex, especially CTMs, and the scientific communities in the developing countries still prefer the more traditional HPC solution. IaaS solution can be opted as an appropriate alternative solution to the HPC, and the CC-based solution for air quality modeling is expected to be more widely applied in the future.

4.4.2. Potential applications of cloud computing in air quality modeling

From the preceding content of this chapter, it is shown that different types of air quality models often require, to a certain extent, different input data, and generate different output datasets. The purposes of the model applications also determine the types of input data required and the types of output data generated. In addition, the data transfer and data management would be model-type-specific. With the increase in the spatial scale, coupled with more refined grid resolution, and an increase in the temporal scales of model applications, the size of input data and model generated output datasets also increases.

In summary, the following parts of the whole modeling process involve the big data management and the potential CC roles:

– input: meteorological pre-processors, geographical static data processing and emission processing. These are processed separately and generate big data; hence, CC could play an important role;

– main process: compilation of input data, calculation and output data writing. The best solution for this remains with HPC, but future development of HPC in cloud can be a breakthrough;

– output: processing (analysis) and storage. A cloud-based solution would be appropriate for both the processing and the storage of the output.

4.5. Case studies of air pollution modeling in Southeast Asia

Selected case studies of air pollution modeling applications in SEA conducted at AIT are presented in this section to highlight the modeling approach for understanding air pollution problems in the region. The case studies also highlight the difference in geographical and time scale, the purpose of model applications and the size of the input and output datasets associated.

4.5.1. Modeling air quality in Vietnam

4.5.1.1. Domain configuration and input data

Vietnam, located on the Indochinese Peninsula, is bordered by China, Laos and Cambodia to the north, northwest and southwest respectively. On the east side, Vietnam is bordered by the East Sea. The country is influenced by its tropical monsoon climate, with typical Southwest (SW) monsoon season prevalent from May to October and Northeast (NE) monsoon season from November to April. The CTM modeling system of WRF/CAMx was applied for the simulation of O_3 and PM air quality in Vietnam for one month of August to represent the rainy season and one month of December to represent the dry season of 2010. The CAMx coarse domain covered Vietnam with a resolution of 12 km × 12 km and a fine domain of the Hanoi Metropolitan Region (HMR) (4 km × 4 km) for PM and the Eastern region of Southern of Vietnam (ERS) surrounding Ho Chi Minh City (HCMC) for O_3 air quality, as presented in Figure 4.3. The emission inventory (EI) database for the year 2010 was prepared for major emission anthropogenic sources (on-road mobile, industry, thermal power plants, residential cooking, biomass open burning and gasoline stations) and biogenic (natural) sources (Huy 2015; Huy and Kim Oanh 2017). Meteorological data at the major airports and meteorological stations in Vietnam and the synoptic weather charts were used to evaluate the WRF performance. Available air quality monitoring data (PM and O_3) in Vietnam were used to evaluate performance of the CAMx/WRF modeling system. Both time series and spatial distribution patterns of the pollutants were considered for the model performance evaluation.

The WRF simulations were done for three domains as shown in Figure 4.3. The vertical structure of the WRF domain consisted of 30 sigma layers, ranging from the ground surface level to the top of 15.797 km. The CAMx domain consisted of 15 vertical layers matching the layer interface of WRF layers. The emission data of 10 different air pollutants were aggregated appropriately to the model species using the CB-IV (Fu *et al.* 2004). The profile speciation for VOC and PM was applied to speciate the original 10 species into 30 species. Then, they were also segregated spatially into 81 × 162 grids (for the CAMx coarse domain of Vietnam), and temporally first into the monthly profile for the two simulated months and then hourly for the model input. This results in a dataset of 23 million points of daily emission data input for the coarse domain alone for two months. Likewise, the processing and computing had to deal with more than 1.3 and 5.9 million of emission data points daily for the fine domain of the HMR and ERS respectively. The models were run on a PC/Linux platform installed at AIT. The initial and boundary conditions for CAMx domain were extracted from the study of Permadi (2013) and Permadi *et al.* (2018) who simulated air quality for the entire SEA domain using CHIMERE/WRF.

The WRF-CAMx output data included hourly values of 12 PM species (e.g. fine and coarse fractions: CCRS, CPRM, FPRM; sulfate-PSO_4; nitrate-PNO_3, ammonium-PNH_4; primary organic aerosol-POA; secondary organic aerosol-SOA_1-SOA_5) and one O_3 to analyze the PM and O_3 concentrations respectively. To get the hourly average concentrations of PM and O_3, more than 245, 14.1 and 61.8 million of hourly data points for Vietnam, HMR and ERS domains respectively were processed for two months. Besides the 12 PM species and one O_3 output, there were 19 other species that made a total of 32 species of the model output dataset. In total, there were more than 604 million hourly data points for the coarse domain, and 34.7 and 152.2 million for the HMR and ERS domain respectively for the two-month simulation.

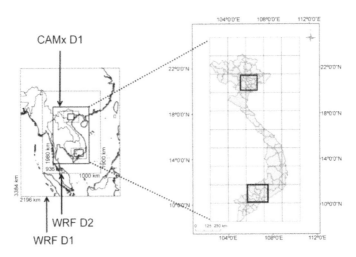

Figure 4.3. *The modeling domain, Vietnam (12 km grid size), Hanoi Metropolitan Region (4 km grid size) and Eastern Region of Southern Vietnam (4 km grid size) (Huy 2015). For a color version of this figure, see www.iste.co.uk/laffly/torus3.zip*

4.5.1.2. Result highlights

Monthly gridded average ground-level O_3 concentrations in the Vietnam domain for August and December 2010 were analyzed, which showed lower O_3 concentrations in the center of HCMC and Hanoi, and this was attributed to the titration effect by NO freshly emitted from the traffic.

In principle, the precursors of O_3 were transported from urban areas to downwind locations, and when passing the area with rich biogenic emissions such as forest, more O_3 can be formed. Accordingly, in August, high ground-level O_3 concentrations were shown in the downwind regions (north and northeast of HCMC; and north and northwest of Hanoi) due to the dominant SW monsoon during the month. For example, the SW monsoon directed the plume of O_3 in HCMC to the provinces of Binh Duong and Dong Nai.

In December, Vietnam was affected by the NE monsoon. A high concentration of O_3 was also seen downwind of Hanoi (Nam Dinh, Ninh Binh and northern central coastal regions). The long-range transport of emissions from China would contribute to the high O_3 levels in northern Vietnam. The O_3 plume from HCMC moved south-westerly and showed high concentrations at Ben Tre, Tra Vinh and south coastal regions. As a way of example, the spatial distribution of O_3 in the Eastern region of Southern Vietnam is presented in Figure 4.4.

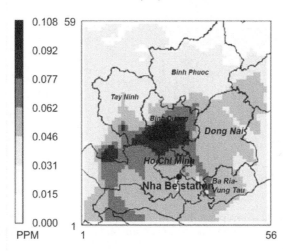

Ozone concentration (ppm)

October, 23, 2010 at 15:00 LST

Figure 4.4. Simulated hourly ground-level O_3 in the ERS domain, Vietnam (Danh et al. 2016) at 15:00 LST on October 23, 2010

The highest hourly concentrations of O_3 in the domain of Vietnam were 143 ppb in August and 162 ppb in December, i.e. they exceeded the National Ambient Air Quality Standard (NAAQS) of one-hour average 100 ppb for O_3. The eight-hour O_3 had the maximum, in August, of 97 ppb (Hanoi), and in December, of 122 ppb (HCMC), both exceeding the eight-hour standard for O_3 of 60 ppb (MONRE 2013). High emissions from local sources such as traffic, open burning and industry in these large urban areas would significantly influence the O_3 concentrations.

Monthly average concentrations of $PM_{2.5}$ (fine particles with an aerodynamic diameter less than 2.5 µm) in both months are presented in Figure 4.5. High levels of PM occurred in the surrounding areas of Hanoi and HCMC respectively that show the influence of the intensive emissions from transportation, industrial and construction activities and the biomass open burning (rice straw field burning) in the Red River and Mekong River Deltas. Cooking activities from urban regions with high population density also considerably contributed to the PM pollution (Huy 2015). As expected, higher PM levels were simulated in the dry month of December as compared to those in the rainy month of August. The PM plumes in August and December were shown to follow the main wind directions of the months.

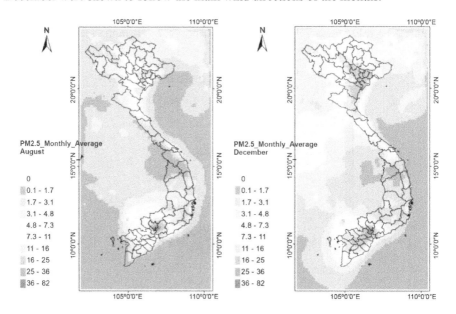

Figure 4.5. *Monthly average of $PM_{2.5}$ for August and December in Vietnam by model (Huy 2015). For a color version of this figure, see www.iste.co.uk/laffly/torus3.zip*

4.5.1.3. Model evaluation

Only fragmented observation data were available in Vietnam for the model performance evaluations. The model performance in ozone simulation was done using the time series and scatter plot of the modeled versus observed O_3 concentrations in August and December available at three stations (Da Nang, Nha Be in HCMC and Nguyen Van Cu in Hanoi) in August and two stations (Nha Be and Nguyen Van Cu) in December. The analysis showed that the model underestimated O_3 concentration at Da Nang and Nha Be stations (both months) and overestimated O_3 concentration at Nguyen Van Cu station (a traffic site). The statistical criteria were examined for these stations using the USEPA-suggested parameters of MNB, MNE and UPA, but only some criteria were satisfied, for example MNB at Nha Be and UPA at Nguyen Van Cu in August, while in December none was satisfied. More observation data were still required for in-depth model performance evaluation.

For PM, a statistical analysis of WRF/CAMx model performance for August and December was conducted, which showed that both MFB and MFE were satisfactorily met for the Da Nang station, but none was met for Nha Be and Nguyen Van Cu stations. It is further noted that the modeled values represent the grid-based average while the monitoring data are point-based; therefore, the differences are expected. Lack of the spatially distributed observed data is a key obstacle to evaluate the model performance for both O_3 and PM. There are also uncertainties in observed data and model results that lead to the discrepancy.

4.5.2. Modeling air quality in the Bangkok Metropolitan Region

4.5.2.1. Domain configuration and input data

The Bangkok Metropolitan Region (BMR) administratively includes Bangkok, the capital city of Thailand, and its five surrounding provinces – Samut Prakan, Nonthaburi, Pathum Thani, Nakhon Pathom and Samut Sakhon. The BMR covers an area of about 7,762 km^2. The WRF-CAMx was used to simulate PM and O_3 air quality in the BMR. Two-way nesting was applied to simulate the interaction between the inner domain and the outer domain. The outer domain thus covered the central part of Thailand and some parts of the Gulf of Thailand (Figure 4.6) and was named as the CENTHAI domain. It had an area of 300×300 km^2 and consisted of 50×50 horizontal grid cells at a 6 km grid resolution. The inner BMR domain had an area of 100×70 km^2 and consisted of 50×35 grid cells at 2 km grid resolution.

Meteorological input data were generated by the WRF simulation at AIT using the Computing on Kepler Architectures (COKA) cluster, a multicore high HPC system installed at the University of Ferrara, Italy, as detailed in Chapter 18 of

Volume 1. The emissions data were prepared from the updated EI for key anthropogenic sources and a natural (biogenic) emission source in the inner BMR domain for 2016. Similar to the case of the simulation for the Vietnam domain above, there were 30 species in the model emission input file to CAMx. The emission data were segregated spatially into 50×35 grid cells of the BMR domain and temporally monthly and then hourly for the simulation period of one year (2016). The emission dataset thus consisted of about 15 million data points (24 hours $\times$ 12 months $\times$ 30 species $\times$ 50×35 grid cells). The WRF-CAMx output data included hourly values of 12 PM species and O_3, i.e. similar to the case of the Vietnam domain above. To get the daily average concentration of PM and O_3, about 500,000 data points (24 hours $\times$ 13 species $\times$ 35 $\times$ 50 grid cells) needed to be processed; hence, about 16 and 200 million data points were used to compute the monthly and annual average concentration respectively.

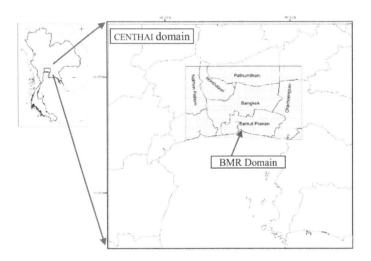

Figure 4.6. *Location and coverage of CENTHAI and the BMR domain*

4.5.2.2. *Result highlights*

The simulated results for PM by WRF-CAMx for 2016, extracted for every month for $PM_{2.5}$ and PM_{10} (particles with an aerodynamic diameter less than 10 μm), showed higher levels in the dry season and lower levels in the wet season, i.e. opposite to the precipitation trend. The monthly average $PM_{2.5}$ in the domain was 11 μg/m^3 in March, 7 μg/m^3 in August and 22 μg/m^3 in November. Spatially, the higher values were found in the center of Bangkok city every month, for example 7–24 μg/m^3 in August and 20–51 μg/m^3 in November. The dispersion plume of $PM_{2.5}$ was influenced by the wind field that in turn reflected the monsoon regime (Figure 4.7).

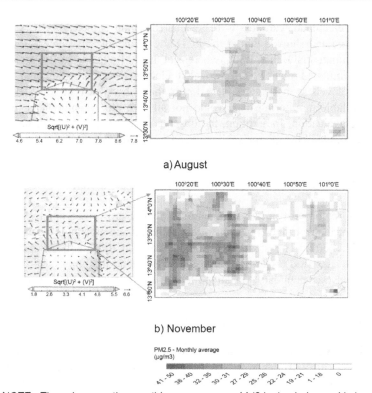

a) August

b) November

PM2.5 - Monthly average
(µg/m3)

NOTE.–The values are the monthly average per grid (2 km); wind speed is in m/s

Figure 4.7. *Monthly wind fields and spatial distribution of grid average PM$_{2.5}$ (Ha Chi 2018). For a color version of this figure, see www.iste.co.uk/laffly/torus3.zip*

4.5.2.3. Model performance evaluation

The WRF-CAMx performance was evaluated using the statistical criteria. The modeled PM$_{2.5}$ and PM$_{10}$ concentrations of hourly (1 hour), daily (24 hour) average, and weekly averages were compared with the observed data collected from the Pollution Control Department (PCD) stations and from a research project on "A Study on Urban Air Pollution Improvement in Asia" conducted by AIT in collaboration with the Japan International Cooperation Agency (JICA) and the Asia Pacific Clean Air Partnership (APCAP) of Japan.

The model performance was shown to be better for some stations than others. The evaluation for hourly PM showed that all the criteria were satisfied for station ST59 (representing the general area of the BMR) for both PM$_{2.5}$ and PM$_{10}$, while for station ST27 (industrial estate), the MFB and MFE for PM$_{10}$ were satisfactorily met. The weekly simulated PM$_{2.5}$ and compositions (nitrate-PNO$_3$, sulfate-PSO$_4$, organic carbon and elemental carbon) were evaluated against the AIT-JICA project monitoring data and showed that at the PCD site (Bangkok city center), the model can better simulate PNO_3 than PSO_4, whereas at the AIT site (sub-urban area), PSO_4 was better simulated than PNO_3. Modeled elemental carbon (EC) and organic carbon (OC) levels in both sites were lower than observed (Ha Chi 2018). The sparsely available monitoring data would not allow a more comprehensive model performance evaluation. In addition, the observed data are point-based, hence may not be fully comparable with the grid-averaged modeled values.

4.5.3. Modeling air quality in the Southeast Asia domain

SEA is a region with a large population and fast-growing economy and is an important contributor to the emissions of air pollution and greenhouse gases in Asia (Zhang *et al.* 2009). The simulation domain covered the Southeast Asia (SEA) region in this case study with the purpose to understand the impacts of emissions, both local and transboundary, on air pollution levels, climate forcing and human health.

4.5.3.1. Configuration and input data

CHIMERE was used to simulate 3D aerosol concentrations in the domain using the meteorological fields generated by the WRF model. The domain extended from southern China (24°N, 95°E) to eastern parts of Indonesia (9°S, 137°E) consisting of 169 × 133 grids with eight vertical layers (from 20 to 5,500 m) and a horizontal grid resolution of 0.25° × 0.25° (~30 × 30 km^2). CHIMERE is equipped with the MELCHIOR 2 chemistry mechanism, which consists of about 120 reactions and 40 chemical species. One-year simulation (January 1–December 31, 2007) was performed with a spin-up period of one week prior to the main simulation period. The details of model configuration are given in Permadi *et al.* (2018).

The emissions input was prepared for three countries (Indonesia, Thailand and Cambodia), while for the rest of the domain, the emissions were taken from the available online gridded EI databases (grid size of 0.5°~50 km) compiled by the Centre for Global and Regional Environmental Research (CGRER) (Zhang *et al.* 2009). The hourly speciated emissions of each species were gridded into 0.25° × 0.25° using the Geographic Information System tool. In total, the emission input included 24 hour × 33 species × 169 × 133 (grids) data points. Other model input data included 3D hourly gridded meteorological parameters for the entire one-year simulation period plus 10 spin-up days and the associated gridded geographical data of the domain, i.e. land cover, albedo, etc., as detailed in Permadi *et al.* (2018). The output data included 3D hourly gridded concentrations of 33 chemical species (i.e. trace gases and aerosol) for one year.

4.5.3.2. Result highlights

The hourly concentrations of 33 species (i.e. NO, NO_2, HONO, CO, SO_2, NH_3, HCL, SULF, CH_4, C_2H_6, NC_4H_{10}, C_2H_4, C_3H_6, C_5H_8, APINEN, OXYL, HCHO, CH_3CHO, CH_3COE, CH_3OH, C_2H_5OH, GLYOX, MGLYOX, MVK, TOL, TMB, PPM_big, PPM_coa, PPM_fin, OCAR_fin, BCAR_fin, PNO_3 and H_2SO_4_fin) were produced by the model for each grid of the domain. The data were then extracted and processed. For example, the spatial distributions of the modeled monthly average PM_{10}, $PM_{2.5}$ and black carbon (BC) are presented in Figure 4.8 for January and August 2007.

The highest monthly average concentrations of PM_{10} in January and August over the domain were 69 and 58 $\mu g/m^3$ respectively, while the corresponding values of $PM_{2.5}$ were 40 and 37 $\mu g/m^3$. The simulated highest hourly PM_{10} in January and August 2007 were 325 and 245 $\mu g/m^3$ respectively, while the corresponding values of $PM_{2.5}$ were 188 and 150 $\mu g/m^3$. In January, in the Northern Hemisphere, NE monsoon transported pollutants from the source regions to the southwest direction, while in the Southern Hemisphere part (Indonesia), the plume moved to the northeast/east direction. The opposite is seen in August where, in the Southern Hemisphere part of the modeling domain, the plumes of PM moved north-westerly and turned into north-easterly after reaching the equator line. In August, the dry months in the southern domain, the PM_{10} and $PM_{2.5}$ plumes, were shown to reflect the effects of biomass open burning (forest fire and crop residue) emissions in Indonesia that originated in the Riau province (Sumatera Island) and the western and southern parts of the Borneo island, and were seen clearly moving northeast-ward. In January, a dry season month in the northern part of the domain, the plumes of PM_{10} and $PM_{2.5}$ were intensified by biomass open burning in the central and northern areas of Thailand, which were seen moving southwest-ward. The simulated maximum monthly average BC concentration in the domain was somewhat higher in January (8.2 $\mu g/m^3$) as compared to August (7.8 $\mu g/m^3$). The BC plumes were generally seen originating from large cities in the domain that confirms the significant influence of the fossil fuel combustion emission, specifically traffic, and other urban activities for all months of the year. During the dry period, BC plumes from the areas were also seen being intensified by biomass open burning emissions but were not as clearly shown as the PM plumes. This may be because biomass open burning contributed more to organic carbon (OC) than to BC emissions.

4.5.3.3. Model evaluation

The daily (24-hour) modeled PM_{10} concentrations were calculated using the hourly output data, and the results were compared with the 24-hour data gathered from the governmental monitoring networks available in three large cities of SEA (i.e. one station in Kuala Lumpur, two stations in Bangkok and one station in Surabaya). For BC, the 24-hour BC measured by the optical method available at several SEA sites under the AIRPET project (Kim Oanh *et al.* 2013b) was used. The statistical evaluation of PM_{10} showed that in all three cities, the MFB and MFE values for 24-hour PM_{10} and BC satisfactorily met the suggested criteria (Permadi *et al.* 2018). The model system was used to analyze the effects of emission reduction strategies in the key sectors in Indonesia and Thailand on BC levels in 2030 and potential co-benefits on air quality (and health) and climate forcing in SEA region (Permadi *et al.* 2018).

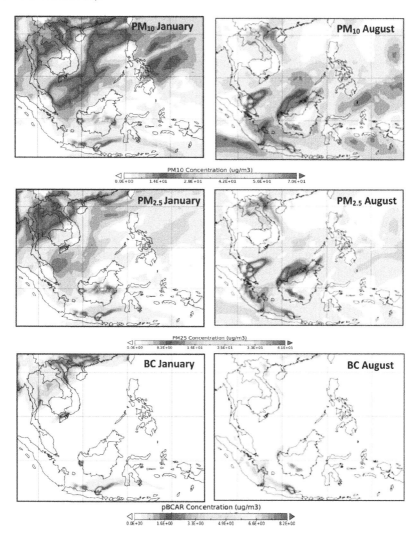

Figure 4.8. *Spatial distribution of monthly average PM_{10}, $PM_{2.5}$ and BC in the selected months, 2007. For a color version of this figure, see www.iste.co.uk/laffly/torus3.zip*

4.6. Summary and conclusion

Atmospheric dispersion modeling is widely used to simulate air quality in various domains. The modeling tool is essential to link the causes (emissions, meteorology) to the effects (air quality and associated effects on health and ecosystems, and climate forcing), hence can be applied to support air quality management activities by various stakeholders, i.e. scientific communities, policy makers and the general public, among others. Many types of atmospheric dispersion modeling systems are available worldwide. Such systems included meteorological models (i.e. MM5, WRF, etc.) that generate meteorological fields to drive the air quality models (i.e. CAMx, CMAQ, GEOS-Chem, CHIMERE, etc.). Several case studies conducted by the AIT air quality research group are presented in this chapter to illustrate the modeling applications and magnitude of input–output data size. These include the urban scale (i.e. BMR Thailand by using WRF/CAMx), the country scale (i.e. Vietnam by using WRF/CAMx) and the regional scale (SEA by using WRF/CHIMERE).

Two important types of input data, i.e. meteorological data and emission data, are required for most of the atmospheric modeling applications. The input data are required for every grid in the domain with a grid size range of 0.10–0.5° for the large regional domain to as small as 2 km or lower for urban and local scale domains. Temporally, the air quality models often require hourly input data for the required pollution species. The number of input species varies with the model system and purpose of the applications; for example, for O_3 and PM, simulations using CTMs normally require more than 20 species, including gases and aerosol. The output datasets normally consist of hourly levels of modeling species for every grid in the domain, not only on the surface layer but also in every vertical layer. This results in the handling and transferring of big datasets where CC could play important roles. The model output quality cannot be better than the input quality; hence, the uncertainty related to meteorology and emission input data should be scrutinized and reduced. Evaluation of the model performance is done both quantitatively and qualitatively to ensure the accuracy of the model output.

Overall, the big datasets of both inputs (meteorology and emissions) and output (simulated air quality) require large storage resources that may be potentially handled by CC. The cloud computing for big dataset management, especially for air quality data has emerged as one of the potential tools for storing, processing and publicizing data in an efficient way.

4.7. References

Bosanquet, C.H. (1936). The spread of smoke and gas from chimneys. *Trans. Faraday Soc.*, 32, 1249.

Boylan, J.W. and Russell, A.G. (2006). PM and light extinction model performance metrics, goals, and criteria for three-dimensional air quality models. *Atmos. Environ.*, 40(26), 4946–4959.

Byun, D.W. and Ching, J.K.S. (1999). Science algorithms of the EPA models-3 community multi-scale air quality (CMAQ) modelling system. *NERL*, Research Triangle Park, North Carolina, USA.

Carter, W.P.L. (2000). Implementation of the SAPRC-99 chemical mechanism into the Models-3 framework. Report, US Environmental Agency, USA.

Daly, A. and Zannetti, P. (2007). Ambient Air Pollution. In *Air Pollution Modelling – An Overview*, Zannetti, P., Al-Ajmi, D., and Al-Rashied, S. (eds). The Arab School for Science and Technology and the EnviroComp Institute, Fremont, CA, USA.

Danh, N.T., Huy, L.N., and Kim Oanh, N.T. (2016). Assessment of rice yield loss due to exposure to ozone pollution in Southern Vietnam. *Sci. Tot. Environ.*, 566–567, 1069–1079.

Dawson, J.P., Racherla, P.N., Lynn, B.H., Adams, P.J., Adams, J., and Pandis, S.N. (2008). Simulating present-day and future air quality as climate changes: Model evaluation, *Atmos. Environ.*, 42, 4551–4566.

Dodge, M.C. (2000). Chemical oxidant mechanisms for air quality modelling: Critical review. *Atmos. Environ.*, 34, 2103–2130.

Emmons, L.K., Walters, S., Hess, P.G., Lamarque, J.F., Pfister, G.G., Fillmore, D., Granier, C., Guenther, A., Kinnison, D., Laepple, T., Orlando, J., Tie, X., Tyndall, G., Wiedinmyer, C., Baughcum, S.L., and Kloster, S. (2010). Description and evaluation of the model for ozone and related chemical tracers, version 4 (MOZART-4). *Geosci. Model Dev.*, 3, 43–67.

Fu, J.S., Jang, C.J., Chen, C., and He, K. (2004). Attachment 8: Project for the MCNC/US: ICAP 2 Project-Task 8 pilot project of national/regional air quality modelling assessment in China (MCNC contract no. 10176.003). Environmental Protection Agency, USA.

Goga, K., Parodi, A., Ruiu, P., and Terzo, O. (2017). Performance analysis of WRF simulations in a public cloud and HPC environment. In *Complex, Intelligent, and Software Intensive Services*, Barolli L., and Olivier T. (eds). Springer, Turin, Italy.

Ha Chi, N.N. (2018). Assessment of particulate matter, surface ozone air quality and associated health burdens in the Bangkok Metropolitan Region using a photochemical grid model. Master Thesis, Asian Institute of Technology, Bangkok, Thailand.

Huy, L.N. (2015). Evaluation of performance of photochemical smog modelling system for air quality management in Vietnam. Master Thesis, Asian Institute of Technology, Bangkok, Thailand.

Huy, L.N. and Kim Oanh, N.T. (2017). Assessment of national emissions of air pollutants and climate forcers from thermal power plants and industrial activities in Vietnam. *Atmos. Pollut. Res.*, 8(3), 503–513.

Jadeja, Y. and Modi, K. (2012). Cloud computing – Concepts, architecture, and challenges. *International Conference on Computing, Electronics and Electrical Technologies*, ICCEET, Tamil Nadu, India.

Jankov, I., Gallus Jr., W.A., Segal, M., Shaw, B., and Koch. S.E. (2005). The impact of different WRF model physical parameterizations and their interactions on warm season MCS rainfall. *Weather Forecast.*, 20(6), 1048.

Kim Oanh, N.T. and Permadi, D.A. (2009). Photochemical smog modelling for ozone air quality management. In *Modelling of Pollutants in Complex Environmental Systems*, vol. I, Hanrahan, G. (ed.). ILM Publications, Hertfordshire, UK.

Kim Oanh, N.T., Permadi, D.A., Zhang, B.N., Huy, T.N.Q., Phuong, N.L., Kanabkaew, T., and Iqbal, A. (2013a). Applications of photochemical smog models for assessment of ozone, particulate matter air quality, and acid deposition in Asian cities. In *Integrated Air Quality Management: Asian Case Studies*, Kim Oanh, N.T. (ed.). CRC Press, Florida, USA.

Kim Oanh, N.T., Pongkiatkul, P., Templonuevo Cruz, M., Nghiem, T.D., Philip, L., Zhuang, G., and Lestari, P. (2013b). Monitoring and source apportionment for particulate matter pollution in six Asian Cities. In *Integrated Air Quality Management: Asian Case Studies*, Kim Oanh, N.T. (ed.). CRC Press, Florida, USA.

Middleton, P., Stockwell, W.R., and Carter, W.P. (1990). Aggregation and analysis of volatile organic compound emissions for regional modelling. *Atmos. Environ.*, 24, 1107–1133.

MONRE (2013). National technical regulation on ambient air quality. Ministry of Natural Resources and Environment, Vietnam [Online]. Available: http://www.monre.gov.vn/ [Accessed 31 May 2018].

Osuri, K.K., Mohanty, U.C., Routray, A., Kulkarni, M.A., and Mohapatra, M. (2012). Customization of WRF-ARW model with physical parameterization schemes for the simulation of tropical cyclones over North Indian Ocean. *Nat. Hazards*, 63, 1337–1359.

Permadi, D.A. (2013). Assessment of efficiency of black carbon emission reduction measures and co-benefit on climate forcing mitigation and air quality improvement in Southeast Asia. PhD Thesis, Asian Institute of Technology, Bangkok, Thailand.

Permadi, D.A., Kim Oanh, N.T., and Vautard, R. (2018). Integrated emission inventory and modelling to assess distribution of particulate matter mass and black carbon composition in Southeast Asia. *Chem. Phys.*, 18, 2725–2747.

Ramanathan, V. and Feng, Y. (2008). Air pollution, greenhouse gases and climate change: Global and regional perspectives. *Atmos. Environ.*, 43, 37–50.

Reynolds, S., Roth, P., and Seinfeld, J. (1973). Mathematical modelling of photochemical air pollution. *Atmos. Environ.*, 7, 1033–1061.

Rohde, H. (1972). A study of the sulphur budget for the atmosphere over northern Europe. *Tellus*, 24, 128.

SAI (1995). User's Guide to the Systems Applications International Mesoscale Model. Systems Applications International, California, USA.

Schmidt, H., Derognat, C., Vautard, R., and Beekmann, M. (2001). A comparison of simulated and observed ozone mixing ratios for the summer of 1998 in Western Europe. *Atmos. Environ.*, 35, 6277–6297.

Schneider, S.H., Krenz, J.H., Glantz, M.H., Salby, L.M., Niiler, P.P., Dickinson, R.E., Aber, J.D., Turco, R.P. (1989). *Climate System Modelling*, Cambridge University Press, London, UK.

Simpson, D. (1993). Photochemical model calculations over Europe for two extended summer periods: 1985 and 1989 model results and comparison with observations. *Atmos. Environ.*, 27A, 912–943.

Stockwell, W.R., Middleton, P., Chang, J.S., and Tang, X. (1990). The second generation regional acid deposition model chemical mechanism for regional air quality modelling. *J. Geophys. Res.*, 95, 16343–16367.

Takemura, T., Okamoto, H., Maruyama, Y., Numaguti, A., Higurashi, A., and Nakajima, T. (2000). Global three-dimensional simulation of aerosol optical thickness distribution of various origins. *J. Geophys. Res.*, 105, 17853–17873.

USEPA (1991). Guideline for the regulatory application of the Urban Airshed Model. Report, United States Environmental Protection Agency, Research Triangle Park, North Carolina, USA.

Zhang, Q., Streets, D.G., Carmichael, G.R., He, K.B., Huo, H., Kannari, A., Klimont, Z., Park, S., Reddy, S., Fu, J.S., Chen, D., Duan, L., Lei, Y., Wang, L.T., and Yao, Z.L. (2009). Asian emissions in 2006 for the NASA INTEX-B mission. *Atmos. Chem. Phys.*, 9, 5131–5153.

5

Particulate Matter Concentration Mapping from Satellite Imagery

5.1. Introduction

Air pollution has become a worldwide environmental issue as a result of the quick pace of industrialization and urbanization, and a lack of comprehensive and effective pollution abatement. According to the Clean Air Initiative Network (Huizenga *et al.* 2004), air pollution levels in many countries, especially in Southeast Asia (SEA), exceed the WHO recommendation or the US Environmental Protection Agency standard. In particular, populous cities in China, India, Thailand and Vietnam have been suffering from some of the highest levels of air pollution in the world (Lelieveld *et al.* 2015). Moreover, emissions from major biomass burning episodes have had negative impacts on air quality, such as from peat, forest and land clearing fires in Indonesia and Malaysia (Mahmud 2013; Gaveau *et al.* 2014; Hayasaka *et al.* 2014; Reddington *et al.* 2014; Vadrevu *et al.* 2014) and crop residue open burning in continental South and Southeast Asia (Streets *et al.* 2003; Yadav *et al.* 2017; Kim Oanh *et al.* 2018; Shi *et al.* 2018).

Aerosols are the solid and liquid particles suspended in the atmosphere. Satellite remote sensing has provided Aerosol Optical Depth (AOD) products which are a measurement of the scattering and absorption of light by atmospheric aerosols. Correlation studies with ground-based measurements have found AOD to be a good proxy for particulate matter ($PM_{2.5}/PM_{10}$) concentration; thus, they have been used to monitor dust pollution from a global to regional scale. Quality of the satellite AOD is validated by a comparison with ground AOD measurements such as the global AERONET network. The reliability of satellite AOD products was shown at

Chapter written by Thi Nhat Thanh NGUYEN, Viet Hung LUU, Van Ha PHAM, Quang Hung BUI and Thi Kim Oanh NGUYEN.

a global scale (Chu *et al.* 2002; Ichoku *et al.* 2002) and over the SEA region (Feng and Christopher 2013; Reid *et al.* 2013; Sayer *et al.* 2013; Asmat *et al.* 2018). As a result, the estimation of $PM_{2.5}/PM_{10}$ concentrations from satellite AOD has been conducted in different SEA countries (Jamil *et al.* 2011; Kanabkaew 2013; Kanniah *et al.* 2014; Sukitpaneenit and Kim Oanh 2014; Trang and Tripathi 2014; Le *et al.* 2014; Nguyen *et al.* 2015; Leelasakultum and Kim Oanh 2017; Macatangay *et al.* 2017; Kamarul Zaman *et al.* 2017).

In this chapter, we present the methodology and experiment to analyze the relationship between satellite AOD to ground PM measurements, in terms of individuality and combination with meteorological conditions. Based on high correlations of satellite AOD and ground PM, PM mapping techniques will be presented to provide PM maps at low-and high-spatial resolutions (i.e. country/city and commune/ward levels respectively).

5.2. Relation of aerosol optical thickness, meteorological variables and particulate matter concentration

Although $PM_{2.5}$ measurements through ground-based stations measure the concentrations with a high level of accuracy and frequency, they have limited geographic coverage. Also, point measurements from ground-based monitoring stations are not necessarily representative of regional concentrations, and regional variability is difficult to assess from point measurements alone (van Donkelaar *et al.* 2010). Recent studies suggest the potential use of satellite remote sensing technologies for mapping and monitoring of pollutants and relating them to ground sources (Badarinath *et al.* 2009, Monks and Bierelle 2011, Kharol *et al.* 2012, Vadrevu *et al.* 2014). Specific to PM, the use of satellite instruments to estimate surface PM concentration is considered an effective way to extend point-based measurements to wide spatial scales (Duncan *et al.* 2014). Satellite-derived PM maps are gradually becoming basic layers for air quality, human health and disaster management (van Donkelaar *et al.* 2011; Anderson *et al.* 2012).

A satellite product of the AOD, which is the measurement of the extinction of light due to interferences with airborne PM or aerosol present in the atmospheric column, is perhaps the most excessively used PM surrogate (Zeeshan and Kim Oanh 2014). Several researchers used AOD or aerosol optical thickness (AOT) derived from satellite data for PM estimation (Chu *et al.* 2003; Wang and Christopher 2003; Engel-Cox *et al.* 2004; Pelletier *et al.* 2007; Badarinath *et al.* 2007; Gupta and Christopher 2008; Schaap *et al.* 2009; Zha *et al.* 2010; Lee *et al.* 2011; Hirtl *et al.* 2014; Ma *et al.* 2014). Methods for estimating PM vary from linear regression (LR) or multiple linear regression (MLR) to nonlinear regression methods such as artificial neural network (ANN), support vector regression (SVR) and self-organizing map (SOM) (Thanh *et al.* 2015). Studies have compared ground level PM concentrations to the AOD observed by Moderate Resolution Imaging Spectroradiometer (MODIS) on board Terra and Aqua Satellites across the globe. These yield varying results with the correlation coefficients (R values) from 0.12 to above 0.9 for $PM_{2.5}$ (particles with an aerodynamic diameter not above 2.5 μm) and from 0.2 to above 0.6 for PM_{10} (particles with an aerodynamic diameter not above 10 μm) (Zeeshan and Kim Oanh 2014).

The main aim of this section is to investigate the potential use of satellite derived AOD on mapping PM. To do that, we first validate the agreement of satellite-derived AOD against ground-based measurement. Then, we study its correlation with PM concentration and meteorological factors. The study areas are in Vietnam and central Thailand.

5.2.1. Data collection

Daily satellite derived AODs are obtained from MODIS and VIIRS satellite instruments at a 10 km spatial resolution (i.e. Optical_Depth_Land_And_Ocean at 0.550 μm of MOD04 in Collection 5.1 and AOD_550_Dark_Target_Deep_ Blue_Combined of MYD04 in Collection 6). Ground-based measurement of AOD is extracted from seven AERONET stations in Vietnam. The Sun photometer on the AERONET site recorded AOD at several wavelengths ranging from 0.34 to 1.6 μm. PM data are provided by six stations of the Center for Environmental Monitoring (CEM) at Vietnam Environment Administration (VEA) for the Vietnam area and 29 stations of the Pollution Control Department (PCD), Ministry of Natural Resource and Environment of Thailand for the Thailand area.

5.2.2. Outlier detection

Data outliers were removed using the method of standard deviation. Observations outside these intervals may be considered as outliers:

$$3\,SD\ method = \bar{X} \pm 3\,SD \qquad [5.1]$$

where $\bar{X}$ is the sample mean and SD is the standard deviation of the dataset.

5.2.3. Data integration

Since satellite and ground datasets have different temporal and spatial characteristics, they need to be integrated for the modeling and testing process of PM estimation. Satellite data are first resampled to the resolution of choice using a bilinear function and integrated using time and location constraints proposed by

(Ichoku *et al.* 2002). Only cloud-free aerosol data pixels with distances to a ground station within a radius of R km are considered. Meanwhile, ground measurements are averaged within a temporal window of T minutes coinciding with the satellite overpasses. The optimal thresholds would be selected by experiments.

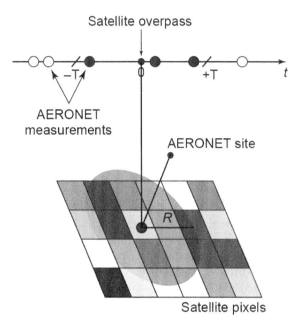

Figure 5.1. *Spatial–temporal window for extracting satellite and ground-based measurements*

5.2.4. *Correlation analysis*

Correlation analysis of two variables (i.e. MODIS/VIIRS AOD and AERONET AOD) is done using quantitative and qualitative methodologies. The first one is performed by analyzing statistic parameters. The latter is conducted by visualizing and analyzing the variation of two data.

Quantitative analysis of the agreement between two variables can be done using several criteria including coefficient of determination (R^2), root mean square error (RMSE) and relative error (RE). Their definitions are as follows:

$$R^2 = \frac{\left(\sum_{t=1}^{n}(x_t - \bar{x})(y_t - \bar{y})\right)^2}{\sum_{t=1}^{n}(x_t - \bar{x})^2 \sum_{t=1}^{n}(y_t - \bar{y})^2}$$ [5.2]

$$RMSE = \sqrt{\frac{\sum_{t=1}^{n}(x_t - y_t)^2}{n}}$$ [5.3]

$$RE = \frac{|x_t - y_t|}{x_t}.100\%$$ [5.4]

where $\bar{x}$ and $\bar{y}$ are the arithmetic mean of two datasets, and n is the number of samples.

5.2.5. Validation of satellite-derived AOD and ground-measured AOD

MODIS/VIIRS products provide AOD at a 0.550 μm wavelength. Meanwhile, AERONET stations provide AOD at several wavelengths but not exactly at any of the MODIS AOD wavelengths. Therefore, the first step is to interpolate the Sun photometer AOD at a specific 0.550 μm wavelength by using AODs at two available closest wavelengths:

$$\tau_{0.55\,\mu m} = \frac{\tau_{0.55\,\mu m}}{e^{-\alpha_{0.44\,\mu m - 0.67\,\mu m} \ln\frac{0.5}{0.55}}}$$ [5.5]

In which $\alpha_{0.44\,\mu m\ -\ 0.67\,\mu m}$ is the Angstrom exponent in the range of 440–675 nm. $\tau_{0.55\mu m}$ and $\tau_{0.5\mu m}$ are AERONET AOD at 550 nm and 500 nm respectively.

Based on correlation coefficient statistics of MODIS/VIIRS AOD and AERONET AOD, data suggested R as 6 km and 12 km for MODIS AOD and VIIRS AOD respectively and T as 15 minutes for AERONET AOD.

Figure 5.2 depicts the correlation of MODIS AOD/VIIRS AOD and AERONET AOD obtained at seven ground stations in Vietnam from 2009 to 2014. The results show that the correlation coefficients between MOD04 and MYD04 to AERONET AOT are 0.867 and 0.887 respectively.

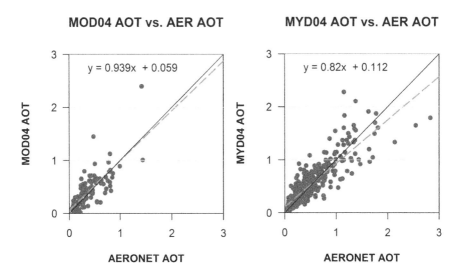

Figure 5.2. *Scatter plots between MOD04-, MYD04- and AERONET-AOT at seven AERONET stations in Vietnam from 2009 to 2014 (source: Nguyen et al. 2015). For a color version of this figure, see www.iste.co.uk/laffly/torus3.zip*

5.2.6. *Relation of particulate matter concentration and meteorological variables*

Meteorological data are collected at CEM air pollution stations for the experiment. The impact of meteorological variations, i.e. temperature (Temp), pressure (Pres), radiation (Rad), wind speed (Wsp) and relative humidity (RH) on the PM of 1, 2.5 and 10 µm diameters in Vietnam, has been evaluated (see Figure 5.3). The results clearly identify the influence of temperature parameters on PM concentrations. Results suggested a stronger influence of temperature on PM than on pressure, radiation, wind speed and relative humidity, and the relationship gradually decreasing from PM_1, $PM_{2.5}$ to PM_{10}. Correlation coefficients (R) of temperature with PM are −0.561, −0.509 and −0.366 for PM_1, $PM_{2.5}$ and PM_{10} respectively.

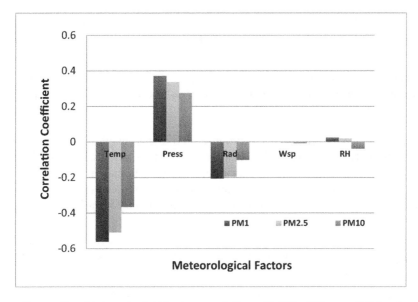

Figure 5.3. *Meteorological factor correlation with PM$_1$, PM$_{2.5}$ and PM$_{10}$ at Phu Tho, Hanoi, Hue and Da Nang stations in Vietnam from December 2010 to September 2014*

In addition, the qualitative analysis of the association between PM and meteorological variables is investigated over Central Thailand. 18 meteorological variables (i.e. sea level pressure (SLP), air temperature, etc.) collected from surface weather stations during the dry seasons were used for synoptic pattern identification. These stations were selected keeping in view the major synoptic processes in the surrounding regions, which can affect the weather in Central Thailand. Nine stations were used including three stations in Thailand (Bangkok, Chiang Mai and Hatyai), three stations in China (Kunming, Wuhan, Xian) and three stations in Cambodia (Phnom Penh), Vietnam (Hanoi) and Sri Lanka (Colombo). In total, 1010 days of data are used. Two stage clustering using IBM SPSS Statistic 21 was applied, producing four meteorologically homogeneous patterns as follows:

– pattern 1 represents a situation with the highest pressure in China and Southeast Asia (SEA). This pattern is also characterized by the lowest temperature and lowest moisture content which is typical when the area is under the influence of a high pressure ridge;

– pattern 2 represents the lowest pressure at all considered weather stations. This pattern presents the influence of the thermal lows over the study area that prevails in the local summer months of February–April;

– pattern 3 has the second lowest pressure recorded in the region. In this pattern, thermal lows are strengthening while the high pressure system is weakening over the study area;

– pattern 4 is quite similar to pattern 3 in terms of average pressure and temperature over Thailand but with the lowest values of dew deficit, visibility and wind speed in Bangkok.

A synoptic pattern represents a combination of meteorological conditions which affects the horizontal and vertical dispersions of the PM once released into the atmosphere, the chemical transformation leading to the formation of secondary PM and may also affect the emission intensity (Kim Oanh and Leelasakultum 2011). To verify this, the mean daily ambient PM_{10} concentrations for each meteorological pattern were analyzed (see Table 5.1).

Pattern	Mean PM10 $\pm$ Standard Deviation ($\mu g/m^3$)	95% confidence interval ($\mu g/m^3$)	Exceedance of NAAQS (days/total days)
1	83 $\pm$ 27	$\pm$3.28	22/261
2	53 $\pm$ 17	$\pm$2.10	3/251
3	73 $\pm$ 24	$\pm$2.79	13/285
4	80 $\pm$ 28	$\pm$3.22	31/290

Table 5.1. *Summary statistics of 24 h PM_{10} in four patterns. Thailand NAAQS for PM_{10} is 120 $\mu g/m^{-3}$, 25 °C at 1 atm (source: Zeeshan and Kim Oanh 2014)*

The average PM_{10} concentration was maximum (83 $\pm$ 27 $\mu g/m^3$) during the prevalence of pattern 1, which is linked to the high pressure system over the study area with more stable atmospheric conditions. Pattern 4 had the second highest average PM_{10} levels (80 $\pm$ 28 $\mu g/m^3$). The presence of the stagnating high pressure with low wind speed over Bangkok prevalent in this pattern may explain the high levels of PM_{10}. It is noted that both pattern 1 and pattern 4 showed a high pressure ridge governing over the study area but the ridge was at different development stages in these two patterns. Pattern 1 had the highest SLP, highest wind speed and zero to negative pressure tendency in the study area indicating that the ridge was at its maximum development in the region that is normally observed in winter. Pattern 4 had relatively high SLP and the lowest wind speed in Bangkok that may indicate the weakened and stagnating stage, with a possibility of ridge strengthening (positive pressure tendency). The meteorological conditions in both patterns were inducing high pollution levels with more vertical dispersion restriction in pattern 1 and more horizontal dispersion restriction in pattern 4. These explained why the PM concentration ranges in the two patterns appeared to overlap with only a small difference in the mean values.

The minimum average daily PM_{10} concentrations $(53 \pm 17 \, \mu g/m^3)$ were observed during the occurrence of pattern 2 which is consistent with the prevalent meteorological conditions with the lowest SLP and highest temperature among the four patterns. Pattern 3 had intermediate PM_{10} levels $(73 \pm 24 \, \mu g/m^3)$.

The above analysis confirms that air temperature and pressure are the two most important determinants for the PM estimation model.

5.2.7. Relation of particulate matter concentration and satellite-derived AOD

The relation of satellite-derived aerosol (MOD04 and MYD04) on PM of 1, 2.5 and 10 μm diameters in Vietnam has been evaluated using correlation coefficient (R). The results clearly identify the strong correlation of aerosol parameters on PM concentrations (see Figure 5.4). The effect on PM at different sizes is similar to the temperature for MOD04 but MYD04 dataset. R of 0.527, 0.522 and 0.429 were obtained for MOD04 and 0.617, 0.482 and 0.592 for MYD04 datasets and PM_1, $PM_{2.5}$ and PM_{10} datasets.

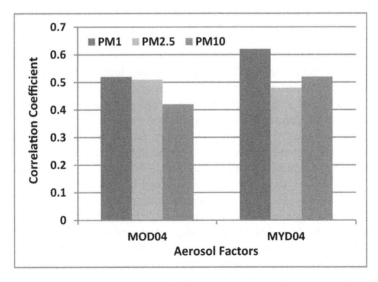

Figure 5.4. MODIS aerosol data correlation with PM_1, $PM_{2.5}$ and PM_{10} at Phu Tho, Hanoi, Hue and Da Nang stations from December 2010 to September 2014 (source: Nguyen et al. 2015)

MODIS satellite aerosol product is also analyzed with PM_{10} data in Central Thailand. In order to validate the MODIS AOD extraction procedure – after excluding all the days with cloud cover more than 3/10 recorded at Bangkok – the Aqua and Terra AOD (0.55 μm) were compared to the interpolated values of AERONET AOD (at 0.55 μm) and overall R^2 was found to be 0.81 with a sample size of 361 matched-up pairs and an RMSE of 0.08. Table 5.2 shows the correlation coefficients between AOD (at 0.47 μm) and PM_{10} concentrations at 22 monitoring stations during the study period for the MODIS Terra and Aqua AOD. These stations are located roadside, within 3–5 m from main roads, and are ambient monitoring stations. Without the consideration of meteorological patterns (lump), R value varied among the stations from 0.28 to 0.55 for Terra and 0.27 to 0.58 for Aqua AOD. Overall, the average R values across stations were 0.34 and 0.31 for Terra and Aqua AODs respectively.

With the consideration of the synoptic patterns, R values were generally improved for all except pattern 2. Pattern 1 had the highest R values at all stations, ranging between 0.38 and 0.68 (average of 0.46) for Terra and 0.33 and 0.68 (average of 0.38) for Aqua. This improvement in R values for pattern 1 may be attributed to the near ground presence of the maximum amount of PM as approximated by the Lidar aerosol backscatter coefficient profiles. The shallow mixing layers, indicated by the Lidar profiles, associated with the presence of a high pressure ridge in this pattern, also enhance the PM–AOD correlation. In addition, the dry air conditions (highest dew deficit) in this pattern may also improve the PM–AOD correlation. In pattern 4, the R value was found to be the second highest for most of the stations, i.e. 0.24–0.72 (average 0.39) for Terra and 0.28–0.85 (average 0.38) for Aqua AOD. The mixing heights for this pattern were also relatively low, and the steeper backscatter coefficient profiles with higher values observed near ground, compared to patterns 2 and 3, may enhance the PM_{10}–AOD correlation. For pattern 3, the overall range of R values was almost similar to that of the lump (combined) case but varied among stations; R was between 0.22 and 0.72 for Terra and 0.23–0.65 for Aqua AOD. In general, the R values for pattern 3 were lesser than those in pattern 4. Note that pattern 3 was found to be cloudy, second to pattern 2, hence reducing the data points (with cloudiness ≤ 3/10) for the analysis. Therefore, after excluding cloudy days, only 71 and 53 days of Terra and Aqua AOD were available, respectively, for PM–AOD comparison. In pattern 2, the R values were minimum and also unexpectedly negative at some stations for both Terra and Aqua AOD, showing poor PM_{10}–AOD relationships. As noted above, the vertical profiles of aerosol backscatter coefficient in this pattern varied widely, and this inconsistency in the vertical aerosol distribution should lead to lower correlations between PM_{10} measured near the ground and the total AOD column. It was noteworthy that pattern 2 was the cloudiest; hence, out of the total 1010 considered days during the study period, pattern 2 had the maximum number of days eliminated due to the cloud screening.

Station	MODIS Terra (1030)					MODIS Aqua (1330)				
	Lump	With pattern consideration				Lump	With pattern consideration			
		1	2	3	4		1	2	3	4
48Ta	0.47 (296)	0.59 (103)	−0.1 (25)	0.54 (77)	0.6 (80)	0.47 (287)	0.68 (107)	0.04 (26)	0.27 (64)	0.66 (70)
11T	0.5 (400)	0.63 (151)	−0.16 (23)	0.72 (102)	0.6 (128)	0.53 (393)	0.53 (150)	−0.01 (21)	0.65 (82)	0.61 (93)
12T	0.48 (352)	0.66 (123)	−0.26 (23)	0.55 (93)	0.62 (110)	0.35 (369)	0.57 (137)	−0.62 (25)	0.41 (85)	0.49 (93)
53Ta	0.47 (387)	0.67 (155)	0.04 (20)	0.35 (89)	0.3 (111)	0.27 (421)	0.44 (156)	0.06 (23)	0.46 (82)	0.4 (110)
54Ta	0.42 (411)	0.52 (148)	0.15 (23)	0.46 (97)	0.42 (120)	0.41 (377)	0.55 (141)	0.1 (24)	0.46 (71)	0.63 (101)
59T	0.39 (165)	0.5 (79)	0.18 (12)	0.33 (34)	0.49 (37)	0.58 (193)	0.58 (96)	0.07 (12)	0.46 (35)	0.85 (34)
61T	0.49 (181)	0.65 (80)	0.51 (11)	0.65 (34)	0.29 (49)	0.45 (243)	0.63 (105)	0.51 (13)	0.52 (34)	0.48 (57)
17T	0.43 (294)	0.59 (101)	−0.05 (14)	0.42 (66)	0.58 (79)	0.46 (293)	0.36 (110)	0.1 (17)	0.63 (72)	0.73 (72)
13T	0.36 (363)	0.56 (147)	−0.25 (20)	0.42 (80)	0.62 (108)	0.42 (336)	0.47 (144)	0.02 (17)	0.44 (76)	0.42 (81)
22T	0.45 (387)	0.61 (150)	−0.13 (26)	0.55 (78)	0.64 (128)	0.32 (373)	0.45 (150)	−0.01 (26)	0.25 (81)	0.49 (98)
20T	0.38 (377)	0.38 (125)	0.36 (20)	0.57 (87)	0.35 (120)	0.38 (396)	0.45 (160)	0.38 (14)	0.44 (94)	0.4 (96)
21T	0.4 (306)	0.55 (107)	0.8 (21)	0.5 (68)	0.32 (99)	0.44 (368)	0.61 (165)	−0.02 (19)	0.38 (78)	0.67 (88)
26T	0.37 (335)	0.64 (115)	−0.04 (28)	0.47 (82)	0.41 (89)	0.4 (315)	0.57 (121)	0.41 (21)	0.36 (65)	0.49 (76)
15T	0.55 (344)	0.66 (146)	−0.49 (17)	0.53 (77)	0.54 (108)	0.33 (351)	0.4 (135)	0.24 (19)	0.23 (81)	0.4 (84)
52Ta	0.54 (348)	0.55 (144)	−0.13 (19)	0.62 (78)	0.72 (106)	0.5 (349)	0.6 (136)	0.43 (21)	0.5 (76)	0.54 (81)
08T	0.29 (297)	0.45 (125)	−0.31 (18)	0.22 (53)	0.6 (91)	0.31 (303)	0.43 (122)	0.38 (18)	0.14 (54)	0.48 (72)

19T	0.43 (385)	0.56 (168)	0.34 (25)	0.43 (80)	0.6 (101)	0.28 (388)	0.33 (154)	0.07 (15)	0.31 (87)	0.47 (95)
27T	0.44 (280)	0.52 (109)	−0.28 (11)	0.53 (60)	0.51 (96)	0.43 (278)	0.63 (103)	−0.28 (11)	0.57 (59)	0.53 (99)
25T	0.35 (340)	0.55 (120)	−0.61 (20)	0.54 (82)	0.24 (112)	0.41 (361)	0.52 (132)	0.36 (22)	0.43 (98)	0.28 (96)
16T	0.28 (282)	0.5 (114)	−0.18 (12)	0.45 (48)	0.39 (75)	0.34 (276)	0.45 (113)	−0.18 (12)	0.26 (53)	0.44 (83)
50Ta	0.42 (316)	0.54 (99)	−0.48 (16)	0.41 (81)	0.57 (107)	0.48 (355)	0.56 (130)	−0.03 (24)	0.59 (75)	0.59 (91)
10T	0.53 (368)	0.68 (136)	−0.16 (22)	0.48 (74)	0.64 (122)	0.36 (398)	0.56 (160)	−0.26 (26)	0.57 (82)	0.4 (83)
Overall	0.34 (7214)	0.46 (2745)	0.08 (426)	0.39 (1620)	0.4 (2176)	0.31 (7426)	0.38 (2927)	0.1 (426)	0.34 (1584)	0.38 (1853)

Table 5.2. *Correlation coefficients between PM_{10} and AOD (MODIS Aqua and Terra) for all 22 stations in Thailand (source: Zeeshan and Kim Oanh 2014)*

5.3. $PM_{2.5}$ mapping from moderate resolution satellite images

Many studies suggest the potential use of satellite AOD for mapping and monitoring of PM. In the above sections, ground-measured PM have a strong correlation with satellite AOD and several meteorological variables. In this section, a procedure for the mapping of PM map from satellite AOD and meteorological variables using the regression model is presented. A case study in Vietnam using MODIS Aqua and Terra is demonstrated.

5.3.1. *Data collection*

The collection of MODIS MOD/MYD AODs, ground-measured PM and meteorological variables for Vietnam are the same as in section 5.2.1. The selection of meteorological variables for the regression model is based on the correlation assessment of each factor to PM at ground level. Monthly meteorological data (i.e. temperature, pressure, relative humidity and precipitation) is considered for the regression model to characterize climate regions, which are collected from 98 ground stations of the National Center for Hydro-Meteorological Forecasting (NCHMF) for temperature, relative humidity and precipitation, from 2005 to 2013. At each meteorological station, temperature and relative humidity are measured at 13:00 hrs but precipitation at 13:00 hrs and 24:00 hrs every day (Vietnam local time).

5.3.2. *Multiple variable regressions*

Multiple linear regression (MLR) is used to estimate PM from the MODIS AOD and other meteorological variables. Multiple variations of MLR models with different sets of meteorological indicators (i.e. temperature, relative humidity and precipitation) are considered. Firstly, the data is standardized into the range of $(-1, 1)$ using min–max scaler:

$$x_i = \frac{x_i - min(X)}{max(X) - min(X)} \tag{5.6}$$

The least square fitting technique determines MLR coefficients based on the least square errors of a model over a training dataset. After that, the Bayesian model average (BMA) technique calculates Bayesian information criterion (BIC) and post probability for each MLR model and selects the one that best minimizes BIC and maximizes posterior probability:

$$p(\theta|y) = \sum_{m_i} p(m_i|y)p(\theta|y, m_i) \tag{5.7}$$

where m_i are a set of candidate models, $p(m_i|y)$ is the posterior probability over model m_i and $p(\theta|y, m_i)$ is the posterior density on model parameters conditional on model m_i.

Finally, Cook's distance (Cook's D) is applied on the selected models to identify and remove the samples that have significant impacts on the estimated coefficients. Cook's distance of observation i (for $i = 1, 2, \dots, n$) is defined as the sum of all the changes in the regression model when observation i is removed from the dataset:

$$D_i = \frac{\sum_{j=1}^{n}\left(\widehat{y_j} - \widehat{y_{j(i)}}\right)^2}{ps^2} \tag{5.8}$$

$\widehat{y_{j(i)}}$ is the fitted response value obtained when excluding i, and $s^2 \equiv (n - p)^{-1}e^T e$ is the mean squared error of the regression model.

5.3.3. *Data interpolation*

The universal Kriging is applied on regression PM maps to interpolate values for the entire region that also included areas impacted by clouds. The spatial correlation of PM values is modeled by fitting the spherical variogram to the experimental semi-variance accounting for all valid geo-locations in a PM image. Several models such as Gaussian, spherical and exponential were tested to fit data. The spherical model is usually considered as the best model with the lowest mean square error between the variogram model and experimental data. Universal Kriging is then applied on each

MOD and MYD $PM_{2.5}$ image to obtain an interpolated map, together with its associated error map.

5.3.4. Evaluation metrics

Four statistical indicators, i.e. Pearson's correlation coefficient (R), coefficient of determination (R^2), RMSE (i.e. absolute error) and relative error (RE) (i.e. percentage error), are used to evaluate predicted PM maps. In addition, mean fractional bias (MFB) and mean fractional error (MFE) defined as follows can be used to assess model performance:

$$MFB = \frac{2}{N} \sum_{i=1}^{N} \frac{M_i - O_i}{M_i + O_i} \times 100$$

$PM: \leq \pm 30\% \ (goal); \ \leq \pm 60\% \ (criteria)$ [5.9]

$$MFE = \frac{2}{N} \sum_{i=1}^{N} \frac{|M_i - O_i|}{M_i + O_i} \times 100$$

$PM: \leq \pm 50\% \ (goal); \ \leq \pm 70\% \ (criteria)$ [5.10]

where N is the number of samples. M_i and O_i are the modeled and observed PM mass concentration respectively. In the above equation, the goal is the level of accuracy close to the best estimation and criteria is the level of accuracy acceptable for standard modeling purposes.

5.3.5. Predictor variables and model selection

The BMA technique suggests five and four regression models for MOD and MYD datasets respectively (see Table 5.2). Each regression model with different variables (i.e. MODIS-derived aerosol – AOTt, MODIS-derived temperature – Tempt, regional monthly temperature/relative humidity/Precipitation – Tempmr, RHmr, Precmr) is evaluated using R^2 and posterior probability of model correction. The best regression models are MOD #1 and MYD #1 which use satellite-derived aerosol (AOT_t) and monthly and regional temperatures ($Temp_{mr}$) as predictor variables and then gain high R^2 and highest posterior probability. The low R^2 for MYD models can be explained by outliers in the MYD dataset. Therefore, Cook's Distance using 4/(n-p-1) threshold is applied on MOD and MYD datasets for MOD#1 and MYD#1 regression models to remove outliers. Table 5.3 presents the regression results of the MOD and MYD regression models. Results suggested R^2 and RE of 0.602 and 33.348% for MOD data and 0.577 and 53.353% for MYD data.

MOD				MYD			
#Sample	R^2	RMSE ($\mu g/m^3$)	RE (%)	#Sample	R^2	RMSE ($\mu g/m^3$)	RE (%)
274	0.602	8.527	33.348	385	0.577	8.777	53.353

Table 5.3. *MOD and MYD regression model results on filtered dataset using 4/(n-p-1) threshold in which n and p are the number of samples and degree of freedom respectively (source: Nguyen et al. 2015)*

5.3.6. Interpolation model

We carried out a 3-fold cross-validation using all valid pixels for each image. Interpolated $PM_{2.5}$ values are compared with regression $PM_{2.5}$ values to evaluate Kriging performance (Table 5.4). For the interpolation model, R^2 and RE are 0.935 and 3.703% on average of a total 128 datasets, which suggests the robustness of our approach.

	MOD				MYD				Total			
Year	#	R^2	RMSE ($\mu g/m^3$)	RE (%)	#	R^2	RMSE ($\mu g/m^3$)	RE (%)	#	R^2	RMSE ($\mu g/m^3$)	RE (%)
2010	4	0.918	1.371	2.402	1	0.929	0.946	2.436	5	0.924	1.158	2.419
2011	11	0.948	1.382	3.434	5	0.901	1.266	3.585	16	0.925	1.324	3.510
2012	10	0.937	1.231	3.118	7	0.950	1.312	4.031	17	0.943	1.272	3.575
2013	31	0.940	1.328	3.485	14	0.925	1.500	4.638	45	0.933	1.414	4.061
2014	29	0.953	1.337	3.696	16	0.945	1.748	6.202	45	0.949	1.542	4.949
Total	85	0.939	1.330	3.227	43	0.930	1.354	4.178	128	0.935	1.342	3.703

Table 5.4. *Results of universal Kriging cross-validation are considered separately by model and year. Overall assessments are calculated on the total dataset (source: Nguyen et al. 2015)*

5.3.7. *Map validation results*

Validation is carried out using 85 MOD- and 43 MYD-derived $PM_{2.5}$ images from December 2010 to September 2014. First, we projected each MODIS image on the Vietnamese grid of 10 km to create a $PM_{2.5}$ map using the regression model. As the percentage of available data ($\geq$ 30%) in each image is limited, the data has been interpolated from valid cells. We extracted $PM_{2.5}$ over four automatic ground stations (i.e. Phu Tho, Hanoi, Hue and Da Nang) which are representative of four regions in Vietnam (North East, Red River Delta, North Central Coast and South Central Coast) respectively and compared them with ground $PM_{2.5}$. Table 5.5 shows different results of MOD and MYD model performances in which the MOD model is slightly dominant. Satellite-derived $PM_{2.5}$ have a moderate correlation and error to ground-based $PM_{2.5}$ (R^2 = 0.427 and RE = 39.957%) for the MOD dataset but lower correlation and error (R^2 = 0.337 and RE = 39.459%) for the MYD dataset.

	#Images	#Samples	R^2	RMSE $(\mu g\ m^{-3})$	RE (%)	MFB (%)	MFE (%)
MOD	85	189	0.427	21.709	39.957	0.491	34.954
MYD	43	96	0.337	17.188	39.458	3.639	34.799
Total	128	285	0.411	20.299	39.789	1.552	34.902

Table 5.5. *Overall validation of satellite-derived $PM_{2.5}$ maps over Phu Tho, Hanoi, Hue and Da Nang. Results are separated by MOD and MYD datasets and accumulated in total (source: Nguyen et al. 2015)*

We also analyzed the results for different locations (Table 5.6). Satellite-derived $PM_{2.5}$ at Phu Tho station has the best correlation (R^2 = 0.412 and RE = 39.693%) in comparison with the ground-based $PM_{2.5}$. At Hanoi station, predicted $PM_{2.5}$ has low quality with R^2 = 0.158 and RE = 36.195%, mainly due to large variations in the Hanoi dataset. A large error was observed at Da Nang station (RE = 45.656% and R^2 = 0.281), while moderate results were obtained for Hue station (RE = 32.747% and R^2 = 0.300). MFBs show that $PM_{2.5}$ is underestimated in Phu Tho, Hanoi and Hue datasets but overestimated in the Da Nang dataset. However, four station's MFBs and MFEs still meet the goals. We attribute the errors to geolocation. For example, all ground stations are located close to roadsides, whereas satellite signals represent an average of 10 km, leading to high errors on satellite-derived $PM_{2.5}$.

Station	#Samples	R^2	RMSE $(\mu g\ m^{-3})$	RE (%)	MFB (%)	MFE (%)
Phu Tho	68	0.412	26.146	39.693	-7.047	36.274
Hanoi	52	0.158	26.448	36.195	-14.485	38.269
Hue	60	0.300	19.786	32.747	-9.323	33.038
Da Nang	105	0.281	10.276	45.656	21.276	33.410

Table 5.6. *Satellite-derived $PM_{2.5}$ is validated with ground-based $PM_{2.5}$ by station (source: Nguyen et al. 2015)*

5.4. PM_{10} mapping from high resolution satellite images

Very high resolution (VHR) instruments onboard satellites (i.e. SPOT series) can provide us with detailed imagery. Unlike moderate resolution satellites that have a specific band to monitor AOD (i.e. MODIS, VIIRS), VHR satellites, however, usually do not equip instruments for AOD monitoring. Thus, the mapping of PM data from VHR satellite requires an extra step to measure AOD. In this section, we present methodology and results for PM_{10} mapping using SPOT images (Luu *et al.* 2016).

5.4.1. Dataset

Data for mapping air environment pollution at a specified time consist of both optical satellite images and pollutant measurements on the ground. Two SPOT4 images captured on a polluted day (i.e. pollution image) and a clean day (i.e. reference image) in 2012 are used to derive relative aerosol (Table 5.7).

	Date	Scene ID	Sun Elevation	Sun Azimuth
Ref. image	16/09/2012	S4_XI270308_16092012_L3A	54.5	117.2
Pol. image	04/05/2012	S4_XI269308_04052012_L3A	61.0	94.8

Table 5.7. *Two SPOT 4 images for air pollution mapping*

Meanwhile, ground PM_{10} measurements for pollution modeling in Hanoi have been provided by Hanoi Centre for Environmental and Natural Resources Monitoring and Analysis (CENMA). Data are PM_{10} captured over 57 hot spots during the period May 2012 to June 2012. Those hot spots are located at the road intersection with high traffic density (Figure 5.5).

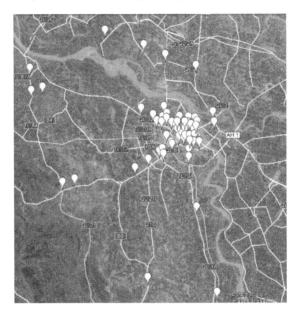

Figure 5.5. *Ground PM stations. For a color version of this figure, see www.iste.co.uk/laffly/torus3.zip*

The standard SPOT products use quantized and calibrated scaled Digital Numbers (DN) representing multispectral image data. To work on SPOT data, DNs are firstly converted to Radiance and Top Of Atmosphere (TOA) reflectance. Then, radiometric normalization is carried out on TOA reflectance, in order to remove the difference in atmospheric conditions and lighting at two different times. After that, relative aerosol is calculated and matched to ground PMs to obtain the PM map.

5.4.2. Radiometric normalization

Data captured by the same satellite sensors have been influenced by a number of factors such as atmospheric and illumination conditions; therefore, it is difficult to compare targets in multi-date scenes. Relative radiometric normalization (RRN) techniques are able to minimize radiometric difference between images caused by inconsistencies of acquisition condition, rather than change in surface reflectance.

In this article, a relative radiometric normalization is implemented. We make an assumption that the relationship between the radiance obtained by a sensor in two different instances from the same regions, with constant reflectivity, can be approximated by a linear function. The Dark Set/Bright Set Normalization method is applied. The brightness area of two images, which is assumed to be time invariant and unaffected by air pollution, is selected. The linear relationship between the spectral reflectance of pixels within the selected area at time t_1 and t_2 is presented as follows:

$$\rho_{t1} = 1.6800127248\, \rho_{t2} - 0.0944640446$$

$$\leftrightarrow \rho_{t1} = F(\rho_{t2}) \tag{5.11}$$

where ρ_{t1} and ρ_{t2} are the reflectance values at time t_1 and t_2 respectively. The linear function F is then applied in the whole satellite image at time t_2.

5.4.3. Relative Aerosol Optical Depth Extraction

In most cases, a Radiative Transfer Model (RTM) is used to construct a Lookup Table (LUT) to act as a map between measurement and physical quantities. Another strategy is to apply RTM calculations directly to satellite data without an LUT. In this section, we provide the procedure to estimate AOD from a pair of SPOT-4 images following the approach of Sifakis and Deschamps (1992).

Optical atmospheric effects influence satellite signals through scattering or absorption processes. Using a clean scene as the reference image, we can assess the spatial variation in the optical depth of a polluted day image, by comparing it with the reference image. A relative calibration procedure is based on the inversion of the atmospheric conversion model. The at-sensor reflectance is expressed as:

$$\rho^* = \rho \frac{T(\vartheta_s)T(\vartheta_v)}{1-\rho S} + \rho_a \tag{5.12}$$

where ρ is the surface reflectance; ρ_a is the atmospheric reflectance; S is the spherical albedo of atmosphere; ϑ_v is the solar zenith angle; ϑ_s is the observation zenith angle; $T(\vartheta_s)$ is the total transmission function on the down-welling path as the sum of $T_{dir}(\vartheta_s)$ and $T_{diff}(\vartheta_s)$, which are the direct and diffuse transmission functions respectively; $T(\vartheta_v)$ is the total transmission function on the up-welling path as the sum of $T_{dir}(\vartheta_v)$ and $T_{diff}(\vartheta_v)$, which are the direct and diffuse transmission functions respectively.

The adjacent effect caused by neighborhood pixels with regard to background average reflectance ρ_e is considered:

$$\rho^* = \rho \frac{T(\vartheta_s)T_{dir}(\vartheta_v)}{1-\rho_e S} + \rho_e \frac{T(\vartheta_s)T_{diff}(\vartheta_v)}{1-\rho_e S} + \rho_a \tag{5.13}$$

Following two assumptions: (1) uniform background contribution to all adjacent pixels of a random group, and (2) atmospheric reflectance is spatial invariable, in regard to our case study which deals with small urban areas, the variation in ρ^* is controlled by:

$$\sigma(\rho^*) = \sigma(\rho)\frac{T(\vartheta_s)T_{dir}(\vartheta_v)}{1-\rho_e S} \qquad [5.14]$$

where $\sigma(\rho^*)$ and $\sigma(\rho)$ is the standard deviation of ρ^* and ρ respectively.

From the Lambert–Bouguer transmission law:

$$T_{dir}(\vartheta_v) = e^{-km} = e^{-\tau} \qquad [5.15]$$

where τ represents the optical depth value. From equations [5.13] and [5.14] and normalized for the angle of incidence ϑ_v, we obtain:

$$\sigma(\rho^*) = \sigma(\rho)\frac{T(\vartheta_s)e^{-\tau/\cos\vartheta_v}}{1-\rho_e S} \qquad [5.16]$$

For the pair of reference and pollution images, a grid overlay is superimposed, dividing the images of the study area into n-pixels array, where n represents different resolutions. Selecting a random array for each of the two compared images respectively $\overline{\rho_1^*}$, $\overline{\rho_2^*}$ are the local mean values; $\sigma_1(\rho^*)$, $\sigma_2(\rho^*)$ are the local standard deviations; and τ_1, τ_1 are the local optical depths. The following assumptions are made for each of the arrays:

Spectral response of the ground in each array is variable in space but not in time.

Atmospheric within each array is variable in time but not in space so that $\sigma(\rho^*)$ will be attributed only by ground spectral variation.

Applying equation [5.15] for a given array of two compared images, we have:

$$\sigma_1(\rho^*) = \sigma(\rho)\frac{T(\vartheta_s)e^{-\tau_1/\cos\vartheta_{v1}}}{1-\rho_e S} \qquad [5.17]$$

$$\sigma_2(\rho^*) = \sigma(\rho)\frac{T(\vartheta_s)e^{-\tau_2/\cos\vartheta_{v2}}}{1-\rho_e S} \qquad [5.18]$$

$T(\vartheta_s)$ may be considered as a constant independent of the temporal variation in optical depth because the variation of its two additional $T_{dir}(\vartheta_s)$ and $T_{diff}(\vartheta_s)$ cancel out each other (Sifakis et al. 1992). The ratio of equation [5.16] over equation [5.17] is

$$\frac{\sigma_1(\rho^*)}{\sigma_2(\rho^*)} = e^{-\frac{\tau_1}{\cos\vartheta_{v1}} + \frac{\tau_2}{\cos\vartheta_{v2}}} \qquad [5.19]$$

For nadir images where observation zenith angle is close to 0, we can accept $\cos\vartheta_{v2} = \cos\vartheta_{v1} = 1$. From equation [5.8], we obtain:

$$\Delta\tau = \tau_2 - \tau_1 = \ln\frac{\sigma_1(\rho^*)}{\sigma_2(\rho^*)} \qquad [5.20]$$

For the reference image taken on a pollution-free day, $\tau_1 \approx 0$, the extracted relative local variation of τ expresses absolute spatial variation of τ_2 on the second image.

The total optical depth τ is the sum of the following partial optical depths:

− optical depth due to molecular absorption τ_m^a;

− optical depth due to particular absorption τ_p^a;

− optical depth due to molecular scattering (i.e. Rayleigh) τ_m^d;

− optical depth due to particular scattering (i.e. Mie scattering) τ_p^d.

Using images acquired by the SPOT sensor which are made through atmospheric windows where absorption by atmospheric gas is minimal, τ_m^a is disregarded. Absorption by particulates τ_p^a is generally negligible in the visible spectrum. Due to the Rayleigh-type scattering caused mainly by natural atmospheric gases, which may also be considered invariable in time within similar atmospheric pressure, τ_m^d is regarded as constant. The variation in optical depth estimated will therefore be represented by τ_p^d, which is generally determined by aerosol concentrated in the lowest portion of the atmosphere.

5.4.4. Least square fitting

Given a training dataset, including PM concentration as the dependent variable and aerosol as the independent variable, the modeling process would investigate an appropriate function f representing the relationship between PM and aerosol with the minimal error ε:

$$PM = f(AOT) + \varepsilon \qquad [5.21]$$

The least square fitting technique determines model parameters based on the least square errors of modeled and measured values in a training dataset.

5.4.5. PM_{10} estimation from SPOT images

Three different grid sizes of 3 by 3, 4 by 4 and 6 by 6 pixels are considered for generating relative AOD maps. Due to the lack of ground PM concentration captured on time with the polluted image, we assume that the derived aerosol map at the time of the pollution day is represented by the average aerosol values during the period from May 2012 to June 2012. The experiment is carried out to investigate the effect of various grid sizes, based on the correlation between extracted AOD and ground PM measurements. Results presented in Table 5.7 show that the correlation of PM on aerosol decreases in the order of increasing array size. The array size of 3 by 3 pixels should be selected because of its maximum correlation, and the resolution obtained is 60 meters. Since ground pollutant sources are traffic hotspots instead of ambient pollution, higher resolution leads to a more accurate pollutant estimation.

Array size (pixel by pixel)	Derived resolutions (m)	# of matched samples	Correlation Coefficient (R)
3	60	60	0.56
4	80	60	0.33
5	100	60	0.22

Table 5.8. *Correlation between satellite-derived aerosol and ground PM data in different resolutions*

The 10-fold cross-validation procedure is used to evaluate the performance of least square fitting with different residual function using a derived 60-meter aerosol map (Table 5.8). We considered correlation coefficient (R), RMSE, and relative error (RE).

	# Samples	R	RMSE	RE
Linear	23	0.430	47.82	13.12
Quadratic	23	0.425	49.67	13.52
Log	23	0.259	55.41	15.34

Table 5.9. *Least square fitting performance on PM estimation*

Regarding the type of residual function, PM can be estimated best by both linear and quadratic functions (R/RMSE = 0.430/47.82 and 0.425/49.67 respectively). The worst case is for using the logarithm function. Based on experiment results, together with the small number of samples, linear least square fitting is selected for PM estimation.

The Standard Deviation method is used to identify the samples that may be considered as outliers. The samples that exceed the threshold given in equation [5.20] are removed from the dataset:

$$\text{Threshold} = \mu \pm 2 \times \sigma \qquad\qquad [5.22]$$

where μ is the mean value of samples and σ is the standard deviation of independent variables.

The derived PM_{10} image is then interpolated using the Kriging technique. The final validation is carried out by synchronization in space of satellite PM_{10} and ground PM_{10}. There are 38 matched samples for consideration. Table 5.9 shows the validation results for the considered dataset. Although the Index of Agreement scores less than 0.5 and correlation coefficient is low at 0.39, the relative error (RE) shows a potential number of 17.85%. The low correlation and index of agreement might be explained by two characteristics of ground truth data. First, they are recorded over a long period of time, not in-time with satellite data. Second, they are recorded at the intersection of roads which always show peak values.

Model	Samples	R	RMSE	RE	Index of Agreement
Linear	38	0.39	82.62	17.85	0.48

Table 5.10. *Correlation between derived PM model and ground PM*

Figure 5.6 shows the estimated PM versus ground PM. Modeled PM was able to replicate ground PM spatial patterns; however, it is limited in capturing maximal or minimal peaks.

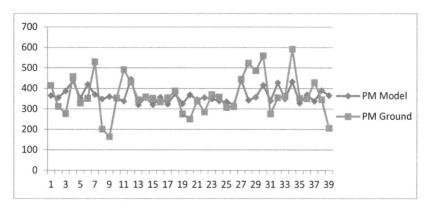

Figure 5.6. *Estimated PM vs ground PM*

Figure 5.7 shows the false color composite PM_{10} map, excluding water, which was obtained by estimation and interpolation. Since ground PM_{10} are measured at traffic crossings with very high PM_{10} concentrations, the estimated PM_{10} should be considered over areas concerning traffic instead of residential areas. A ground survey carried out around the peak areas, indicated on the pollution map, reveals some important air pollution sources. The areas of Gia Lam and Dong Anh areas at the north side of the city suffered air pollution from the industrial zone and very high traffic highway (road width > 6m). The air pollution from the source could spread out through the whole area due to the flat topography, with few high buildings.

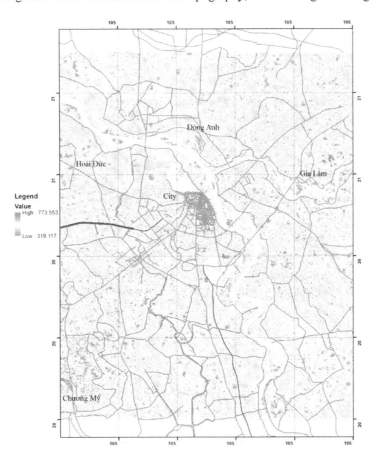

Figure 5.7. *PM map over Hanoi at a resolution of 60 meters. For a color version of this figure, see www.iste.co.uk/laffly/torus3.zip*

In the city area, traffic is the main source of air pollution due to the rapid increase in the number of vehicles. However, due to the dense number of high buildings, the largest emissions are mainly located on the road network. These areas also suffered pollution from agricultural activities. During the harvest season, field burning of agricultural and residues rice straw is intensive. This source is significant during the dry seasonal at the time of study (May to June), and the emissions spread widely from the rural areas (Chuong My, Hoai Duc, Dong Anh, Gia Lam, etc.) toward the city.

5.5. Conclusion

In this chapter, we have summarized the approach for PM concentration mapping using satellite images. Ground PM measurements have shown strong relationships with meteorological data and satellite-derived AOD, especially in terms of different synoptic patterns. It provides firm basics for PM mapping from satellite images and meteorological factors. The methodology and experiment to estimate $PM_{2.5}$ maps at a 10 km resolution using moderate resolution satellite images (MODIS AOD) were presented. Moreover, PM_{10} mapping from high resolution satellite images (SPOT 4) was described, although the approach required an additional step for aerosol calculation. The research results highlight the potential of using satellite images for ground PM mapping, especially in the SEA area where ground measurements are very limited.

5.6. References

Asmat, A., Jalal, K.A., and Deros, S.N.M. (2018). Aerosol properties over Kuching, Sarawak from satellite and ground-based measurements. In *Land-Atmospheric Research Applications in South and Southeast Asia*, Vadrevu, K. P., Ohara, T., and Justice, C. (eds). Springer International Publishing, Cham. Available at: https://doi.org/10.1007/978-3-319-67474-2_21

Chu, D.A., Kaufman, Y.J., Ichoku, C., Remer, L.A., Tanre, D., and Holben, B.N. (2002). Validation of MODIS aerosol optical depth retrieval over land. *Geophysical Research Letters*, 29(12), 4–7.

Feng, N. and Christopher, S.A. (2013). Satellite and surface-based remote sensing of Southeast Asian aerosols and their radiative effects. *Atmospheric Research*, 122, 544–554. Available at: https://doi.org/10.1016/j.atmosres.2012.02.018

Gaveau, D.L.A., Salim, M.A., Hergoualc'h, K., Locatelli, B., Sloan, S., Wooster, M., Marlier M.E., Molidena, E., Yaen, H., DeFries, R., Verchot, L., Murdiyarso, D., Nasi, R., Holmgren, P., and Sheil, D. (2014). Major atmospheric emissions from peat fires in Southeast Asia during non-drought years: Evidence from the 2013 Sumatran fires. *Scientific Reports*, 4, 6112.

Hayasaka, H., Noguchi, I., Putra, E.I., Yulianti, N., and Vadrevu, K. (2014). Peat-fire-related air pollution in Central Kalimantan, Indonesia. *Environmental Pollution*, 195, 257–266. Available at: https://doi.org/https://doi.org/10.1016/j.envpol.2014.06.031

Huizenga, C., Ajero, M., and Fabian, H. (2004). Benchmarking urban air quality management in Asian cities. *Presented at 13th World Clean Air and Environmental Protection Congress and Exhibition*, London, UK.

Ichoku, C., Chu, D.A., Mattoo, S., Kaufman, Y.J., Remer, L.A., Tanre, D., Slutsker, I., and Holben, B.N. (2002). A spatio-temporal approach for global validation and analysis of MODIS aerosol products. *Geophysical Research Letters*, 29(12), 1–4.

Jamil, A., Makmom, A.A., Saeid, P., Firuz, R.M., and Prinaz, R. (2011). PM10 monitoring using MODIS AOT and GIS, Kuala Lumpur, Malaysia. *Research Journal of Chemistry and Environment*, 15(2), 1–5.

Kamarul Zaman, N.A.F., Kanniah, K.D., and Kaskaoutis, D.G. (2017). Estimating particulate matter using satellite based aerosol optical depth and meteorological variables in Malaysia. *Atmospheric Research*, 193 (October 2016), 142–162. Available at: https://doi.org/10.1016/j.atmosres.2017.04.019

Kanabkaew, T. (2013). Prediction of hourly particulate matter concentrations in Chiang Mai, Thailand using MODIS aerosol optical depth and ground-based meteorological data. *EnvironmentAsia*, 6(2), 65–70.

Kanniah, K.D., Kamarul Zaman, N.A.F., Lim, H.Q., and Md. Reba, M.N. (2014). Monitoring particulate matters in urban areas in Malaysia using remote sensing and ground-based measurements. *Proc. SPIE 9242, Remote Sensing of Clouds and the Atmosphere XIX; and Optics in Atmospheric Propagation and Adaptive Systems XVII*, 92420J (17 October 2014). Available at: https://doi.org/10.1117/12.2067029.

Kim Oanh, N.T. and Leelasakultum, K. (2011). Analysis of meteorology and emission in haze episode prevalence over mountain-bounded region for early warning. *Science of the Total Environment*, 409(11), 2261–2271. Available at: https://doi.org/10.1016/j.scitotenv.2011.02.022

Kim Oanh, N.T., Permadi, D.A., Dong, N.P., and Nguyet, D.A. (2018). Emission of toxic air pollutants and greenhouse gases from crop residue open burning in Southeast Asia. In *Land-Atmospheric Research Applications in South and Southeast Asia*, Vadrevu, K.P., Ohara, T., and Justice, C. (eds). Springer International Publishing, Cham, 47–66. Available at: https://doi.org/10.1007/978-3-319-67474-2_3

Le, T.H., Nguyen, T.N.T., Laskob, K., Ilavajhalac, S., Vadrevub, P.K., and Justice, C. (2014). Vegetation fires and air pollution in Vietnam. *Environmental Pollution*, 195, 267–275.

Leelasakultum, K. and Kim Oanh, N.T. (2017). Mapping exposure to particulate pollution during severe haze episode using improved MODIS AOT-PM$_{10}$ regression model with synoptic meteorology classification. *GeoHealth*, 1(4), 165–179. Available at: https://doi.org/10.1002/2017GH000059.

Luu, V.H., Man, D.C., Luong, C.K., Bui, Q.H., and Nguyen, T.N.T. (2016). Air pollution mapping from high spatial resolution satellite images: A case study in Hanoi. *Proceedings of the 2nd International Joint Conference IJCC*, 2016, 130–135.

Macatangay, R., Bagtasa, G., and Sonkaew, T. (2017). Non-chemistry coupled PM_{10} modeling in Chiang Mai City, Northern Thailand: A fast operational approach for aerosol forecasts. *Journal of Physics: Conference Series*, 901(1), 12037.

Mahmud, M. (2013). Assessment of atmospheric impacts of biomass open burning in Kalimantan, Borneo during 2004. *Atmospheric Environment*, 78, 242–249. Available at: https://doi.org/https://doi.org/10.1016/j.atmosenv.2012.03.019.

Nguyen, T.T.N., Bui, H.Q., Pham, H.V, Luu, H.V, Man, C.D., Pham, H.N., Le, H.T., and Nguyen, T.T. (2015). Particulate matter concentration mapping from MODIS satellite data: A Vietnamese case study. *Environmental Research Letters*, 10(9), 095016. Available at: https://doi.org/10.1088/1748-9326/10/9/095016.

Reddington, C.L., Yoshioka, M., Balasubramanian, R., Ridley, D., Toh, Y.Y., Arnold, S.R., and Spracklen, D.V. (2014). Contribution of vegetation and peat fires to particulate air pollution in Southeast Asia. *Environmental Research Letters*, 9(9). Available at: https://doi.org/10.1088/1748-9326/9/9/094006.

Reid, J.S., Hyer, E.J., Johnson, R.S., Holben, B.N., Yokelson, R.J., Zhang, J., Campbell, J.R., Christopher, S.A., Di Girolamo, L., Giglio, L., Holz, R.E., Kearney, C., Miettinen, J., Reid, E.A., Turk, F.J., Wang, J., Xian, P., Zhao, G., Balasubramanian, R., Chew, B.N., Janjai, S., Lagrosas, N., Lestari, P., Lin, N.-H., Mahmud, M., Nguyen, A.X., Norris, B., Oanh, N.T.K., Oo, M., Salinas, S.V., Welton, E.J., and Liew, S.C. (2013). Observing and understanding the Southeast Asian aerosol system by remote sensing: An initial review and analysis for the Seven Southeast Asian Studies (7SEAS) program. *Atmospheric Research*, 122, 403–468. Available at: https://doi.org/10.1016/j.atmosres.2012.06.005.

Sayer, A.M., Hsu, N.C., Bettenhausen, C., and Jeong, M.J. (2013). Validation and uncertainty estimates for MODIS Collection 6 "deep Blue" aerosol data. *Journal of Geophysical Research Atmospheres.*, 118(14), 7864–7872. Available at: https://doi.org/10.1002/jgrd.50600.

Shi, Y., Matsunaga, T., Yamaguchi, Y., Li, Z., Gu, X., and Chen, X. (2018). Long-term trends and spatial patterns of satellite-retrieved $PM_{2.5}$ concentrations in South and Southeast Asia from 1999 to 2014. *Science of the Total Environment*, 615, 177–186. Available at: https://doi.org/10.1016/j.scitotenv.2017.09.241.

Streets, D.G., Yarber, K.F., Woo, J.-H., and Carmichael, G.R. (2003). Biomass burning in Asia: Annual and seasonal estimates and atmospheric emissions. *Global Biogeochemical Cycles*, 17(4). Available at: https://doi.org/10.1029/2003GB002040.

Sukitpaneenit, M. and Kim Oanh, N.T. (2014). Satellite monitoring for carbon monoxide and particulate matter during forest fire episodes in Northern Thailand. *Environmental Monitoring and Assessment*, 186(4), 2495–2504. Available at: https://doi.org/10.1007/s10661-013-3556-x.

Trang, N.H. and Tripathi, N.K. (2014). Spatial correlation analysis between particulate matter 10 (PM$_{10}$) hazard and respiratory diseases in Chiang Mai Province, Thailand. *ISPRS Archives*, XL-8(1), 185–191. Available at: https://doi.org/10.5194/isprsarchives-XL-8-185-2014.

Vadrevu, K.P., Lasko, K., Giglio, L., and Justice, C. (2014). Analysis of Southeast Asian pollution episode during June 2013 using satellite remote sensing datasets. *Environmental Pollution*, 195, 245–256. Available at: https://doi.org/https://doi.org/10.1016/j.envpol.2014.06.017.

Yadav, I.C., Linthoingambi Devi, N., Li, J., Syed, J.H., Zhang, G., and Watanabe, H. (2017). Biomass burning in Indo-China peninsula and its impacts on regional air quality and global climate change – A review. *Environmental Pollution*, 227, 414–427. Available at: https://doi.org/https://doi.org/10.1016/j.envpol.2017.04.085.

Zeeshan, M. and Kim Oanh, N.T. (2014). Assessment of the relationship between satellite AOD and ground PM$_{10}$ measurement data considering synoptic meteorological patterns and Lidar data. *Science of the Total Environment*, 473–474, 609–618. Available at: https://doi.org/10.1016/j.scitotenv.2013.12.058.

6

Comparison and Assessment of Culturable Airborne Microorganism Levels and Related Environmental Factors in Ho Chi Minh City, Vietnam

6.1. Introduction

Microorganism-based air pollution is usually in a closed relationship with human activities (Qian et al. 2012; Aaron and Marr 2015; Aaron et al. 2015). Ambient microorganism standards are not being implemented in Vietnam yet. Microorganism or bioaerosol is an important factor which leads to diseases and negative effects (Shokri et al. 2010; Jyotshna and Brandl 2011), and it will affect humans in hot and humid climate conditions (Pasquarella et al. 2000). The environment contains dust particles, and this is an advantage factor to enhance the development of microorganisms (Pengrui et al. 2018). The economic process related to environmental issues has become a large problem, and the air pollution is a serious issue in Ho Chi Minh City (Hung et al. 2015). However, microorganism pollution is not considered much yet, and there are no extended studies of microbial development and its distribution which affects urban air quality. The airborne microbial contribution depends on the specific local position and environmental conditions. An ambient environment usually has a large microbial concentration like bacteria and fungi (Robert et al. 2011). These microorganisms are caused from soil, water, humans, animals and plants, and follow the wind in order to move to many different sites (Robert et al. 2011; Beata et al. 2015). In some cases, the bacterial level is affected by wastes from livestock farms (Elliott et al. 1976;

Chapter written by Tri Quang Hung NGUYEN, Minh Ky NGUYEN and Ngoc Thu Huong HUYNH.

Pillai and Ricke 2002). Characteristics of airborne microorganisms impact the air quality and environment (Zhengsheng *et al.* 2018). The previous studies examined microorganism levels like bacteria and fungi in urban and household environments (Mancinelli and Shulls 1978; Pastuszka *et al.* 2000; Hargreaves *et al.* 2003; Sophia 2013). The dust could bring microorganisms and especially microorganisms that are able to live long-term in airborne environments. Besides, these microorganisms also have a strong relationship with environmental factors such as light, temperature, humidity, the CO_2 level, etc. (Zhou *et al.* 2016; Anne *et al.* 2018). The above environmental factors have an important role and determine the microbial quantity and components. Microorganisms can cause adverse human health effects (Linda *et al.* 1998; Ruiping *et al.* 2013). Exposure to biological agents (bacteria and fungi) might be associated with public health issues such as infectious diseases and allergies (Douwes *et al.* 2003). Also, there is a strong relationship between air humidity and health effects (Peder 2018), as well as the relationship between fungi level, health issues and diseases (Jose *et al.* 2017). Furthermore, big data management can resolve and deal with environmental monitoring issues. Through the application of big data and cloud storage in environmental monitoring, the researcher can find data to provide a valid basis for an area and/or global environmental protection. Big data allows users to combine datasets from disparate data or meta-analysis to understand and analyze deeper information from these studies. The big data can be usefully developed in the fields of science data network to statistically search, compare, classify and cluster, etc. The study *"Comparison and assessment of culturable airborne microorganism levels and related environmental factors in Ho Chi Minh City, Vietnam"* aims to determine and assess the specific status of the important environmental factors that affect microorganism levels in Ho Chi Minh City, Vietnam. This chapter contributes to data from various environment conditions and microorganisms in Ho Chi Minh City, Vietnam. Within the context of the development of rapid big data, the characteristics of microorganisms in Ho Chi Minh City will be of great use in the development of science data.

6.2. Materials and methods

6.2.1. *Studying sites*

This study focuses on some important sites in Ho Chi Minh City, Vietnam (Table 6.1). Sampling includes three sites: one trend site (Faculty of Forestry – NLU) and two impact sites (Rang Dong Building – NLU and LinhTrung Export Processing Zone, Thu Duc district, Ho Chi Minh City).

Sites	Characteristics and monitoring purposes	
Faculty of Forestry, Nong Lam University of Ho Chi Minh City	– Characteristics: it has many plants, is a quiet area and is less impacted by human activities – Purposes: trend assessment	
Rang Dong Building, Nong Lam University of Ho Chi Minh City	– Characteristics: it has a large student population, medium plant level, cool space – Purposes: human impact and health issue assessment	
LinhTrung Export Processing Zone	– Characteristics: it is located along 1A National highway, is an important road connecting Dong Nai Province, Ho Chi Minh City and Binh Duong Province, has high vehicle levels – Purposes: a vehicle impact and health issue assessment	

Table 6.1. *Summary of the characteristics of the studied areas. For a color version of this table, see www.iste.co.uk/laffly/torus3.zip*

6.2.2. Sampling

Two different sampling methods to collect fungi and bacteria were used, namely the active method and passive deposition. In active monitoring, a microbiological air sampler draws a known volume of air through an EMS-6 collection device where the sampling flow volume is 28.3 L min^{-1}. The quantity of microorganisms present is measured by counting the number of CFUm^{-3} of air. Each sample was collected in 3 minutes for fungi and 2 minutes and 30 seconds for bacteria. In passive monitoring, the concentration of bacteria and fungi was determined using the conventional sedimentation method with standard Petri dishes. Results are expressed in CFU m^{-2}h^{-1} (Pasquarella *et al.* 2000). Petri dishes are left open to the air according to the 1/1.5/1 scheme (for 1 hour, 1.5 m above the floor, 1 m away from walls or obstacles) and containing agar media (Tryptic Soy Agar).

A total of three replicates for fungi and bacteria in each sampling site were collected. After sample collection, the agar plates were transported to the laboratory and incubated at $37\pm1°C$ for 24 hours for bacteria and at $25\pm1°C$ for 24–72 hours for fungi (Macher 1999; Christian *et al.* 2012). Concerning fungi and bacterial assessments, two periods were conducted in winter and summer (Table 6.2). A total of 1,344 air samples (672 samples from each season) were collected for bacterial and fungi analyses.

Sites	Dry season			Wet season		
	Period	Time	N	Period	Time	N
Faculty of Forestry, NLU	23/04–25/04/2017		168	13/08–15/08/2017		168
Rang Dong Building (indoor), NLU	07/05–09/05/2017	7:00 11:00	168	10/09–12/09/2017	7:00 11:00	168
Rang Dong Building (outdoor), NLU	07/05–09/05/2017	15:00 18:00	168	17/09–19/09/2017	15:00 18:00	168
LinhTrungEPZ	14/05–16/05/2017		168	17/09–19/09/2017		168
	Total		672	Total		672

Table 6.2. *Sampling process in Ho Chi Minh City*

6.2.3. *Identification of microorganisms*

In this study, colonies were examined and identified by biochemical reactions, as well as PCR technology. The PCR was performed for the quantification of culturable airborne microorganisms in air samples. The rapid identification of bacteria and fungi using molecular techniques is 16SrRNA gene sequencing and the ITS region.

6.2.4. *Statistical analysis*

Statistical analyses were performed using the SPSS software (version 13.0 for Windows). The Pearson correlation coefficient was employed to evaluate the relationship between bacterial and fungi levels. A paired t-test was used to compare the bacterial and fungi datasets for the two sampling types. The criteria for significance in the procedure were $p<0.05$ and $p<0.01$. For each type of culturable microorganism, a general linear model procedure was applied.

The multiple regression model analysis was used to examine the relationships among quantitative variables such as air temperature, light, humidity, CO_2 level and wind velocity during sampling with microbial concentrations. Besides, principal component analysis (PCA) is a statistical procedure for identifying a smaller number of uncorrelated variables, which resolves the components that best explain the variance in the data (Hotelling 1933; Wold *et al.* 1987). PCA was carried out to characterize the ambient microorganism concentration and its variation. In order to enhance the interpretability of the factors, a varimax rotation was applied to the significant factors with an initial eigenvalue >1.0 (Guo *et al.* 2004).

6.3. Results and discussions

6.3.1. *Results of environmental factors in Ho Chi Minh City*

Temperature, light, relative humidity, carbon dioxide level (CO_2) and wind velocity are shown by sampling sites in Table 6.3.

Items	Dry season (n = 72)				Wet season (n = 72)			
	Min	Max	Mean	SD	Min	Max	Mean	SD
Temp, °C	26.2	37.8	30.8	2.057	26.3	39.1	30.4	2.380
Light, lux	0.0	18,600.0	2,558.9	3,708.29	0.0	16,880.0	2,533.1	3,541.23
Humidity, %	51.0	89.0	72.0	7.87	47.1	91.3	73.7	8.927
CO_2, ppm	318.0	826.0	450.3	74.25	355.0	849.0	433.3	69.11
Wind, ms^{-1}	0.0	5.9	0.57	1.16	0.0	6.4	0.32	1.010

Table 6.3. *Descriptive statistics of environmental factors in Ho Chi Minh City*

The average temperature in a dry season is 30.8±2.057 °C, and the fluctuation is about 26.2–37.8 °C. A wet season temperature varied from 26.3 to 39.1 °C and was equal to 30.4±2.380 °C on average. Results of light levels are 2,558.9±3,708.297 lux and 2,533.1±3,541.232 lux in dry and wet seasons respectively. An average relative humidity in a wet season is higher than that in a dry season with averages of 73.7±8.927% and 72.0±7.878%. The CO_2 level ranges from about 318.0–826.0 ppm (dry season) and 355.0–849.0 ppm (wet season). The results showed that the CO_2 concentration trend in the dry season is greater than that in the wet season. Regarding wind velocity, it was on average 0.57±1.168 m s^{-1} (dry season) and 0.32±1.010 m s^{-1} (wet season).

6.3.2. *Results of monitoring on culturable microorganism levels in ambient air*

Multiple studies have also been performed on the appearance of airborne bacteria. Abdul Hameed *et al.* (2009) studied airborne bacterial and fungal composition in Egypt. In this study, we analyzed the relative abundance and diversity of microbial communities in three sites in Ho Chi Minh City, Vietnam. In addition, the paired t-test was used to compare the bacterial and fungi dataset for the two sampling types, which are presented in Table 6.4. In general, the wet season's fungal levels are higher than in dry season in the condition of different sampling methods. In contrast, the wet season's bacterial levels are greater than in the dry season's (Figures 6.1 and 6.2). Results of the fungal level of the active sampling method are found to be higher than those of the passive methods in the wet season. Meanwhile, in the dry season, the fungal level results showed that the passive method is greater than the active method. Bacterial levels in Rang Dong Building illustrate that indoor levels are higher than the outdoors level in both seasons. Generally, fungal spore counts seem to be the highest in summer, both indoors and outdoors (Garrett *et al.* 1998). The fungi and their spores are more resilient than bacteria, being able to withstand greater stresses owing to ultraviolet radiation (Cox 1989; Karra and Katsivela, 2007). Bacterial level results also showed that the passive sampling method is better than the active sampling method.

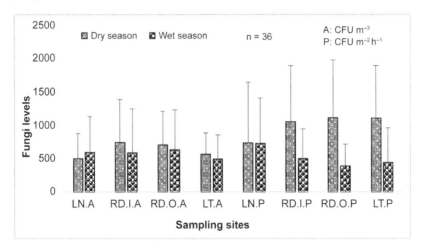

Figure 6.1. *Average fungal levels in Ho Chi Minh City. NOTES.– (i) LN-Faculty of Forestry of NLU; RD-Rang Dong Building of NLU; LT-LinhTrungEPZ. (ii) A-Active; P-Passive. I-Indoor; O-Outdoor*

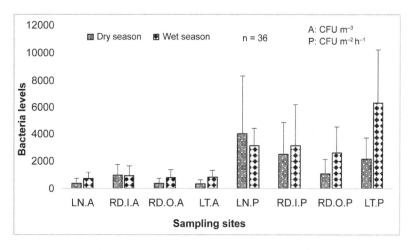

Figure 6.2. *Average bacterial levels in Ho Chi Minh City*

Fungal levels during the dry season at the Faculty of Forestry (LN) varied from 493.97±384.935CFU m^{-3} (active method) and 731.25±912.815CFU m^{-2} h^{-1} (passive method). At Rang Dong Building (RD), indoor active monitoring of fungal concentration is higher than the outdoor level, and these results are in contrast to the passive monitoring method. There are many students at this Building and pathogenic fungi can be hazardous to humans (Julian 2009). It could be explained as the influence of bacterial transportation on microbial communities from the outside environments (Nobuyasu *et al.* 2014). Results of bacterial and fungal identifications are shown in Tables 6.4 and 6.5. The indoor microbiome was known as a complex system, and there was a seasonal effect on the fungal concentration in both indoor and outdoor environments (Rachel *et al.* 2013). Furthermore, the fungal levels of the passive method were greater than those of the active method. Especially at LinhTrungEPZ, fungal monitoring results are different with mean values 563.08±320.507CFU m^{-3} (active method) and 1,102.94±787.559 CFU m^{-2} h^{-1} (passive method). Similar to fungal levels, airborne bacterial concentration showed that the passive method is higher than the active method ($p < 0.01$), and it is a clear confirmation by paired sample test (Table 6.6). Besides, a statistically significant difference was detected between the concentrations of bacterium at LN.A and LN.P ($p < 0.01$). The microorganism levels (bacteria and fungi) shown at sites in Ho Chi Minh City were affected by human factors at Rang Dong Building, as well as vehicle activities at LinhTrungEPZ. Also, these results showed that they were higher than at the Faculty of Forestry (NLU). In a school environment, aerosol particles are one of the pollutants that can decrease indoor air quality. Due to microorganism concentration, airborne bacteria and fungi can be the cause of a variety of health effects (Husman 1996).

Species	Fungi
A3	*Aspergillus fumigatus*
A5	*Aspergillus oryzae*
P6	*Penicillium janthinellum*
T1	*Trichoderma reesei*
F1	*Fusarium solani*
S1	*Syncephalastrum monosporum*
R1	*Rhizopus microsporus*

Table 6.4. *Results of fungal identification*

Species	Bacteria
17b	*Bacillus siamensis*
18b	*Micrococcus luteus*
31c	*Virgibacillus halodenitrificans*
15e	*Brachybacterium conglomeratum*

Table 6.5. *Results of bacterial identification*

	Dry season				Wet season			
Paired samples test	Fungi		Bacteria		Fungi		Bacteria	
	t	Sig.	t	Sig.	t	Sig.	t	Sig.
Pair 1 LN.A-LN.P	−1.637	0.111	−10.197	0.000	−0.901	0.374	−5.161	0.000
Pair 2 RD.I.A-RD.O.A	0.418	0.679	1.014	0.318	−0.609	0.546	4.393	0.000
Pair 3 RD.I.P.RD.O.P	−0.361	0.720	0.893	0.378	0.695	0.492	3.435	0.002
Pair 4 LT.A-LT.P	−4.170	0.000	−9.029	0.000	2.346	0.025	−4.187	0.000
Pair 5 RD.I.A-RD.I.P	−1.921	0.063	−4.663	0.000	1.398	0.171	−3.941	0.000
Pair 6 RD.O.A-RD.O.P	−2.679	0.011	−5.551	0.000	0.618	0.541	−7.593	0.000

Table 6.6. *The paired t-tests used to compare the bacterial and fungi dataset for the two sampling types*

In the wet season in Ho Chi Minh City, the results showed that the fungal levels at the Faculty of Forestry fluctuate from 12 to 1,779 CFU m^{-3} (active) and 0 to 2,548 CFU m^{-2} h^{-1} (passive) respectively. In this season, there were sometimes low fungal levels that were equal to zero, approximately. Results of the active fungal level showed that the Rang Dong Building's outdoor levels were higher than the indoor environment with average values 628.83 (SD = 600.823) and 583.28 (SD = 663.610) CFU m^{-3} of air. According to Rachel et al. (2013), the outdoor air fungi dominate the patterning of indoor air. In contrast to the passive sampling method, the outdoor's fungal levels were lower than the results of the indoor environment (Figure 6.2). Therefore, indoor air pollution can cause health problems and increase sources of disease (Jantunen et al. 1997). In LinhTrungEPZ, the average results of fungal concentration in wet season were low with 490.83; SD = 361.361CFU m^{-3} (active) and 436.42; SD = 520.050CFU m^{-2} h^{-1} (passive) respectively. Regarding the wet season in Ho Chi Minh City, the results showed that the bacterial concentration was high at the Rang Dong Building and the Faculty of Forestry. Especially, the passive bacterial levels were high with 1,097.00 (SD = 1,065.028) and 2,186.89 (SD = 1,542.359) CFU m^{-2} h^{-1} regarding indoor and outdoor environments respectively. The difference between the bacterial and fungi concentrations was subjected to statistical analysis, and the outcomes of the t-tests are summarized in Table 6.6. A statistically significant difference was observed between the LT.A and LT.P, especially concerning the bacterium and fungi in the dry season (p<0.01). Similarly, there are statistically significant differences among t-test pairs such as RD.I.A-RD.I.P, RD.O.A-RD.O.P, RD.I.A-RD.O.A and RD.I.P-RD.O.P (p<0.01) related to both bacterial and fungi concentrations.

6.3.3. Comparison and assessment of environmental factor effects on culturable microorganism levels

6.3.3.1. Correlation analysis between environmental factors and culturable microorganism level

The concentration of microorganisms in ambient air and its qualitative composition is very much dependent on different atmospheric factors (Lin and Li 2000). Examination of the relationship between environmental factors and culturable microorganism levels (bacteria and fungi) with the different sampling methods is shown below. The study's results showed the existence of the strong correlation among independent variables almost and microorganism levels (p<0.05).

The correlation coefficient of bacterial sampling types obtained $R = 0.575$ ($p<0.01$), especially the existence of the good relationship between bacterial concentration and CO_2 level, light and temperature ($p<0.01$). These important factors can lead to their appearance in airborne environments. Regarding the result of active monitoring methods, there was positive correlation between bacterial levels and CO_2 concentration with $R = 0.674$, $p<0.01$. The relationship among indoor bacteria and environmental factors such as humidity and season was also carried out by Anne et al. (2018). Similarly, results also illustrated that the correlation coefficients of the passive bacterial level with temperature and light were 0.562 and 0.466 ($p<0.01$) respectively. The strong relationship between temperature and light, and humidity was shown by Pearson correlation coefficients 0.572 ($p<0.01$) and -0.928 ($p<0.01$). In addition, the correlation coefficients of light with humidity and CO_2 concentration were -0.592 ($p<0.01$) and -0.564 ($p<0.01$) respectively. Although the negative correlation of relative humidity and bacteria is consistent with the previous study conducted by Tong and Lighthart (2000), it was not confirmed by this study ($p>0.05$). Also, in 2004, Jones and Harrison's (2004) study showed the positive correlation between bacterial concentration and windy speed. In this study, however, there is no relationship for statistical significance between bacterial levels and windy velocity ($p>0.05$).

	Bacteria (active)	Bacteria (passive)	Temp	Light	Humidity	CO_2	Wind
Bacteria (active)	1	0.575(**)	0.347	−0.383	−0.448	0.674(**)	0.487
Bacteria (passive)	0.575(**)	1	0.562(**)	0.466(**)	−0.594	0.516	0.594
Temp	0.347	0.562(**)	1	0.572(**)	−0.928(**)	−0.368	−0.251
Light	−0.383	0.466(**)	0.572(**)	1	−0.592(**)	−0.564(**)	0.272
Humidity	−0.448	−0.594	−0.928(**)	−0.592(**)	1	0.441(*)	0.210
CO_2	0.674(**)	0.516	−0.368	−0.564(**)	0.441(*)	1	−0.316
Wind	0.487	0.594	−0.251	0.272	0.210	−0.316	1

**Correlation is significant at the 0.01 level (two-tailed). *Correlation is significant at the 0.05 level (two-tailed).

Table 6.7. Correlation coefficients showing the effect of meteorological factors on bacterial concentrations

The relationship between fungal concentration and some important factors such as CO_2, humidity, light, wind velocity and temperature is shown in Table 6.8.

	Fungi (active)	Fungi (passive)	Temp	Light	Humidity	CO_2	Wind
Fungi (active)	1	0.585(**)	−0.430	−0.621(**)	0.531	0.634(*)	−0.379
Fungi (passive)	0.585(**)	1	−0.504	−0.491	0.660(**)	0.618(*)	0.419
Temp	−0.430	−0.504	1	0.693(**)	−0.907(**)	−0.515	0.412
Light	−0.621(**)	−0.491	0.693(**)	1	−0.601(**)	−0.633(**)	0.539(**)
Humidity	0.531	0.660(**)	−0.907(**)	−0.601(**)	1	0.484	−0.527(*)
CO_2	0.634(*)	0.618(*)	−0.515	−0.633(**)	0.484	1	−0.385
Wind	−0.379	0.419	0.412	0.539(**)	−0.527(*)	−0.385	1

**Correlation is significant at the 0.01 level (two-tailed). *Correlation is significant at the 0.05 level (two-tailed).

Table 6.8. *Correlation coefficients showing the effect of meteorological factors on fungal concentrations*

Positive correlation coefficients between active and passive bacterial sampling methods were R = 0.585 ($p<0.01$). The study results also showed that the active fungal levels indicate the positive correlation coefficient with CO_2 level (R = 0.634, $p<0.05$) and negative correlation coefficient with light factor (R = −0.621, $p<0.01$). Meanwhile, the results of passive monitoring fungal levels obtained show the positive correlation with CO_2 concentration, as well as the humid factor ($p<0.05$). Therefore, the study results show the effects of mainly environmental factors like the humidity and CO_2 level on fungal levels in ambient air.

Most studies confirmed the positive correlation between fungal levels and temperatures (Sabariego *et al.* 2000; Khan and Wilson 2003; Erkara *et al.* 2008). In this study, similarly, there exists a strong relationship between temperature with light, as well as humidity, whose correlation coefficients were 0.693 ($p<0.01$) and −0.907 ($p<0.01$) respectively. Besides, light and other factors (humidity, CO_2, wind) related to each other with correlation coefficients were (R = −0.601, $p<0.01$) and (R = −0.633, $p<0.01$) and wind velocity (R = 0.539, $p<0.01$) respectively.

6.3.3.2. *Linear regression models and the effects of environmental factors on culturable microorganism level*

6.3.3.2.1. Active sampling model

Several authors have reviewed the influence of meteorological factors on bacteria and fungi in the atmosphere (Jones and Harrison 2004). In order to identify the factors that affect the diversity of airborne bacteria, the study gathered environmental and meteorological information. In addition, meteorological conditions in summer showed high humidity and high winds, which may contribute to the movement of ground bacteria into airborne bacteria. In this study, the concentration of CO_2 and wind significantly affected bacterial levels ($p<0.05$), while light significantly affected fungi levels ($p<0.01$). Tables 6.9 and 6.10 showed linear regression models of the effects of environmental factors (temperature, light, humidity, CO_2 level and wind velocity) on the microorganism level with different sampling methods.

The linear regression models regarding the effects of environmental factors on the bacterial level showed an important impact of CO_2 and wind levels, with standardized coefficients (β) being 0.698 ($p<0.001$) and 0.519 ($p<0.05$) respectively. The aerosol dissemination of bacteria into different types of atmosphere can also affect the survival characteristics of the microorganism populations. Additionally, these problems are summarized by Burch and Levetin (2002), who also discussed the significant influence of meteorological conditions like wind speeds, cold fronts and air pressure, which may drive airborne fungal spores. The result of the linear regression model illustrated a positive relationship between active sampling bacterial levels with CO_2 concentration and wind velocity. In contrast, the results of the fugal levels' linear regression model showed that light plays important roles in the airborne environment ($\beta = -0.549$, $p<0.01$). However, in environmental conditions, light contains ultraviolet radiation which can be a harmful to bacteria (Walker and Ko 2007).

Model	Bacteria					Fungi				
	Unstandardized coefficients		Standardized coefficients	t	Sig.	Unstandardized coefficients		Standardized coefficients	t	Sig.
	B	Std. error	Beta			B	Std. error	Beta		
Constant	2,131.282	1,878.219		1.135	0.257	-865.100	1,685.687		-0.513	0.608
Temp	-45.242	40.552	-0.282	-1.116	0.266	35.085	36.230	0.345	0.968	0.334
Light	-0.105	0.101	-0.231	-0.439	0.661	-0.237	0.112	-0.549	-3.494	0.001
Humidity	-19.742	10.091	-0.301	-1.956	0.051	3.468	9.080	0.254	0.382	0.703
CO_2	5.065	0.452	0.698	6.785	0.000	0.538	1.456	0.472	1.181	0.238
Wind	61.809	28.718	0.519	2.152	0.032	-11.086	28.549	-0.223	-0.388	0.698

Table 6.9. Linear regression models of the effects of environmental factors on the microorganism level (active sampling)

6.3.3.2.2. Passive sampling model

Environmental conditions such as relative humidity, temperature and wind velocity had a significant effect on the type of populations and number of microorganisms in the air (Harrison *et al.* 2005). Multiple regression models are used to predict the effects of environmental factors on the levels of culturable bacteria and fungi in Ho Chi Minh City. Moreover, airborne bacteria are important biological components of the aerosols and have a closed relationship with human health (Ruiping *et al.* 2013). Meteorological elements are the main reason and they have an important effect on airborne bacterial communities (Quan *et al.* 2017). Also, the effects of humidity have a large role regarding microorganism concentration (Zhou *et al.* 2016). In this study, the effects of temperature and humidity showed that the significant impacts related to urban bacterial levels ($p<0.05$) with standardized coefficients (β) were 0.635 ($t = 2.511$, $p = 0.013$) and 0.541 ($t = 2.083$, $p = 0.038$) respectively. Linear regression results of the relationship between humidity and fungal concentrations are also obtained with similarly standardized coefficients which were 0.663 ($t = 2.549$, $p<0.05$). In general, the temperature and humidity factors have a positive ratio and impact on dense microorganism levels. The study results showed the roles and effects of environmental factors on the airborne microorganism's appearance. Temperature and humidity significantly affected bacterial levels, while the fungi level was just significantly affected by humidity ($p<0.05$). Similarly, temperature and relative humidity are also known to be important factors in the life and growth of microbial populations (Wright *et al.* 1969). The other study also demonstrated that the airborne bacterial communities were dependent on the air fluxes, which occurred due to seasonal variations (Fierer *et al.* 2008).

Thus, standardized coefficients (β) from the active linear regression model showed the environmental factors that affected bacteria levels including CO_2 concentration and wind velocity. Concerning fungi levels, the light factor had important roles and led to their appearance in ambient air. Meanwhile, passive sampling methods showed significantly important factors such as temperature and humidity (bacteria and fungi).

Model	Bacteria					Fungi				
	Unstandardized coefficients		Standardized coefficients	t	Sig.	Unstandardized coefficients		Standardized coefficients	t	Sig.
	B	Std. error	Beta			B	Std. error	Beta		
Constant	−22,899.992	10,273.950		−2.229	0.027	−4,789.951	2,465.487		−1.943	0.053
Temp	556.918	221.822	0.635	2.511	0.013	88.198	52.991	0.251	1.664	0.097
Light	0.167	0.159	0.385	1.134	0.258	−0.214	0.116	−0.464	−0.889	0.375
Humidity	114.969	55.198	0.541	2.083	0.038	33.848	13.280	0.663	2.549	0.011
CO_2	3.819	2.471	0.521	0.331	0.741	0.885	2.667	0.582	1.328	0.185
Wind	194.768	157.090	0.473	1.240	0.216	41.451	41.756	0.360	0.993	0.322

Table 6.10. Linear regression models of the effects of environmental factors on the microorganism level (passive sampling)

6.3.4. *Principal component analysis of microorganism groups*

Principal component analysis (PCA) is a statistical procedure for identifying a smaller number of uncorrelated variables. It aims to reduce the dimensionality for a large set of data (Hotelling 1933). PCA is carried out on the correlation matrix, and only the components that have an eigenvalue greater than one are included in the evaluation of data. To facilitate the evaluation of the multidimensional maps of principal component (PC) loadings, PCA is an exploratory tool to investigate patterns in the studied data.

6.3.4.1. *Principal component analysis of bacterial populations*

Hypothetical bacterial populations were used to show that such analysis can be used to compare collections of bacterial concentration taken at different periods or from different conditions and sources (Gary 1975). To understand the compositional differences or similarities, PCA was conducted for all measured samples. The obtained varimax-rotated factor scores of samples are shown in Table 6.11. According to the PC loading plots, the spectral differences that contributed to the discrimination of the three groups were related to different conditions. This method proved to be reliable to identify the sources and dispersal patterns of airborne bacteria (Lighthart *et al.* 2009). The result of the bacterial levels' PCA showed three principal components which explained 62.882% of the cumulative variance regarding eigenvalues equal to 1.068. The Kaiser–Meyer–Olkin Measure of Sampling Adequacy (KMO) was fairly high and was obtained at a value of 0.597. The PC loadings computed by PCA are compiled in Table 6.11. Three hypothetical variables explained the majority of total variance with 37.118% loss of information. Most of the varieties had high loadings in the first two PCs. Along the PC-1 axis accounting for 25.735% of the variance involves LT.P, LT.A and RD.O.P with positive score values (Figure 6.3). Along the PC-2 axis accounting for 23.803% of the variance involves RD.O.A, RD.I.A, RD.I.P and LN.A with positive score values (Figure 6.3). Along the PC-3 axis accounting for 13.344% of the variance involves LT.P and LN.P with positive score values, and RD.O.A with a negative score value (Table 6.11). PC-1 examined "vehicle impacts" and included the areas affected by LinhTrungEPZ's transport activities and outside the zone of the Rang Dong Building (NLU) with mainly the passive sampling method. PC-2 was examined effects related to "human impacts" including the inside and outside areas of the Rang Dong Building (NLU); a part of the ozone belongs to the Faculty of Forestry (NLU) with the active sampling method. These impacts show that, in the non-industrial indoor environments, the most important source of airborne bacteria is related to the presence of humans (Stetzenbach 2007). PC-3 examined "integrated impacts" including a zone at the Faculty of Forestry (NLU), a part outside the Rang Dong Building (NLU) and LinhTrungEPZ's with mainly the passive sampling method. Thus, the principal component loading results show the distribution among the studied areas by the different impacts due to socio-economic activities. However, in many case studies, it is difficult to determine the source of the increased bacteria such as emissions or other sources (Burrows *et al.* 2009). Some of the most important anthropogenic sources are related to transport activities. The factors of transportation were discovered to be contributors in microbial concentration (Pathak and Verma 2009). The presence of human activities can also affect the air quality, and these factors may be associated with microbial growth conditions, which may cause serious problems. Therefore, the large number of humans in public places in urban areas such as LinhTrungEPZ or school environments may be the key for natural pathogen transmission (Robertson *et al.* 2013).

No.	Variables	Principal component		
		PC-1	PC-2	PC-3
1	LT.P	**0.967**	−0.030	**0.251**
2	LT.A	**0.732**	−0.097	−0.102
3	RD.O.P	**0.387**	0.132	−0.176
4	RD.O.A	0.242	**0.682**	**−0.383**
5	RD.I.A	−0.046	**0.612**	0.163
6	RD.I.P	−0.109	**0.542**	−0.040
7	LN.A	0.073	**0.487**	0.005
8	LN.P	−0.011	0.016	**0.313**

Table 6.11. *Principal component loading of bacteria*

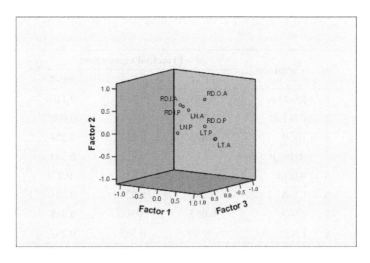

Figure 6.3. *Plotting bacteria as PC loadings by three major PC components*

6.3.4.2. *Principal component analysis of fungi populations*

Lewi *et al.* (2005) applied the matrix used for PCA and applied in order to calculate the abundance and the variety-dependent distribution of fungal species. In this study, three groups of fungal samples were also recognized based on the PCA of weight and component loss data (Figure 6.4). Regarding fungal levels, PCA showed three principal components with eigenvalues equal to 1.202 and explained 62.844% of cumulative variance. Results of the Kaiser–Meyer–Olkin Measure of Sampling Adequacy (KMO) were good and equivalent to 0.644. Eight variables (fungal items) dominated three PCs, as shown in Table 6.12 and Figure 6.4.

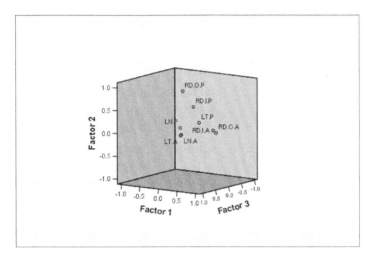

Figure 6.4. *Plotting fungi as PC loadings by three major PCs*

No.	Variables	Principal component		
		PC-1	**PC-2**	**PC-3**
1	RD.O.A	**0.858**	0.058	0.110
2	RD.I.A	**0.764**	0.101	0.096
3	LT.P	**0.473**	**0.257**	**0.221**
4	RD.O.P	0.121	**0.931**	**0.344**
5	RD.I.P	0.117	**0.527**	−0.074
6	LT.A	**0.267**	0.024	**0.641**
7	LN.A	0.063	−0.028	**0.318**
8	LN.P	−0.005	0.105	**0.263**

Table 6.12. *Principal component loading of fungi*

On the basis of the data in Figure 6.4, the fungal concentrations were divided into three groups. The PCA results of fungal concentration achieved three principal components and involves PC-1, PC-2 and PC-3. As depicted in Figure 6.4, the PC-1, PC-2 and PC-3 explained 62.844% of the variance overall. The first ordinal axis was positively correlated with RD.O.A (0.858), RD.I.A (0.764), LT.P (0.473) and LT.A (0.267). The second ordinal axis was positively correlated with LT.P (0.257), RD.O.P (0.931) and RD.I.P (0.527). The third ordinal axis was positively correlated with LT.P (0.221), RD.O.P (0.344), LT.A (0.641), LN.A (0.318) and LN.P (0.263). First, PC-1 involves the outside and inside zones of the Rang Dong Building (NLU), the vehicle area along LinhTrungEPZ with mainly the active sampling method and identified "integrated impacts of human and transport activities". Second, PC-2 represents the passive sampling method of outside and inside zones of the Rang Dong Building, as well as a part of the LinhTrung area examined "human impacts". Finally, PC-3 includes LinhTrungEPZ's transport zone, the Faculty of Forestry (NLU) and a part outside the Rang Dong Building examined "vehicle impacts" with the typical passive sampling method. Thus, it could be said that the basic solution of PCA has usefully applied and explained the variance in the datasets (Wold *et al.* 1987; Pasquarella *et al.* 2000).

In summary, the comparison of microorganism sampling methods has shown bacterial and fungal levels to be different. The active sampling method is more relevant for the assessment of effects related to indoor human activities. This system is applicable when the concentration of microorganisms is not very high, such as in indoor ambient or silent areas like hospitals (Blomquist 1994; Pasquarella *et al.* 2008). In contrast, the passive sampling method should be used with the evaluation of effects related to transport or integrated impacts.

6.4. Conclusion

In this study, an investigation of culturable airborne bacterial and fungi levels was conducted in Ho Chi Minh City. Generally, the dry season's fungal levels are higher than the wet season's in different sampling methods. Conversely, the wet season's bacterial concentration is greater than the dry season's. Over the different seasons (dry and wet seasons), the study results showed that indoor bacterial levels are higher than outdoor levels at the Rang Dong Building. Fungal and bacterial levels were affected by human (Rang Dong Building) and transport reasons (LinhTrungEPZ). These results were greater than the zone belonging to the Faculty of Forestry (NLU), which less impacted by human activities.

The correlation coefficient of bacterial sampling types obtained $R = 0.575$ ($p<0.01$), especially, the existence of the good relationship between bacterial concentration and CO_2 level, light and temperature ($p<0.01$). These important factors can lead to their appearance in the atmosphere. Positive correlation coefficients between active and passive bacterial sampling methods were $R = 0.585$ (p<0.01). The results showed that the active fungal levels do not only indicate the positive correlation coefficient with CO_2 level ($R = 0.634$, p<0.05) but also the existence of negative correlation coefficients with light factor ($R = -0.621<0$, p<0.01).

The linear regression model of active sampling bacterial levels confirmed the positive relationship with CO_2 and wind velocity. Meanwhile, the fungal level regression model showed the light element role as an important factor which leads to its appearance in the atmosphere (p<0.01). According to the passive method, temperature and humidity were significant factors and impacted the bacterial concentration of the airborne environment in urban spaces (p<0.05). The linear regression model between the fungal level and humidity illustrated similar results with standardized coefficients (β) equal to 0.363 (t = 2.549, p<0.05).

Bacterial levels' PCA results showed three principal components which explained 62.882% of cumulative variance with eigenvalues equal to 1.068. Regarding fungal levels, PCA recommended three principal components with eigenvalues obtained 1.202 and explained 62.844% of cumulative variance. PCs named related to human impacts, transport impacts and integrated impacts respectively.

Thus, the study results showed culturable microorganism concentration in Ho Chi Minh City over the different seasons. In general, the microorganism levels fluctuated and were affected by mainly environmental factors such as humidity, temperature and CO_2 concentration. The findings of this study can provide a useful reference for future health studies, policy making and helpful urban planning in Ho Chi Minh City. Besides, the big microorganism data provides a new methodology for data management and a smart key for understanding the environmental issues. These databases can be stored and transferred into environmental data with a standardized information system.

6.5. References

Aaron, J.P. and Marr, L.C. (2015). Sources of airborne microorganisms in the built environment. *Microbiome*, 3(1), 78–87.

Aaron, J.P., Garcia, E.B., and Marr, L.C. (2015). Total virus and bacteria concentrations in indoor and outdoor air. *Environ. Sci. Technol. Lett.*, 2(4), 84–88.

Abdul Hameed, A.A., Khoder, M.I., Yuosra, S., Osman, A.M., and Ghanem, S. (2009). Diurnal distribution of airborne bactria and fungi in the atmosphere of Helwan area, Egypt. *Sci. Total Environ.*, 407(24), 6217–6222.

Anne, M.M., Moslehi-Jenabian, S., Islam, M.Z., Frankel, M., Spilak, M., and Frederiksen, M.W. (2018). Concentrations of Staphylococcus species in indoor air as associated with other bacteria, season, relative humidity, air change rate, and *S. aureus*-positive occupants. *Environ. Res.*, 160, 282–291.

Beata, G., Skóra, J., Stępień, Ł., Szponar, B., Otlewska, A., and Pielech-Przybylska, K. (2015). Assessment of microbial contamination within working environments of different types of composting plants. *J. Air Waste Manag. Assoc.*, 65(4), 466–478.

Blomquist, G. (1994). Sampling of biological particles. *Analyst*, 119, 53–56.

Burch, M. and Levetin, E. (2002). Effects of meteorological conditions on spore plumes. *Int. J. Biometeorol.*, 46, 107–117.

Burrows, S.M., Elbert, W., Lawrence, M.G., and Pöschl, U. (2009). Bacteria in the global atmosphere-part 1: Review and synthesis of literature data for different ecosystems. *Atmos. Chem. Phys.*, 9, 9263–9280.

Christian, N., Marcotrigiano, V., and Montagna, M.T. (2012). Air sampling procedures to evaluate microbial contamination: A comparison between active and passive methods in operating theatres. *BMC Public Health*, 12, 594–599.

Cox, C.S. (1989). Airborne bacteria and viruses. *Sci. Prog.*, 73, 469–499.

Douwes, J., Thorne, P., Pearce, N., and Heederic, D. (2003). Bioaerosol health effects and exposure assessment: Progress and prospects. *Ann. Occup. Hyg.*, 47, 187–200.

Elliott, L.F., Mccalla, T.M., and Deshazer, J.A. (1976). Bacteria in the air of housed swine units. *App. Environ. Microbiol.*, 32, 270–273.

Erkara, I.P., Asan, A., Yilmaz, V., Pehlivan, S., and Okten, S.S. (2008). Airborne *Alternaria* and *Cladosporium* species and relationship with meteorological conditions in Eskisehir City, Turkey. *Environ. Monit. Assess.*, 144, 31–41.

Fierer, N., Liu, Z., Rodríguez-Hernández, M., Knight, R., Henn, M., and Hernandez, M.T. (2008). Short-term temporal variability in airborne bacterial and fungal populations. *Appl. Environ. Microbiol.*, 74, 200–207.

Garrett, M.H., Rayment, P.R., Hooper, M.A., Abramson, M.J., and Hooper, B.M. (1998). Indoor airborne fungal spores, house dampness and associations with environmental factors and respiratory health in children. *Clin. Exp. Allergy*, 28, 459–467.

Gary, D. (1975). Principal component analysis of intraspecific variation in bacteria. *Appl. Microbiol.*, 30(2), 282–289.

Guo, H., Wang, T., and Louie, P.K.K. (2004). Source apportionment of ambient non-methane hydrocarbons in Hong Kong: Application of a principal component analysis/absolute principal component scores (PCA/APCS) receptor model. *Environ. Pollut.*, 129, 489–498.

Handley, B.A. and Webster, A.J. (1995). Some factors affecting the airborne survival of bacteria outdoors. *J. Appl. Bacteriol.*, 79(4), 368–378.

Hargreaves, M., Parappukkaran, S., Morawska, L., Hitchins, J., He, C., and Gilbert, D. (2003). A pilot investigation into association between indoor airborne fungal and non-biological particle concentrations in residential houses in Brisbane, Australia. *Sci. Total Environ.*, 312, 89–101.

Harrison, R.M., Jones, A.M., Biggins, P.D., Pomeroy, N., Cox, C.S., Kidd, S.P., Hobman, J.L., Brown, N.L., and Beswick, A. (2005). Climate factors influencing bacterial count in background air samples. *Int. J. Biometeorol.*, 49, 167–178.

Hotelling, H. (1933). Analysis of a complex of statistical variables into principal components. *J. Educ. Psychol.*, 24, 498–520.

Hung, N.T.Q., Lam, N.H., Le, H.A., Phuoc, L.B., and Hai, V.D. (2015). Assessment of air pollution (PM10 and BTEX) in Ho Chi Minh City in 2014. *VNU J. Sci. Nat. Sci. Technol.*, 31(2), 172–178.

Husman, T. (1996). Health effects of indoor-air microorganisms. *Scand. J. Work Environ. Health*, 22(1), 5–13.

Jantunen, M., Jaakkola, J.J.K., and Krzyzanowski, M. (1997). Assessment of Exposure to Indoor Air Pollutants. WHO Regional Publications, Copenhagen.

Jensen, P.A. and Schafer, M.P. (1998). Sampling and characterization of bioaerosols. NIOSH Manual of Analytical Methods. NIOSH Publication.

Jones, M. and Harrison, R.M. (2004). The effects of meteorological factors on atmospheric bioaerosol concentrations – A review. *Sci. Total Environ.*, 326, 151–180.

Jose, J.L., Joseph, H.S., and David, M.U. (2017). Commensal fungi in health and disease. *Cell Host Microbe.*, 22(2), 156–165.

Julian, W.T. (2009). The effect of environmental parameters on the survival of airborne infectious agents. *J. R. Soc. Interface*, 6, 737–746.

Jyotshna, M. and Brandl, H. (2011). Bioaerosols in indoor environment – A review with special reference to residential and occupational locations. *Open Environ. Biol. Monit. J.*, 4, 83–96.

Karra, S. and Katsivela, E. (2007). Microorganisms in bioaerosol emissions from wastewater treatment plants during summer at a Mediterranean site. *Water Res.*, 41, 1355–1365.

Khan, N.N. and Wilson, B.L. (2003). An environmental assessment of mold concentrations and potential mycotoxin exposures in the greater Southeast Texas area. *J. Environ. Sci. Health A Tox. Hazard. Subst. Environ. Eng.*, 38, 2759–2772.

Laura, P., Sampedro, G., Herrera, J.J., and Cabo, M.L. (1996). Effect of carbon dioxide atmosphere on microbial growth and quality of salmon slices. *J. Sci. Food Agri.*, 72(3), 348–352.

Lewi, P.J. (2005). Spectral mapping, a personal and historical account of an adventure in multivariate data analysis. *Chemometr. Intell. Lab. Syst.*, 77(1–2), 215–223.

Lighthart, B., Shaffer, B.T., Frisch, A.S., and Paterno, D. (2009). Atmospheric culturable bacteria associated with meteorological conditions at a summer-time site in the mid-Willamette Valley, Oregon. *Aerobiologia*, 25(4), 285–295.

Lin, W.H. and Li, C.S. (2000). Association of fungal aerosols, air pollutants, and meteorological factors. *Aerosol Sci. Technol.*, 32(4), 359–368.

Linda, D.S. (1998). Microorganisms and indoor air quality. *Clin. Microbiol. Newsl.*, 20(19), 157–161.

Macher, J. (ed.) (1999). *Bioaerosols: Assessment and Control*. ACGIH, Cincinnati, OH.

Mancinelli, R. and Shulls, W. (1978). Airborne bacteria in an urban environment. *Appl. Environ. Microbiol.*, 35, 1095–1101.

Nobuyasu, Y., Park, J., Kodama, M., Ichijo, T., Baba, T., and Nasu, M. (2014). Changes in the airborne bacterial community in outdoor environments following Asian dust events. *Microbes Environ.*, 29(1), 82–88.

Pasquarella, C., Pitzurra, O., and Savino, A. (2000). The index of microbial air contamination. *J. Hosp. Infect.*, 46, 241–246.

Pasquarella, C., Albertini, R., Dall'aglio, P., Saccani, E., Sansebastiano, G.E., and Signorelli, C. (2008). Air microbial sampling: The state of the art. *Ig Sanita Pubbl.*, 64, 79–120.

Pastuszka, J., Paw, U., Lis, D., and Wlazlo, A. (2000). Bacterial and fungal aerosol in indoor environment in Upper Silesia, Poland. *Atmos. Environ.*, 34, 3833–3842.

Pathak, A.K. and Verma, K.S. (2009). Aero-bacteriological study of vegetable market at Jabalpur. *Iran J. Environ. Health. Sci. Eng.*, 6, 187–194.

Peder, W. (2018). Indoor air humidity, air quality, and health – An overview. *Int. J. Hyg. Environ. Health*, 221(3), 376–390.

Pengrui, D., Dua, R., Rena, W., Lua, Z., Zhanga, Y., and Fu, P. (2018). Variations of bacteria and fungi in PM2.5 in Beijing, China. *Atmos. Environ.*, 172, 55–64.

Pillai, S.D. and Ricke, S.C. (2002). Bioaerosols from municipal and animal wastes: Background and contemporary issues. *Can. J. Microbiol.*, 48, 681–696.

Qian, J., Hospodsky, D., Yamamoto, N., Nazaroff, W.W., and Peccia, J. (2012). Size-resolved emission rates of airborne bacteria and fungi in an occupied classroom. *Indoor Air*, 22, 339–351.

Quan, Z., Deng, Y., Wang, Y., Wang, X., Zhang, H., Sun, X., and Ouyang, Z. (2017). Meteorological factors had more impact on airborne bacterial communities than air pollutants. *Sci. Total Environ.*, 601–602, 703–712.

Rachel, I.A., Miletto, M., Taylor, J.W., and Bruns, T.D. (2013). Dispersal in microbes: Fungi in indoor air are dominated by outdoor air and show dispersal limitation at short distances. *ISME J.*, 7, 1262–1273.

Robert, M.B., Sullivan, A.P., Costello, E.K., Collett, J.L., Knight, R., and Fierer, N. (2011). Sources of bacteria in outdoor air across cities in the midwestern United States. *Appl. Environ. Microbiol.*, 77(18), 6350–6356.

Robertson, C.E., Baumgartner, L.K., Harris, J.K., Peterson, K.L., Stevens, M.J., Frank, D.N., and Pace, N.R. (2013). Culture-independent analysis of aerosol microbiology in a metropolitan subway system. *Appl. Environ. Microbiol.*, 79, 3485–3493.

Ruiping, L., Xiao, P., She, R., Han, S., Chang, L., and Zheng, L. (2013). Culturable airborne bacteria in outdoor poultry-slaughtering facility. *Microbes Environ.*, 28(2), 251–256.

Sabariego, S., Diaz de la Guardia, C., Alba, F. (2000). The effect of meteorological factors on the daily variation of airborne fungal spores in Granada (southern Spain). *Int. J. Biometeorol.*, 44, 1–5.

Shokri, H., Khosravi, A.R., Naseri, A., Ghiasi, M., and Ziapour, S.P. (2010). Common environmental allergenic fungi causing respiratory allergy in North of Iran. *Int. J. Vet. Res.*, 4(3), 169–172.

Sophia, H. (2013). Some fungi in the air. *Microbes Infection*, 15(4), 255–258.

Stetzenbach, L.D. (2007). Introduction to aerobiology. In *Manual of Environmental Microbiology*, Hurst, C.J., Crawford, R.L., Garland, J.L., Lipson, D.A., Mills, A.L., and Stetzenbach, L.D. (eds). ASM Press, Washington, DC.

Tong, Y. and Lighthart, B. (2000). The annual bacterial particle concentration and size distribution in the ambient atmosphere in a rural area of the Willamette Valley, Oregon. *Aerosol Sci. Technol.*, 32, 393–403.

Valley, G. (1928). The effect of carbon dioxide on bacteria. *Q. Rev. Biol.*, 3(2), 209–224.

Walker, C.M. and Ko, G. (2007). Effect of ultraviolet germicidal irradiation on viral aerosols. *Environ. Sci. Technol.*, 41, 5460–5465.

Wold, S., Esbensen, K., and Geladi, P. (1987). Principal component analysis. *Chem. Intell. Lab. Syst.*, 2, 37–52.

Wright, T.J., Greene, V.W., and Paulus, H.J. (1969). Viable microorganisms in an urban atmosphere. *J. Air Pollut. Control Assoc.*, 19(5), 337–341.

Zhengsheng, X., Li, Y., Lu, R., Li, W., Fan, C., Liu, P., Wang, J., and Wang, W. (2018). Characteristics of total airborne microbes at various air quality levels. *J. Aerosol Sci.*, 116, 57–65.

Zhou, J., Fang, W., Cao, Q., Yang, L., Chang, V.W.C., and Nazaroff, W.W. (2016). Influence of moisturizer and relative humidity on human emissions of fluorescent biological aerosol particles. *Indoor Air*, 26, 587–598.

Application of GIS and RS in Planning Environmental Protection Zones in Phu Loc District, Thua Thien Hue Province

7.1. Introduction

In Vietnam, environmental protection planning (EPP) is a concept legalized in 2014's Environmental Protection Law to guide development planning based on an informed decision-making process that relies on quantitative analysis of socio-economic and environmental conditions. The rise of EPP is a response to growing concerns about the general environmental situation in Vietnam after decades of rapid economic development. In fact, the country has significantly reduced poverty and increased the standard of living for its population during the last 40 years thanks to a series of reforming economic policies. However, the economic development process is not without ecological degradation, pollution and the depletion of natural resources that lead to social impact such as inequality and displacement.

EPP is a complex process due to the involvement of not only ecological variables such as vegetation cover, geology and hydrometeorology but also socio-economic variables of current status and planning for the future. In this study, the authors attempt to use GIS and RS to create a map for EPP by zoning the study area, taking into account both the natural environmental and socio-economic variables. The study area, the Phu Loc District in Thua Thien Hue Province, Central Vietnam, is a rural area where there has been a long history of human modification of the natural landscape and resources (Figure 7.1).

Chapter written by Quoc Tuan LE, Trinh Minh Anh NGUYEN, Huy Anh NGUYEN and Truong Ngoc Han LE.

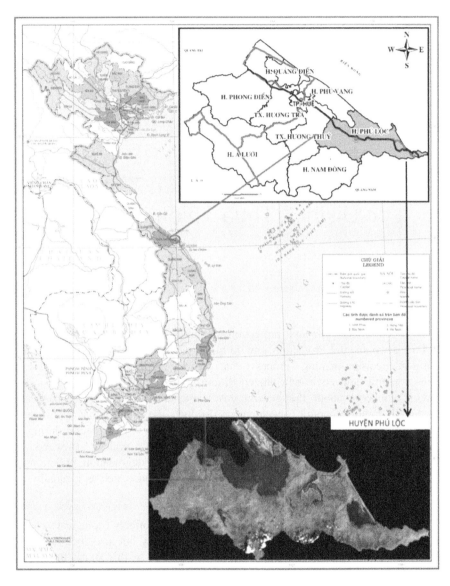

Figure 7.1. *Phu Loc District, Thuan Thien Hue Province, Vietnam.*
For a color version of this figure, see www.iste.co.uk/laffly/torus3.zip

Phu Loc District encompasses an area of 72,092 ha, accounting for 14% of the natural area of Thua Thien Hue Province. Notable landscapes in Phu Loc District include mountains covering the south, running to the sea and circling a blackish lagoon and a narrow basin. Local economy ranges from forestry in mountainous communes in the south, aquaculture in the blackish lagoon to fishery and tourism in the coastal area. The paddy area, which has been a traditional farming system in the coastal basin, is gradually being replaced by shrimp and fish aquaculture ponds. In the last 20 years, tourism has become a vital economy in the local area in the form of a beach resort along the coast.

The development of Phu Loc District has resulted in not only the degradation of natural ecological systems such as the transformation of natural forest area to planted forest, leading to biodiversity loss in the mountainous area, the contamination of the blackish water lagoon but also conflicts between different stakeholders in natural resource exploitation and management. A map for EPP in Phu Loc District is, therefore, necessary, to help decision-makers to consider environmental factors in the development process. In other words, it is expected that there could be a balance between economic development and environmental conservation. This chapter also illustrates the possible application of remote sensing big data in environmental protection.

7.2. Materials and research methods

7.2.1. *Materials*

The following data is used in this research:

– terrain map of Phu Loc District 1:25.000, Coordination system VN2000 produced by MONRE in 2004;

– GIShue datasets: GIShue is a 2005–2011 project aiming to create a database for Thua Thien Hue Province in seven layers: boundary, terrain, names, geographical objects, hydrology, transportation map and surface cover;

– remote sensing images from Landsat 7 ETM+ and Landsat 5 TM with a 30 m resolution during the period from 1989 to 2013 for Path 124, 125 and Row 49. These images are used to interpret vegetation cover and temporal change in vegetation cover in Phu Loc District;

– socio-economic statistics for Phu Loc District in 2000–2013 from provincial and district statistical reports and district socio-economic development in 2005–2013.

7.3. Research methods

7.3.1. Research approach

In this study, the authors employ a catchment area approach. A catchment area can be understood as an area of land where all the surface water from rain or melting snow converges at a lower elevation and exits through a basin, which is the surface area of natural land that any falling precipitation will focus onto, and exits through a single point from which water joins a water body such as a river, lake or lagoon (Huy Anh *et al.* 2012a).

If the interactions between river basin and other geographic entities are to be considered, the catchment area is considered as a geographical space in which the surface water and the underground water flow and interact with other resources and human activities.

A catchment area is an open system and always interacts with the atmosphere through atmospheric circulations and hydrological cycles. Hundreds of catchment areas receive an amount of water from the rain for the use of humans and maintenance of the ecosystem function.

In summary, a catchment area is an appropriate approach in making an EPP map because it takes into account the integrated management of multiple resources, such as water, land, forest and others existing in the basin. It aims to strike a balance between the socio-economic benefits and the sustainability of the catchment area environment.

7.3.2. Research methods

7.3.2.1. Data collection

Secondary data include official documents at all levels from central to local, existing research results both in Vietnam and internationally.

7.3.2.2. Data analysis

Mapping using GIS application is the main approach. This is a set of important methods and brings about efficiency in the process of mapping, planning, geographic resource assessment, environmental monitoring and warning. In addition, GIS modules help to develop standardized geographic information systems, natural and socio-economic environmental factors for environmental planning and management.

A remote sensing method is used for satellite image analysis (Landsat 5-TM, 7-ETM+) to develop vegetation cover, DEM, coastline change and vulnerability to natural disaster information in the study area. ArcGIS 10.2 software and Mapinfo 10 software are the main software in this analysis.

7.3.2.3. Mapping process

Step 1: Phu Loc District Territory Map is established based on the basin approach with the analysis of natural conditions including geology, geomorphology and hydro-meteorology data in combination with interpretation of the Landsat images. Accordingly, Phu Loc District is divided into three catchment areas: Cau Hai, Bu Lu, Lap An Lagoon.

Step 2: An Environmental Zoning Map is created based on the Phu Loc territory map in conjunction with the general evaluation of the natural conditions, economic – social and environmental changes in Phu Loc District.

Step 3: An environmental Protection Planning Map is constructed by taking into account district socio-economic planning until 2030 based on the Environmental Zoning Map.

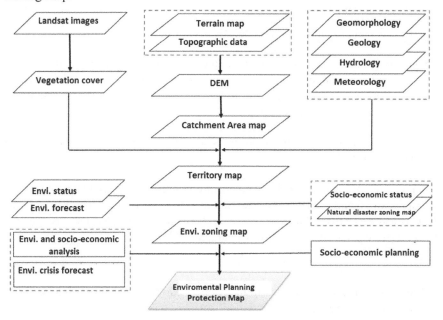

Figure 7.2. *Constructing process of environmental protection planning map*

7.3.3. Results and discussion

7.3.3.1. Characteristics of research area

Geological features: according to the previous researches, in Phu Loc District, the main rock formation is volcanic and sedimentary from the Neoproterozoic to the Cenozoic period (Vietnam Office of Geology 1994).

Topographic features: based on topographic classification, the terrain type group divides the geomorphological map of the district into seven types (Institute of Geography 2005):

– low altitude area of 300–1000 m: result of recent tectonic activity;

– uplift hill of 50–200 m: result of recent tectonic activity;

– stabilized hilly basin of less than 50 m;

– water surface of annual rivers and stream flows;

– coastal plain including the surface of a modern eroded slope;

– plain with sand dunes;

– riverine and maritime fluvial plain.

Climate: annual average temperature in the mountainous area: 20°C; in the plain: 25.2°C; absolute maximum temperature in the mountainous area: 43°C; in the plain: 44°C; absolute minimum temperature in the mountainous area: 8.8°C; in the plain: 11.2°C (Institute of Geography 2005).

Hydrology surface water: the main rivers are the Nong River, Truoi River, Bu Lu River and Cau Hai River.

Vegetation: vegetation in the northern area includes species belonging to the Leguminosae family, the Fagaceae family, the Lauraceae family and the Melaleucaadre family, while in the southern area, the species are of the Dipterocarpaceae family (Institute of Geography 2005).

7.3.3.2. Natural disasters

Tsunami: In theory, a tsunami from a remote earthquake may reach a height of 1.5–5 m in the Central Coast.

Floods: Phu Loc is at the rainfall center of Thua Thien Hue province, resulting in frequent flooding in the vicinity of Cau Hai, Loc An, Lang Co.

Landslide: According to a survey conducted in 2011 and 2012, landslides occur mainly along traffic roads, especially Phuoc Tuong Pass, Phu Pass Gia, Hai Van Pass and Provincial Road 14B.

Typhoons and tropical depressions: In the period 1891–2000, there were 79 events affecting Thua Thien Hue province including Phu Loc District.

Climate change and sea level rise: According to Vietnam 2011 climate change scenarios, Thua Thien Hue province would suffer a 60–71 cm in sea level rise (Huy Anh *et al.* 2012b).

7.3.4. Environmental protection planning map

According to the resulted EPP Map, Phu Loc District is divided into four zones:

Strict conservation zone: these are zones where the main functions are the conservation of genetic resources, protection of biodiversity, areas of national parks and nature reserves. Phu Loc District has six protection and preservation zones that cover an area of 17,006.58 ha, accounting for 21.85% of the total planning area, including: Hai Van – Son Cha: C.I.V.2; Biodiversity conservation area north of Bach Ma (A.I.1); Strict protection zone of Bach Ma National Park core area (A.I.2); Forest protection and restoration of upper Bu Lu River (B.I.1); Forest protection and biodiversity conservation in Hai Van (C.I.1); Chan May Protected Area (B.II.2).

Enhanced management zone: this accounts for an area of 29,284.64 ha (37.62%) of the plan, including areas currently for agricultural, forestry and aquaculture production that are showing early signs of pollution. Management in this zone must take into account the sustainable use of natural resources and economic activities in harmony with environmental protection.

This zone consists of 10 areas: enhanced protection coastal waters to a depth of 6 m A.IV.1, C.IV.1, B.IV.1; enhanced environmental management in northern production areas A.III.1, A.III.2; enhanced environmental management in coastal agricultural production areas A.III.7; enhanced environmental management solutions in Xuan Loc A.II.1; enhanced management and protection area for biodiversity and aquaculture sustainability in coastal lagoons (Cau Hai lagoon and Lap An lagoon) with zones A.III.5, C.II.2; agricultural and fishery production along Cau Hai lagoon A.III.4.

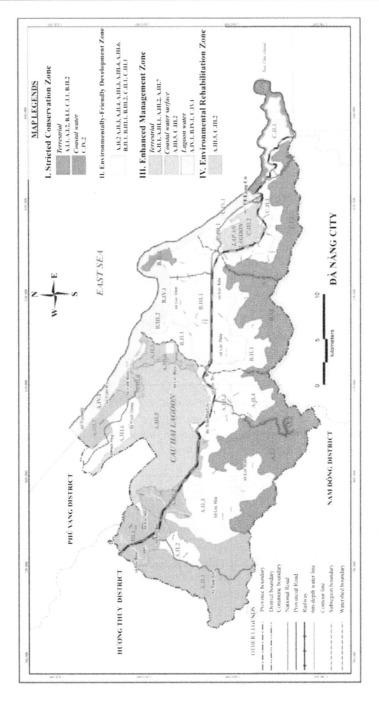

Figure 7.3. *Environmental protection planning map for Phu Loc District. For a color version of this figure, see www.iste.co.uk/laffly/torus3.zip*

Environmentaly-friendly development zone: this encompasses 29,755.9 ha (38.22%) of the planned area, including the areas that apply the relevant regulations for land use change, development activities. EIA/SEA is needed to control the impact from development activities on the environment.

Phu Loc District has identified 11 areas: two of which are high-end resorts and eco-tourism resorts, namely, Laguna B.III.1 and Lang Co Tourism Complex (C.C.III.1); eight areas whose main functions are to develop industry, handicraft, the urban area and eco-tourism such as: Urban environmental protection zones A.III.6, A.III.3; Environmental protection area of Chan May – Lang Co economic zone B.III.2; Green belt of Chan May-Lang Co economic zone B.II.1, C.II.1; Environmental Protection in the Buffer Zone of Bach Ma National Park A.II.3, A.II.4, A.II.2;

Environmental rehabilitation zone: this includes areas that have been degraded and will be rehabilitated, such as post-production titanium mines, sites frequently affected by floods and sea level rise and areas of degraded natural forest. Phu Loc District has identified two areas with an area of 1,800.29 hectares, accounting for 2.31% of the planned area: rehabilitating natural forests in Vinh Phong mountain (A.II.5) and to renovate and rehabilitate coastal protection forests and coastal protection works (A.III.8).

Item	Environmental protection planning	Code	Area (Ha)	Percentage
1	Strict conservation zone (6)			
	Terrestrial	A.I.1, A.I.2, B.I.1, C.I.1, B.II.2	16,129.00	20.72
	Coastal water	C.IV.2	877.58	1.13
2	Environmentaly-friendly development zone (11)	B.III.2, C.III.1, A.III.3, A.III.6, B.II.1, C.II.1, B.III.1, A.II.3, A.II.4, A.II.2, A.III.4	29,755.90	38.22
3	Enhanced management zone (9)			
	Terrestrial	A.II.1, A.III.1, A.III.2, A.III.7	13,583.20	17.45
	Coastal water surface	A.IV.1, B.IV.1, C.IV.1	4,529.65	5.82
	Lagoon water	A.III.5, C.III.2	11,171.79	14.35
4	Environmental rehabilitation zone (2)	A.II.5, A.III.8	1,800.29	2.31

Table 7.1. *Area for environmental protection planning in Phu Loc District*

7.4. Conclusion

The EPP map divides Phu Loc District into four development zones. These are strict conservation zone (21.85%), environmentaly-friendly development zone (38.22%), enhanced management zone (37.62%) and environmental rehabilitation zone (2.31%). The authors expect that the map will provide local decision-makers with a visual and quantitative tool to support the planning of socio-economic development. Nonetheless, given the volume of data available for this task, especially remote sensing data, the current methods can be considered as rudimentary, as it is still too dependent on the subjective processing of technicians and equipment which can only deal with a limited volume of data. It is suggested that human and physical resources should be invested to be able to process the currently available amount of remote sensing data so that the resulting EPP map can be more accurate and informative.

7.5. References

Huy Anh, N., Thang, L.V., Phai, V.V. (2012a). Environmental zoning in Phu Loc District, Thua Thien Hue, Vietnam, *Vietnam National University Natural Science Journal*, 28(5S), 1–11.[In Vietnamese].

Huy Anh N., Thang L.V., Kien D.T. (2012b). Remote sensing and GIS application to build landcover map of Chan May – Lang Co area, Phu Loc district, Thua Thien Hue province, *J Sci, Hue Univ*, 77(8), 5–14. [In Vietnamese].

Institute of Geography (2005). General Survey of Natural Conditions and Resources of Phu Loc District, Thua Thien Hue. Vietnam, Research Report, Hà Nội.

MONRE (2011). *Climate Change Scenario and Sea Level Rise*. Cartography Publisher, Hanoi. [In Vietnamese].

Vietnam Office of Geology (1994). *Geological Map of Thua Thien Hue Province 1:50.000*. Hanoi. [In Vietnamese].

8

Forecasting the Water Quality and the Capacity of the Dong Nai River to Receive Wastewater up to 2020

8.1. Introduction

Dong Nai province is located in the southern key economic region, one of the provinces with economic growth, high investment attraction, rapid industrial development, including industry and services and agriculture. It has launched many industrial parks and clusters, such as Bien Hoa 1, Bien Hoa 2, Amata, Loteco and Tam Phuoc. According to a report of the Department of Natural Resources and Environment in 2015, the Dong Nai province has 31 industrial zones and 27 industrial parks which have built wastewater treatment plants. Besides the wastewater from the industrial park, it also receives a huge amount of wastewater from hospitals and residential areas (CEME Dong Nai province 2010, 2013).

With the processes of economic and social development, the surface waters are directly threatened by the waste generated from everything from daily activities (urban, residential areas, etc.) to development activities, such as industries (industrial, manufacturing factories, etc.), husbandry and fisheries, which is being discharged almost directly into water sources. Contaminated surface water affects the self-cleaning ability of the water system, causing a decline in water quality, which also greatly affects human health and the environment, resulting in a negative impact on the socio-economic development process. This is a great challenge for the socio-economic development of the Dong Nai province (Do Tien Lanh 2010).

Chapter written by Quoc Tuan LE, Thi Kieu Diem NGO and Truong Ngoc Han LE.

Therefore, assessing the quality of present water sources, calculating the load of pollutants into the river, as well as forecasting the water quality and the capacity of the Dong Nai River to receive wastewater in 2020 are important to offer unified management solutions, synchronization and partition of discharge to ensure water quality and socio-economic development. This study is essential to serve the exploitation, usage and protection of water resources the Dong Nai River sustainably for the whole province. Furthermore, enormous data from the water quality forecasting can integrate Big Data to challenge data capturing, data storage, data analysis, research, sharing, transfer, visualization, querying, updating, information privacy and data sources. Then, the Big Data from the Dong Nai River quality will be implicated for many fields such as industrial activities, agricultural production, household water supply and release.

8.2. Materials and methods

8.2.1. *Assessing the water quality and partitioning the receiving zone*

The surface water quality assessment is carried out according to Decision No. 879/QĐ-TCMT, dated 01/07/2011, by the General Department of Environment, on the issuance of the manual calculation of water quality indicators in order to rapidly assess the surface water quality. To determine the quality of each section of the river, water quality index (WQI) values of each river section and WQIs of each monitoring site are calculated (Vietnam Environment Administration 2011).

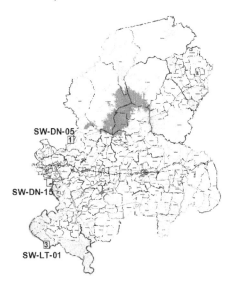

Figure 8.1. *Sites for MIKE 11 application. For a color version of this figure, see www.iste.co.uk/laffly/torus3.zip*

In addition, a comparison of the pollutant concentration with 08-MT: 2015/BTNTM was used to assess concentrations of some pollutants. Application of Decision No. 16/QĐ-UBND, dated 03/19/2010, by People's Committee of Dong Nai Province, for partition of receiving industrial wastewater and emission in the Dong Nai province helps determine the regulations for each section of the Dong Nai River (People's Committee of Dong Nai province 2010), and previous results were used to confirm sections in partitioning of wastewater receiver (SDWRPI 2013).

8.2.2. *MIKE 11 modeling*

MIKE 11 software (Danish Hydraulic Institute 2007) is applied for forecasting water quality and the wastewater-receiving capacity up to 2020. The updated data on the pollution load into the river can forecast the wastewater-receiving capacity of the Dong Nai River up to 2020. Predictive models of water quality were built for the Dong Nai River based on the hydraulic model, the sources of the waste (CEME Dong Nai province 2013), concentration scenarios, and the flow of the waste stream.

The whole 29 streams with more than 40 compute nodes and River Network tools are used for the Mike 11 model to perform hydraulic diagram calculations. Cross-sectional data of models including measurements of the 357 cross sections have been transferred to the digital terrain data format used in Mike 11.

The upper margin of the hydraulic model includes: (1) margin at section 0: the discharge of Tri An hydropower and average flow of Be river; (2) margin of flow on La Buong river: the average of the monthly flow for many years (1978–2000) at hydrological stations; and (3) margin of flow of Nuoc Trong stream: average flow for years $Q_{average} = 5.58$ (m^3/s).

The lower margin of the hydraulic model includes: (1) margin of water levels in Vung Tau (transmission calculation on entrance Long Tau, Dong Tranh, Soai Rap) and (2) margins of flow the same as the upper margin.

8.3. Results and discussion

8.3.1. *The water quality of the Dong Nai River*

Analysis of the monitoring data collected from the Department of Natural Resources and Environment of the Dong Nai province through 2011, 2012 and 2013 (CEME Dong Nai province 2010, 2013) at the 19 monitoring sites according to Decision No. 16/2010/QĐ-UBND, dated 03/19/2010, for partition of receiving industrial wastewater and emission in Dong Nai province to determine the regulations for each section of Dong Nai river was used to assess the quality of the Dong Nai River in each section as follows: section 1: from Nam Cat Tien Wharf to Ferry 107, Phu Ngoc Commune, Dinh Quan District; section 2: from the lower of Tri An reservoir, confluence of Be River and Dong Nai River, Vinh Cuu District to Ba Mieu Wharf, Bien Hoa City; section 3: from Hoa An Bridge, Hoa An Commune, Bien Hoa City to Dong Nai Bridge, Long Binh Tan Ward, Bien Hoa City; section 4: from the lower of Dong Nai Bridge, Long Binh Tan Ward, Bien Hoa City to confluence of Cai Mep and Go Gia Rivers, Phuoc An Commune, Nhon Trach District.

The data monitoring and calculation of WQIs show that the water quality of the Dong Nai River basically meets the regulations for each purpose of water use. The water quality of the Dong Nai River in sections 1 and 2 meets the regulations for water supply. Section 3 also meets the regulations for water supply, but sometimes in the rainy season (in months 7, 8 and 9 of the assessment), the water quality showed a significant decline. Section 4 meets the regulations for irrigation and aquatic conservation.

8.3.2. *Waste sources to the Dong Nai River*

The Dong Nai River receives most of the wastewater from factories, urban areas, residential areas and major industrial parks in the Dong Nai province. According to the data obtained from the Department of Natural Resources and Environment of the Dong Nai province, the Dong Nai River receives wastewater at a rate of 215,477 m^3/day (CEME Dong Nai province 2013), which is the highest ever received. This constitutes wastewater from health facilities (average flow 2,467 m^3/day), urban and residential areas (89,070 m^3/day), livestock operations (about 586 m^3/day), markets, supermarkets and trade centers (589 m^3/day), 11 industrial zones (56,268 m^3/day) and manufactories (about 66,497 m^3/day) (see Table 8.1). In industrial zones, there are wastewater treatment plants where wastewater is controlled before being released to the Dong Nai River. Wastewater from the other sources is not treated and is released directly into the river, especially from urban regions and agricultural sectors (husbandry), which mainly affect the water quality of the Dong Nai River.

No.	Waste sources	Total flow	Flow (Q m^3/day)			
		Q m^3/day	Section 1	Section 2	Section 3	Section 4
1	Health facilities	2,467	16	61	1,820	570

2	Factories outside industrial parks	66,497	2,441	17,710	23,910	22,436
3	Domestic activities	89,070	319	1,297	86,519	935
4	Husbandry activities	586	39	198	25	324
5	Markets	589	5	194	280	110
6	Industrial parks	56,268	24	4,600	40,908	10,736
	Total	**215,477**	**2,844**	**24,060**	**153,462**	**35,111**

Table 8.1. *Waste sources to the Dong Nai River*

8.3.3. *Waste load to Dong Nai river*

According to the quality analysis and relevant calculations for the concentration of pollutants, there are some selected parameters: BOD_5, COD, total N, total P and TSS. The load of pollutants in the wastewater that entered the Dong Nai River in 2013 is presented in Table 8.2.

No.	Waste sources	Q in 2013 (m^3/day)	Load (kg/day)				
			BOD$_5$	COD	Total N	Total P	TSS
1	Health facilities	2,467	35	113	41	12	145
2	Factories outside industrial parks	66,497	1,190	4,360	1,850	79	4,030
3	Domestic activities	89,070	5,700	3,296	1,158	89	9,709

4	Husbandry activities	586	151	333	170	41	245
5	Markets	589	89	100	31	19	121
6	Industrial parks	56,268	800	2,579	1,073	114	3,393
	Total	215,477	7,965	10,781	4,323	354	17,643

Table 8.2. Load of pollutants in wastewater in 2013

8.3.4. Forecasting load to the Dong Nai River in 2020

To forecast the Dong Nai River's water quality for 2020, three given scenarios and their pollution loads of waste sources were proposed and calculated. Five parameters of water quality were selected: BOD, COD, total nitrogen, total phosphorus and TSS, to calculate and build predictive models. The following three scenarios are based on the actual conditions of the provincial planning and economic development.

Scenario 1. The quality of wastewater into the Dong Nai River as current: the obligation for the legal regulations of waste generators; maintaining the management of environmental protection and the increasing economy as planned. Therefore, wastewater flow increases with economic development; collection and treatment of wastewater are not changed much, the wastewater systems continue their current operation, large urban areas do not have developed domestic wastewater treatment, livestock waste is mostly untreated before being discharged into the receiver and the concentration of contaminants does not change. The estimated pollutant loads by 2020 are presented in Table 8.3.

No.	Waste sources	Q in 2020 (m³/day)	Load (kg/day)				
			BOD$_5$	COD	Total N	Total P	TSS
1	Health facilities	5,297	56	271	47	32	429
2	Factories outside industrial parks	108,058	1,934	7,089	3,004	130	6,548

3	Domestic activities	125,326	12,783	14,287	1,792	226	16,982
4	Husbandry activities	59,409	15,328	33,744	17,217	4,182	24,803
5	Markets	1,296	200	316	77	49	292
6	Industrial parks	320,498	4,551	14,679	6,122	641	19,358
	Total (Scenario 1)	**619,884**	**34,852**	**70,386**	**28,259**	**5,260**	**68,412**
1	Health facilities	5,297	265	530	265	53	530
2	Factories outside industrial parks	108,058	5,403	16,209	4,322	648	10,806
3	Domestic activities	125,326	6,266	12,533	1,253	1,253	12,533
4	Husbandry activities	59,409	2,970	5,941	1,782	356	5,941
5	Markets	1,296	65	194	52	8	130
6	Industrial parks	320,498	16,025	48,075	12,820	1,923	32,050
	Total (Scenario 2)	**619,884**	**30,994**	**83,482**	**20,494**	**4,241**	**61,990**
1	Health facilities	5,297	159	265	159	32	265
2	Factories outside industrial parks	108,058	1,837	4,538	1,189	216	3,026
3	Domestic activities	125,326	3,760	6,266	627	752	6,266
4	Husbandry activities	59,409	1,782	2,970	891	238	2,970
5	Markets	1,296	39	65	39	8	65
6	Industrial parks	320,498	9,615	24,037	6,410	1,282	16,025
	Total (Scenario 3)	**619,884**	**17,192**	**38,141**	**9,315**	**2,528**	**28,617**

Table 8.3. *Load of pollutants in wastewater to 2020 in scenarios (1, 2 and 3)*

Scenario 2. Suppose that by 2020, water flow has increased as estimated, and wastewater from urban areas, production establishments, animal husbandry and health facilities are treated to meet 08-MT:2015/MONRE (column B, see Appendix 8.5) before being discharged into the Dong Nai River.

Scenario 3: Based on the planning of social and economic development in the Dong Nai province, environmental protection activities are implemented in the province according to the Environmental Protection project of Dong Nai province until 2020.

The calculated results show that the load of pollutants flowing into the Dong Nai River in scenario 3 is the lowest, which indicates that it is the perfect scenario for the future. Thus, the amount of pollutants discharged will rise until 2020, and if there is no method to reduce and regulate the discharge of wastewater into water receiver, the Dong Nai River will be under stress of pollution.

8.3.5. *Water quality forecasting*

The calculation results for the load of waste sources into the Dong Nai River shows that scenario 3 is the most ideal, where pollution load into the river is the lowest. Assessment of the current state of the river's water quality indicated that it has reached the quality for water use. Therefore, current research is focused on developing predictive models for scenarios 1 and 2 up to 2020. The load-receiving sites have been analyzed and evaluated for pursuing the water use purpose, with site 1 and site 2 compared against standard 08-MT:2015/BTNMT (column A2) and site 3 compared against standard 08-MT:2015/MONRE (column B2).

According to the model results, the concentration of TSS in the location and the scenario is as follows: Under scenario 1: at sites 1 and 2, the highest TSS concentrations in the range of 40–60 mg/L exceed the regulations at the start and end of the months of the rainy season, and the remaining months meet the standards; at site 3, the highest concentration of TSS in March (230 mg/L) exceeds permitted standards, and the remaining months meet the standard. Under scenario 2: at sites 1 and 2, the highest concentrations of TSS in the range of 40–60 mg/L exceed the regulations at the start and end of the months of the rainy season, and the remaining months meet the standards; at site 3, the highest TSS concentrations in the range of 59–61 mg/L meet the regulations and are lower than in scenario 1.

Therefore, in the case of the management under scenario 2, the maximum load of TSS at sites 1 and 2 in the dry season (from January to June) ranges from the minimum (1,000 tons/day) to the maximum in October (7,000 tons/day) and the average maximum load for the whole year is 3,500 tons/day. In the rainy season,

TSS concentrations exceeded the standard 08-MT: 2015/BTNMT (column A2), which should not be allowed for TSS load. At site 3, the maximum load reached 3,200 tons/day in January, with an average value of 1,800 tons/day. The maximum load generally tended to increase during the rainy season. At site 3, due to the strong tides, the maximum load fluctuates.

The result of the modeling scenarios shows that the Dong Nai River is still able to receive BOD, TSS, total N and total P. Note that in scenario 1, the concentrations of TSS and COD waste in the dry season from the Dong Nai Bridge 1 km downstream to Long Tau area exceeded the standards. This section is no longer capable of receiving TSS and COD. From the results of scenario 1, if the management of waste discharge and pollution control remain the same as present, pollutant concentrations will be high, and water quality will be contaminated (with COD, TSS over the standard level).

In scenario 2, by 2020, with good management and the wastewater treatment in good operation, standards 08-MT: 2015/BTNMT (column B) will be reached, and water quality will be better and achieve the purposes of water use. Therefore, scenario 2 is the best choice for environmental management.

8.3.6. *Partition for water receiving of the Dong Nai River*

Based on the modeling results for water quality of scenario 2 by 2020, there are partitions of discharge areas as follows:

– Region 1, from the Tri An Dam to Dong Nai Bridge 1 km downstream: the capacity of receiving wastewater with total BOD: 1,000 tons/day, COD: 2,100 tons/day, TSS: 3,500 tons/day, total N: 600 tons/day and total P: 22 tons/day.

– Region 2, from Dong Nai Bridge (1 km downstream) to the Dong Nai River lower basin, the capacity of receiving maximum BOD: 500 tons/day, COD: 900 tons/day, TSS: 1,800 tons/day, total N: 300 tons/day and total P: 1.4 tons/day.

Based on the partition for receiving wastewater, authorities have licensed discharging wastewater into the Dong Nai River.

8.4. Conclusion

The load of pollutants into the Dong Nai River is huge. According to statistics, the total daily discharge of wastewater into the river about 215,477 m^3, the largest source from the industrial zones and Bien Hoa City. This is the main reason causing the decline in water quality.

Under scenario 2, the forecast shows that by 2020, the water quality of the Dong Nai River and from Tri An Dam to Dong Nai Bridge meets the standards and achieves the purpose of water supply within the parameters of BOD, COD, total N and total P. However, at the beginning of the rainy season and the end of the rainy season, TSS exceeds the standards and does not meet water supply purposes. Water quality in the Dong Nai River lower basin, Nhon Trach district, achieves the purpose of navigation and aquatic life protection.

In order to protect the water quality of the Dong Nai River, it is necessary to implement of the proposed solutions. In particular, in order to implement the priority measures to collect and treat all wastewater from urban centers, based on the partitions of wastewater receiving, localities in the Dong Nai River basin need a common water using purpose and regulations on wastewater discharge for each area accordingly.

Big Data from the Dong Nai River opens the capabilities of the users and their tools, and expanding capabilities makes Big Data an environmental target. For some organizations (private sectors, public sectors, investors), facing hundreds of gigabytes of data for the first time may trigger a need to reconsider data management options. For others, it may take tens or hundreds of terabytes before data size becomes a significant consideration. Getting Big Data from the Dong Nai River watershed and water quality encourages organizations to find out the best ways or methods to orientate their own implementations.

8.5. Appendix

The classification of A1, A2, B1 and B2 are from the 08-MT:2015/MONRE standard for surface water sources, to assess and control water quality. They serve different water use purposes and are arranged in descending levels, according to quality:

	A	B
1	**A1** Suitable for domestic water supply purposes after the application of normal treatment, conservation of aquatic plants and animals and other purposes, such as those for levels A2, B1 and B2.	**B1** Suitable for irrigation or other purposes requiring similar water quality, or purposes such as those for level B2.
2	**A2** Suitable for domestic water supply purposes with suitable treatment technology, or purposes such as those for levels B1 and B2.	**B2** Suitable for transportation/navigation and other purposes with low water quality requirements.

8.6. References

Center for Environmental Monitoring and Engineering of Dong Nai province (CEME Dong Nai province) (2010). Environmental Monitoring of Water Quality of Dong Nai River, Dong Nai Province in 2010.Report. CEME, Dong Nai province.

Center for Environmental Monitoring and Engineering of Dong Nai province (CEME Dong Nai province) (2013). Environmental Monitoring of Surface Water Quality in Dong Nai Province in 2012 and 2013. Report. CEME, Dong Nai province.

Danish Hydraulic Institute (2007). Mike flow model, Hydrodynamic module: Scientific Documentation.

Do Tien Lanh, N.D.C. (2010). Integrated Management of Water Resources in Dong Nai River Basin, KC08-10 Program. Project report. Ministry of Science and Technology.

Ky Phung N. (2009). Determining the Maximum Load for the Building of Discharge Limits on the Saigon River (from Thu Dau Mot to Nha Be). Research report.

Magoulas, R., and Lorica, B. (2009). *Introduction to Big Data. Release 2.0. Vol. 11.* O'Reilly Media, Sebastopol.

Ngoc Anh, N., and Duc Dung, D. (2006). Research, assessing the exploitation status for planning and management of surface water in Dong Nai province. Provincial project report. Dong Nai Department of Science and Technology.

People's Committee of Dong Nai province (2010). Decision No. 16/QĐ-UBND dated 03/19/2010 for partition of receiving industrial wastewater and emission in Dong Nai province to determine the regulations for each section of Dong Nai river.

Reichman, O.J., Jones, M.B., and Schildhauer, M.P. (2011). Challenges and opportunities of open DatainEcology. *Science*, 331(6018), 703–705.

Targio Hashem Abaker, I., Yaqoob, I., Badrul Anuar, N., Mokhtar, S., Gani, A., and Ullah Khan, S. (2015). The rise of "Big Data" on cloud computing: Review and open research issues. *Information Systems*, 47, 98–115.

The Southern Division for Water Resources Planning and Investigation (SDWRPI) (2013). Investigation and assessment of wastewater discharge and receiving capacity in Dong Nai province. Project report.

Vietnam Environment Administration (2011). Decision No. 879/QĐ-TCMT dated 01/07/2011 by the General Department of Environment on the issuance of the manual calculation of water quality indicators in order to assess rapidly the surface water quality.

Water Resource Management

9.1. Introduction

Water resource management (WRM) is the process of planning, developing and managing water resources across all users in terms of both water quantity and water quality. Integrated water resource management (IWRM), on the other hand, is the coordinated approach of the above processes of not only water, but integrated with land and other related resources [ROG 03]. The goal of IWRM is to maximize economic and social welfare without compromising the sustainability of the environment and affected ecosystems. This means ensuring sufficient water of adequate quality for drinking and sanitation services, food production, energy generation and industry, while safeguarding appropriate water for environmental flows, and maintaining healthy water-dependent ecosystems [AKB 10]. WRM also includes the management of risks related to water, such as floods, droughts and water pollution. One of the main goals of both WRM and IWRM is to ensure global water security through building capacity, adaptability and resilience in future planning and management of water resources. These outcomes become more critical across the backdrop of our rapidly growing population, increasing urbanization, changing dietary habits and uncertainties in climatic changes.

Due to the increasing and competing demands of the world's water resources, ongoing management and resolution of issues related to WRM have resulted in the recognition of the need for interdisciplinary research and management approaches [CRO 14]. Hydrology, an important field of research in WRM, is important in understanding and managing our water resources. Thus, hydrological modeling can give us a better understanding of water resources in both water quantity and water quality, which are vital for allocation across competing demands. Although the problems with water security are at a global scale, many challenges are location- and

Chapter written by Imeshi WEERASINGHE.

time-specific and can vary depending on the impacts of, for example, glacier dynamics, economic and population growth, floods and/or droughts and agricultural practices, among many others [ROG 03]. Each of these impacts affects different physical processes that are part of the hydrological cycle shown in Figure 9.1.

9.1.1. *The hydrological cycle*

The hydrological cycle, also known in layman's terms as the water cycle, describes the continuous circulation of water in and around the Earth's surface. As the name suggests, the water moves in a continuous cycle, with the most important processes being precipitation, interception, evaporation, transpiration, surface runoff, percolation and condensation. The total amount of water within the hydrological cycle remains essentially constant, and the distribution among the various processes is continuously changing [CHA 92].

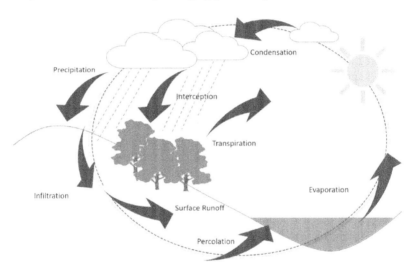

Figure 9.1. *Hydrological cycle processes*

Evaporation is one of the largest processes in the cycle. It is the transfer of water from the liquid state on the earth's surface to the gaseous or vapor state in the earth's atmosphere. The main source of evaporation arises from water bodies; however, evaporation also occurs from soils and other surfaces, as well as snow and ice, which is known as sublimation, the process of converting water from the solid state directly to vapor [DEF 04]. *Transpiration*, on the other hand, is the process of evaporation of water through stomata in plants. The combined effect of transpiration from plants and evaporation from water bodies, soils, bare surfaces, snow and ice is called evapotranspiration or total evaporation. The transition from the vapor state to the liquid state is called *condensation*, and through this process water is released into the atmosphere in the form of *precipitation* [ENC 04]. The released precipitation is distributed in four main processes: part is returned to the atmosphere by evaporation, some is caught by plants and trees by a process called *interception* and then transpired, another portion is percolated into the soil through *infiltration* and the remainder flows directly to a water body as *surface runoff*. The part of the precipitation that has been infiltrated can further flow through the soil into streams through a process called *percolation*. All the mentioned processes can be found in Figure 9.1, to see how the hydrological cycle functions.

9.1.2. *Hydrological models*

Hydrological models are simplified conceptual representations of a part of or the entire hydrological cycle and its processes in order to predict the system behavior and understand the modeled processes. Models have different parameters that help to characterize the physical behavior of a catchment. Hydrological models can be categorized into lumped or distributed models and deterministic or stochastic models. Deterministic models use unique physically based parameter input values, whereas stochastic models use a parameter space resulting from probability distributions [DEV 15]. Lumped models do not take spatial variability into account and take the entire river basin as a single unit, while distributed models take spatial variability into account by dividing the catchment into small units so that parameters, inputs and outputs can vary spatially, thus considering spatial processes.

9.2. Hydrological models for water resource management

With the ability to measure the quantity and quality of water in a given study area using simple or more complex representations of a part of the hydrological cycle, hydrological models are tools that can be used to provide relevant information to decision-makers [CHO 88]. One of the many benefits of hydrological models is their ability to conduct scenario analyses, thus being able to predict the impacts of natural and anthropogenic changes on water resources, using different temporal and spatial resolutions. An initial challenge of using hydrological models for WRM lies in the selection of an appropriate model for a given location with its specific characteristics. Selecting a model can depend on, for instance: required model outputs, availability of data, modeled processes, GUIs and cost, to name but a few. Within the context of this chapter, the analyzed hydrological model is the Soil and Water Assessment Tool (SWAT).

9.2.1. *Soil and Water Assessment Tool (SWAT)*

The Soil and Water Assessment Tool (SWAT) is a continuous-time, semi-distributed and process-based river basin scale model [SRI 10, NIE 11] that operates at a daily, monthly or yearly time-step. The main purpose of its design was to evaluate the impact of management options on water resources, sediment and agricultural chemical yields in ungauged basins [GAS 07, SRI 94]. The main features of the model include the weather, hydrology, soil properties, plant growth characteristics, nutrients, pesticides, bacteria and pathogens and land management [GAS 07]. The model functions such that a basin is delineated from a digital elevation map (DEM) and, optionally, a stream network. Once the basin is defined, it is divided into sub-basins according to the sections of the streams. These are then further subdivided into hydrological response units (HRUs), which consist of unique land use, slope and soil characteristics. This process is shown in Figure 9.2.

Figure 9.2. *Initial processes in the SWAT model. For a color version of this figure, see www.iste.co.uk/laffly/torus3.zip*

Climate inputs are also required by SWAT to simulate the HRU hydrological water balance, including daily precipitation, maximum and minimum temperature, solar radiation, relative humidity and wind speed data. These inputs may be inputted using observed records, generated inputs or a combination of both. The required weather inputs depend on different methods used for simulating ET and calculating infiltration. Relative humidity is only required if the Penman–Monteith [MON 65] or the Priestley–Taylor [PRI 72] ET calculation methods are used, whereas sub-daily precipitation is required if the Green–Ampt [GRE 11] method is used for calculating infiltration [GAS 07]. In addition, average air temperature is used in the calculation of precipitation if simulated as snowfall, whereas minimum and maximum temperature is used in the calculation of daily soil and water temperatures [GAS 07]. Also, as detailed in [GAS 07], generated weather inputs are calculated from 13 monthly climate variables derived from long-term measured weather records. The hydrological balance is simulated for each HRU, and outputs can be derived for HRU, sub-basin and basin levels. The outputs include evapotranspiration, surface runoff, percolation, interception, return flow, recharge and lateral flow.

Other possibilities of the SWAT model include estimation of crop yields and/or biomass, simulation of conservation and water management practices and estimation of HRU level and in-stream pollutant losses. Flow and pollutant loss routing can also be simulated where flows are summed from all HRUs to the sub-basin level and routed through the stream system using either the variable storage [WIL 69] or Muskingam [NEI 11] routing methods. Pollutants such as sediment, nutrients and pesticides are also summed at the sub-basin level, and the resulting losses are routed through channels, ponds, wetlands and/or reservoirs at the basin outlet [GAS 07]. For a more detailed description of the SWAT model and its capabilities, see [GAS 07].

9.2.2. Geographical information systems (GIS) and the SWAT model

The most common method of using the SWAT model is through GIS interfaces, with the two most popular GIS tools being ArcGIS and QGIS. Plugins can be installed on both platforms in order to use ArcSWAT or QSWAT. These interfaces enable the user to easily go through each of the steps in creating a SWAT model. Other GIS-based interfaces also exist, such as MapWindow-SWAT, but they are less commonly used.

9.3. Setting up of a SWAT model for the Blue Nile basin

There are three phases involved using SWAT+ for water management: preprocessing, setting up the model and post-processing. Figure 9.3 shows the steps involved for setting up a SWAT+ model. Steps 1–3 are performed using SWAT+, and steps 4 and 5 are performed using a different program, SWAT+ Editor [CHA 18]. Data inputs required for the development of a SWAT+ model are a digital elevation map (DEM), land use and soil maps and climate data (precipitation, minimum and maximum temperature, relative humidity, solar radiation and wind speed).

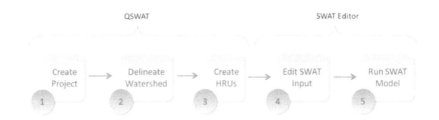

Figure 9.3. *Steps for setting up a SWAT model in QSWAT [CHA 18]*

As an example, a Blue Nile basin model was set up to assess the hydrology balance of the basin. Table 9.1 shows the data used during the setting up of the Blue Nile SWAT model.

Data type	Data source	Description
Digital elevation map (DEM)	Shutter Radar Topography Mission (SRTM)	Resolution: 90 × 90 m²
Soil map	Food and Agriculture Organization (FAO)	Resolution: 1,000 × 1,000 m²
Land use map	European Space Agency (ESA)	Resolution: 300 × 300 m² Period: 2009
Weather data (precipitation, min. and max. temperature, solar radiation, relative humidity and wind speed)	EartH2Observe, WFDEI and ERA-Interim data Merged and Bias-corrected for ISIMIP (EWEMBI) dataset	Resolution: 0.5 × 0.5 degrees Period: 1979–2016

Table 9.1. *Data used for setting up the Blue Nile SWAT model*

In order to create streams and delineate the watershed, the DEM is required, along with the selection or input of an outlet, the outlet snap distance (300 m) and the watershed threshold which was set to 250,000 cells. After delineating the watershed is complete, the following can be viewed in QSWAT where the sub-basins and stream network can be seen (Figure 9.4).

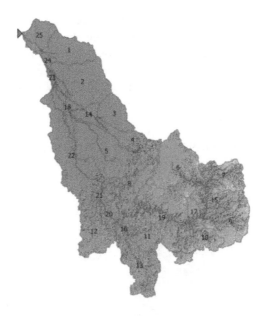

Figure 9.4. *Output of step 2 in QSWAT. Delineate watershed. For a color version of this figure, see www.iste.co.uk/laffly/torus3.zip*

The next step is to create HRUs which requires both a land use and soil map and the associated tables that link the land use and soil categories from the maps to the SWAT databases. These should be prepared during the preprocessing stage. Input settings used for the HRU creation were slope classes of 0, 10, 50, 9999; HRU creation method of filter by land use; HRU threshold type of % and HRU threshold for soil of 0, land use of 15 and slope of 10.

Step 4 is conducted using a different program called SWAT Editor, which inputs the weather data and extracts database tables to ASCII files, which are required for the model to run. The final step is to run the SWAT model, which is also conducted in SWAT Editor. The settings to run depend on which outputs we require, at what time-step, and the properties of our computer. For the running of the Blue Nile model, the following settings were used: starting date – January 1, 1979; ending date – December 31, 2013; daily time-step; NYSKP – 1 (warm up period); SWAT.exe Version – 64-bit, release.

Once the program has been run, the outputs that are desired can be selected to be viewed through SWAT Editor and then the SWAT Check program was run.

SWAT Check is a stand-alone program that processes SWAT output to analyze the mass balance within the basin. The results are shown in Figure 9.5. A quick check of the model is to see whether the mass balance closes. Therefore, using equation [9.1], we see there is a difference in mass balance of 45.77 mm. After this is complete, we can also visualize the output using the QSWAT interface:

$$P = ET + SR + Revap + Perc \tag{9.1}$$

where: P = precipitation = 1,029.7 mm; ET = evapotranspiration = 308.9 mm; SR = surface runoff = 181.96 mm; Revap = revap from aquifer = 17.21; Perc = percolation = 475.86.

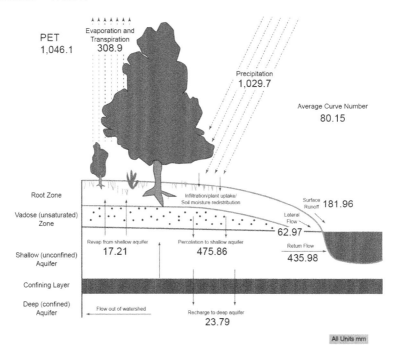

Figure 9.5. *Mass balance for the Blue Nile using SWAT Check. For a color version of this figure, see www.iste.co.uk/laffly/torus3.zip*

9.4. Scenario analysis using SWAT

One of the main objectives of the development of SWAT was to evaluate different management options on the hydrology of a basin. Given this objective, SWAT is actually an idea model for conducting different scenario analyses. Many studies have been conducted using SWAT for different management, land use and climate change scenarios, with several review papers analyzing some of these studies [GAS 07, DOU 10, TUP 11, GAS 14]. In the following sections, a few examples of studies conducted are mentioned to give an overview of the capabilities of the model.

9.4.1. Management scenarios

A study conducted in India simulated the return flow after the introduction of canal irrigation in Andhra Pradesh [GOA 06], looking at different scenarios for planning and management, while [SAN 05] demonstrated a new canal irrigation method that could be used for different conservation scenarios [GAS 07]. [BRE 08] looked at the impacts of global change on nitrogen dynamics in catchments, which they grouped broadly into land management, land use, climatic change and nitrogen deposition. An important area of research is looking at the impact of pesticide, which was the focus of a study by [GEV 08] who applied different pesticide management scenarios to a small catchment in Belgium [KRY 08].

9.4.2. Land use scenarios

[HER 00] investigated the impact of land cover change and rainfall spatial variability on basin hydrology in a small basin in Arizona, USA, using SWAT. Another study by [MAN 11] looked at the sensitivity of the model outputs to land use/cover change using three different hypothetical scenarios for a sub-catchment of the Mara river basin in Kenya, whereas [PIK 03] looked at the hydrological effects of specific land use changes for a basin in Greece. With sustainable land use practices gaining much traction in the recent past, SWAT applications in these areas have also increased. [TON 09] found impacts on flow, sediments and nutrients with a shift in land use from predominantly agriculture to mixed rural and residential lands for a catchment in California, USA, and study in Iran by [GHA 10] on land use change impacts for changes during the years 1967, 1994 and 2007 to the main hydrological components within the basin [GEB 15].

9.4.3. Climate change scenarios

There are two manners in which climate change impacts can be simulated in SWAT: (1) by accounting for the effects of increased atmospheric CO_2 concentrations on plant development and transpiration and (2) by changing the climatic inputs [GAS 07]. Impact assessment studies are a fast growing trend in the application of SWAT with 3 in 2001, 77 in 2013 and 83 in 2014 [KRY 15].

Studies on the impacts of historical climate trends compared with future climate change projects have been conducted by [MUT 02] on the San Jacinto river basin, Texas, for 2040–2059 and by [GOA 06] for 12 major river basins in India for 2041–2060 [GAS 07]. [PIN 14] and [JEO 14] conducted climate impact studies on stream health for basins in Poland and north-central Texas respectively looking at projections for 2040–2069. [ZAB 14] looked at climate change impacts on runoff and sediment yields for the Axiola basin looking at the future period between 2011 and 2100.

9.5. Cloud computing and SWAT

SWAT has been using cloud or grid computing infrastructures in various ways. The most popular and probably also the most efficient, with a high speedup potential, is the use of cloud and grid infrastructure during the parameter calibration process or for sensitivity and uncertainty analysis [GOR 12, ZHA 16, ECR 14]. In these cases, the model needs to be run many times, often needing many thousands or millions of simulations. In a few cases only, the SWAT model itself is run in parallel for single simulations [YAL 14]. This is especially meaningful for large-scale applications. Such an application is more complicated to execute, and the speedup is also lower. Finally, cloud computing is also offered for the decision of support systems or for the visualization of model results [DIT 14].

9.6. References

[AKB 10] AKBARI M., DROOGERS P., DEHGHNISANIJ H., "The role of modelling in Integrated Water Management (A case study in Zayandeh Rud Basin", *4th International Conference on Water Resources and Arid Environments*, Riyadh, Saudi Arabia, December 2010.

[ALB 00] ALBERO B., *L'autoformation en contexte institutionnel, du paradigme de l'instruction au paradigme de l'autonomie*, L'Harmattan, Paris, 2000.

[BRE 08] BREUER L., VACHE K., JULICH S. *et al.*, "Current concepts in nitrogen dynamics for mesoscale catchments", *Hydrological Sciences Journal*, vol. 53, pp. 1059–1074, 2008.

[CHA 18] CHAWANDA C., GEORGE C., THIERRY W. *et al.*, "Easy to use workflows for catchment modelling: Towards reproducible model studies", *Environmental Modelling and Software*, (under review), 2018.

[CHA 92] CHAHINE M., "The hydrological cycle and its influence on climate", *Nature*, vol. 359, p. 373, 1992.

[CHO 88] CHOW V., MAIDMENT D., MAYS I., *Applied Hydrology*, McGraw-Hill, New York, 1988.

[CRO 14] CROKE B., BLAKERS, R., EL SAWAH S. *et al.*, "Marrying hydrological modelling and integrated assessment for the needs of water resource management", *Proceedings of International Commission on Water Resource Systems*, Bologna, Italy, 2014.

[DEF 04] DEFRIES R., ESHLEMAN K., "Land-use change and hydrologic processes: A major focus for the future", *Hydrological Processes*, vol. 18, pp. 2183–2186, 2004.

[DEV 15] DEVIA G., GANASRI G., DWARAKISH G., "A review of hydrological models", *Aquatic Procedia*, vol. 4, pp. 1001–1007, 2015.

[DIT 14] DITTY J., ALLEN P., DAVID O. *et al.*, "Deployment of SWAT-DEG as a web infrastructure utilising cloud computing for stream restoration", *Proceedings of 7th International Congress on Environmental Modelling and Software: Bold Visions for Environmental Modelling*, San Diego, California, 2014.

[DOU 10] DOUGLAS-MANKIN K., SRINIVASAN R., ARNOLD J., "Soil and water assessment tool (SWAT) model: Current developments and applications", *Transactions of the ASABE*, vol. 53, pp. 1423–1431, 2010.

[ECR 14] ECRAN M., GOODALL J., CASTRANOVA A. *et al.*, "Calibration of SWAT models using the Cloud", *Environmental Modelling and Software*, vol. 62, pp. 188–196, 2014.

[ENC 18] ENCYCLOPAEDIA BRITANNICA, EDITORS, "Water Cycle", *Encyclopedia Britannica*, https://www.britannica.com/science/water-cycle, accessed 19 October 2018.

[GAS 07] GASSMAN P., REYES M., GREEN C. *et al.*, "The soil and water assessment tool: Historical development, applications and future research directions", *Transactions of the ASABE*, vol. 50, pp. 1211–1250, 2007.

[GAS 14] GASSMAN P., SADEGHI A., SRINIVASAN R., "Application of the SWAT model special section: Overview and insights", *Journal of Environmental Quality*, vol. 43, pp. 1–8, 2014.

[GEB 15] GEBREMEDHIN K., AMBA S., LAKSHMAN N., "Performance evaluation of SWAT model for land use and land cover change in semi-arid climatic conditions: A review", *Hydrology Current Research*, vol. 6, 2015.

[GEV 08] GEVAERT V., VAN GRIENSVEN A., HOLVOET K. *et al.*, "SWAT developments and recommendations for modelling agricultural pesticide mitigation measures in river basins", *Hydrological Sciences Journal*, vol. 53, pp. 1075–1089, 2008.

[GHA 10] GHAFFARI G., KEESSTRA S., GHODOUSI J. *et al.*, "SWAT-simulated hydrological impact of land-use change in the Zanjanrood basin, Northwest Iran", *Hydrological Processes*, vol. 24, pp. 892–903, 2010.

[GOA 06] GOASAIN A., RAO S., BASURAY D., "Climate change impact assessment on hydrology of Indian river basins", *Current Science*, vol. 90, pp. 346–353, 2006.

[GOR 12] GORGAN D., BACU V., MIHON D. *et al.*, "Grid based calibration of SWAT hydrological models", *Natural Hazards and Earth Systems Science*, vol. 12, pp. 2411–2423, 2012.

[GRE 11] GREEN H., AMPT G., "Studies on soil physicals: 1. The flow of air and water through soils", *Journal of Agricultural Science*, vol. 4, pp. 1–24, 1911.

[HER 00] HERNANDEZ M., MILLER S., GOODRICH D. *et al.*, "Modelling runoff response to land cover and rainfall spatial variability in semi-arid watersheds", *Environmental Modelling and Assessment*, vol. 64, pp. 285–298, 2000.

[JEO 14] JEONG J., KANNAN N., ARNOLD J., "Effects of urbanisation and climate change on stream health in north-central Texas", *Journal of Environmental Quality*, vol. 43, pp. 100–109, 2014.

[KRY 08] KRYSANOVA V., ARNOLD J., "Advances in ecohydrological modelling with SWAT – A review", *Hydrological Sciences Journal*, vol. 53, pp. 939–947, 2008.

[KRY 15] KRYSANOVA V., SRINIVASAN R., "Assessment of climate and land use change impacts with SWAT", *Regional Environmental Change*, vol. 15, pp. 431–434, 2015.

[MAN 11] MANGO L., MELESSE A., MCCLAIN M. *et al.*, "Land use and climate change impacts on the hydrology of the upper Mara river basin, Kenya: Results of a modelling study to support better resource management", *Hydrology and Earth Systems Sciences*, vol. 15, p. 2245, 2011.

[MON 65] MONTIETH L., "State and movement of water in living organisms", *Proceedings of 19th Symposium on Evaporation and the Environment,* Swansea, UK, 1965.

[MUT 02] MUTTIAH R., WURBS R., "Modelling the impacts of climate change on water supply reliabilities", *Water International*, vol. 27, pp. 407–419, 2002.

[NIE 11] NIETSCH S., ARNOLD J., KINITRY J. *et al.*, The Soil and Water Assessment Tool: Theoretical Documentation Version 2009, User Manual, Riyadh, Texas Water Resources Institute, Texas A&M University, 2011.

[PIK 03] PIKOUNIS M., VARANOU E., BALTAS E. *et al.*, "Application of the SWAT model in the Pinios river basin under different land use scenarios", *Global Nest: The International Journal*, vol. 5, pp. 71–79, 2003.

[PIN 14] PINIEWSKI M., LAIZÉ C., ACREMAN M. *et al.*, "Effect of climate change on environmental flow indicators in the Narew basin, Poland", *Journal of Environmental Quality*, vol. 43, pp. 155–167, 2014.

[PRI 72] PRIESTLEY B., TAYLOR R., "On the assessment of surface heat flux and evaporation using large-scale parameters", *Transactions of the ASABE*, vol. 12, pp. 81–92, 1994.

[ROG 03] ROGERS P., HALL A., *Effective Water Governance*, Elanders Novum, Sweden, 2003.

[SAN 05] SANTHI C., MUTTIAH J., ARNOLD J. *et al.*, "A GIS-based regional planning tool for irrigation demand assessment and savings using SWAT", *Transactions of the ASABE*, vol. 48, pp. 137–147, 2005.

[SRI 94] SRINIVASAN R., ARNOLD J., "Integration of basin-scale water quality model with GIS", *Journal of the American Water Resource Association*, vol. 30, pp. 453–462, 1994.

[SRI 10] SRINIVASAN R., ZHANG X., ARNOLD J., "SWAT Ungauged: Hydrological budget and crop yield predictions in the upper Mississippi river basin", *Transactions of the ASABE*, vol. 53, pp. 1533–1546, 2010.

[TON 09] TONG S., LIU A., GOODRICH J., "Assessing the water quality impacts of future land use changes in an urbanising watershed", *Civil Engineering and Environmental Systems*, vol. 26, pp. 3–18, 2009.

[TUP 11] TUPAD P., DOUGLAS-MANKIN K., LEE T. *et al.*, "Soil and water assessment tool (SWAT) hydrological/water quality model: Extended capability and wider adoption", *Transactions of the ASABE*, vol. 54, pp. 1677–1684, 2011.

[WIL 69] WILLIAMS J., "Flood routing with variable time or variable storage coefficient", *Transactions of the ASABE*, vol. 12, pp. 100–103, 1969.

[YAL 14] YALEW S., PILZ T., SCHWEITZER C. *et al.*, "Dynamic feedback between land use and hydrology for ecosystem services assessment", *Proceedings of 7th International Congress on Environmental Modelling and Software: Bold Visions for Environmental Modelling*, San Diego, California, 2014.

[ZAB 14] ZABALETA A., MEAURIO M., RUIZ E. *et al.*, "Simulation climate change impact on runoff and sediment yield in a small watershed in the Basque country, northern Spain", *Journal of Environmental Quality*, vol. 43, pp. 235–245, 2014.

[ZHA 16] ZHANG D., CHEN X., YAO H. *et al.*, "Moving SWAR model calibration and uncertainty analysis to an enterprise Hadoop-based cloud", *Environmental Modelling and Software*, vol. 84, pp. 140–148, 2016.

10

Assessing Impacts of Land Use Change and Climate Change on Water Resources in the La Vi Catchment, Binh Dinh Province

10.1. Introduction

Soil and water resources in many countries are currently under severe pressure due to human intervention, and the changing of runoff patterns caused by climate and land use changes. A population growth and human-induced development have accelerated the speed of land use/cover changes that in turn affect hydrological processes. In addition, climate change may affect many aspects of natural ecosystems. Hence, comprehending climate change impacts on hydrological conditions is essential to enable more efficient soil and water resources development.

The La Vi catchment is selected as a study area as shown in Figure 10.1. At present, there are many critical issues for soil and water resource management in the catchment (The Government of Vietnam, 2006). These problems range from hydrological variability (including floods and droughts) to environmental degradation (including pollution of waterways and deforestation of catchments), erosion and resultant sedimentation of reservoirs, over-exploitation of groundwater, conflicts over the use of water for different purposes and transboundary conflicts (inter-district).

Chapter written by Kim Loi NGUYEN, Le Tan Dat NGUYEN, Hoang Tu LE, Duy Liem NGUYEN, Ngoc Quynh Tram VO, Van Phan LE, Duy Nang NGUYEN, Thi Thanh Thuy NGUYEN, Gia Diep PHAM, Dang Nguyen Dong PHUONG, Thi Hong NGUYEN, Thong Nhat TRAN, Margaret SHANAFIELD and Okke BATELAAN.

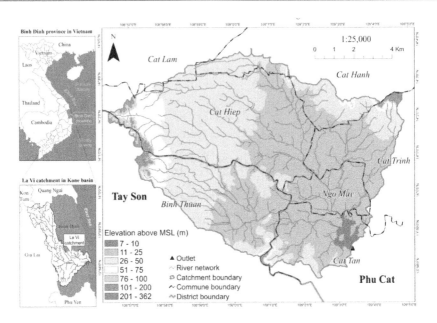

Figure 10.1. *Research site. For a color version of
this figure, see www.iste.co.uk/laffly/torus3.zip*

Therefore, to make suitable adaptation plans for soil and water resources use in this catchment, decision-makers need to understand the extent of the potential impact of both climate change and human activity (land use/land cover change) on local soil and water resources. So far, few studies have quantified the combined potential future impacts of climate and land use/land cover change on hydrology in the Vietnam (Ty *et al.* 2012; Loi 2015), but no study has assessed the impact on hydrology in the La Vi catchment as a big data.

The overall objective of this study is to investigate changes in stream flow and hydrological processes resulting from land use change, and climatic variation in the La Vi catchment. For the moment, we are performing modeling of an ungauged basin; hence, no calibration or validation is possible.

10.1.1. *Background of the study/related literature*

The Intergovernmental Panel on Climate Change report reaffirmed that "global warming" is occurring (IPCC 2007). Climate change leads to changes in precipitation and temperature, which affects the hydrological cycle and thus changes the stream flow, and modifies the transformation and transport characteristics of sediment as well as water pollutants (Tu 2009). Therefore, climate change is an important factor influencing hydrological conditions. A variety of studies have been performed on the impact of climate changes on hydrology (Zhang *et al.* 2007; Githui *et al.* 2009; Kim and Kaluarachchi 2009; Boyer *et al.* 2010; Bauwens *et al.* 2011), most of which indicated that variation of stream flow is closely associated with changes in temperature and precipitation. In the studies of climate change, the outputs of general circulation models (GCMs) are used to generate the future climate conditions for a study area and then a hydrological model is used to estimate the climate change impact on the runoff behavior. In addition to climate information, land use information is essential in watershed hydrology. The effects of land use are directly linked to changes in hydrological components in a watershed, such as evapotranspiration, surface runoff, groundwater and stream flow. Many previous studies around the world have demonstrated that land use significantly affects hydrological processes (Mueller *et al.* 2009; Cai *et al.* 2011; López-Vicente *et al.* 2011; Nie *et al.* 2011). Generally, hydrological models are commonly used to investigate the influences of land use change on runoff and the studies of land use change are often conducted with the assumption that the climate would keep the same for the simulation period.

In the face of potential climate and land use changes, studies of the impact of climate and land use change on hydrology and sediment yield are essential. Understanding the responses of hydrological processes and sediment yield to climate and land use changes is important for planning and managing water resources (Zhang *et al.* 2008). Many studies have addressed the change in hydrology with impacts of climate and land use changes (Wang *et al.* 2008; Li *et al.* 2009; Ma *et al.* 2009; Mango *et al.* 2011; Li *et al.* 2012), but few have investigated the impact on sediment yield at a basin scale. In general, regional impacts of climate change and land use affect hydrology and sediment yield which varies from place to place and an awareness needed for how this impacts on local catchments (Wang *et al.* 2013).

Three-quarters of Vietnam is in the upland with complex topography and steep slopes. Forests play an important role in environmental protection (Lung 1995). However, under the pressure of economic development, the demand for agricultural land and other sectors has been expanding. Natural forests, mostly distributed in highland areas, are destroyed, leading to decreased land cover and rapidly declining soil quality. Therefore, this country is facing soil erosion, especially in the highland areas. Moreover, Vietnam has experienced such climate changes as rising air temperatures and variable precipitation. From 1958 to 2007, the annual average temperature increased by 0.5–0.7°C. Annual precipitation decreased in Northern Vietnam, but increased in Southern Vietnam. For the entire country, rainfall decreased an average of 2% over the past 50 years (1958–2007) (MONRE 2009). These changes have significantly affected the availability of water resources and sediment yield in Vietnam.

Some studies were performed to investigate the impact of land use change and climate change on hydrology in Vietnam. For example, Yohannes (2009) assessed the effects of land use change on water balance and crop production in Tat Hamlet Watershed, Hòa Bình province, over 20 years using the Land Use Change Impact Assessment (LUCIA) tool. Hung *et al.* (2010) used the SWAT (Soil and Water Assessment Tool) model to evaluate the impacts of different re-forested area scenarios (25 and 50% of total 2005-year forested area in the river basin) on the hydrological regime of the upper part of Ma river basin, northwest of Vietnam. Binh *et al.* (2010) examined the effects of land use changes scenarios (built based on crop conversion) on runoff discharge and sediment yield from Song Cau catchment in Northern Vietnam. On the other hand, most studies are related to climate change are primarily based on climate change scenarios for Vietnam (MONRE 2009) or on outputs from individual GCMs. There are many examples: Kawasaki *et al.* (2010) used the output from the Japanese Meteorological Agency GCM for IPCC SRES A1B scenario and the hydrological model HEC-HMS (Hydrologic Modeling System) to consider the climate change impact on water resources in the central highland of Vietnam; Thai and Thuc (2011) used the MIKE 11-NAM hydrological model and climate change scenarios from the Vietnam Ministry of Natural Resources and Environment (MONRE 2009). These data were downscaled from GCMs by the MAGICC/SCENGEN model to evaluate the impact of climate change on the flow in the Hong-Thai Binh (located in North Delta) and the Dong Nai river basins (located in the Central Highland and South Delta). The climate scenarios from MONRE (2009) were developed only for Vietnam's seven climate zones: Northwest, Northeast, North Delta (Red River Delta), North Central Coast, South Central Coast, Central Highlands and South Delta (Mekong River Delta). Therefore, it is unable to accurately reflect the specific local details of climate change in Vietnam (MONRE 2010).

The methods of assessing the hydrological and sediment effects of environmental change include paired catchment, statistical analysis and hydrological modeling (Li *et al.* 2009; Li *et al.* 2012). Among these approaches, the hydrological modeling method is most suitable for use in scenario studies. Widely used hydrological models in studies on the impact on hydrology and sediment yield include the Hydrologic Simulation Program–Fortran, the Soil and Water Assessment Tool (SWAT), WaTEM/SEDEM and the Water Erosion Prediction Project. The SWAT model is selected for the present study because it is widely used to assess hydrology and water quality in agricultural catchments around the world. Another reason for this selection is its availability and user-friendliness in handling input data (Arnold *et al.* 1998).

10.1.2. Description of study area

10.1.2.1. Geographical location

The La Vi catchment is one of the main tributaries to the Kon River. It originates in the Sông Kôn rooted western mountainous district and Hoai An, An Lao district altitude of 600–700 m, which flows from the northwest to southeast.

The La Vi catchment covers an area of about 10,000 hectares (ha) flowing through the territory of the Phu Cat district, in the Binh Dinh province, The area stretches from 13° 57' to 14° 05' North latitude and from 108° 55' to 109° 06' East longitude.

10.1.2.2. Topography

The physical topography of the area is diversified and quite complex, including mountains, hills, highland and lagoon. In general, the catchment has the following types of topography: Phu Cat diverse terrain tends to tilt from west to east, which is characterized by mountainous terrain and coastal lagoons; plain rice cultivation, concentrated in riverside villages Con and La Tinh river; low mountains – hill planting crops and forest trees and the coastal lagoon of Cat Minh, Cat Khanh, Cat Thanh – the La Vi catchment with average elevation ranging from 7 to 325 m, which flows from the northwest to southeast.

10.1.2.3. Climate

Geographic location and topography of Binh Dinh province have dominated the process of forming climate characteristics. Binh Dinh province is located in the center of Vietnam, so the area is known to have humid tropical monsoons. The province's land surface has many high mountains; bare hills interspersed narrow valley plains are important factors leading to the formation of the thermal regime, rain, wind, sun, radiation, evaporation and special types of weather. The total annual rainfall in Phu Cat district is about 2,808.3 mm.

10.1.2.4. Hydrology

La Vi River flows through the Cat Hiep commune, Cat Tan commune, Cat Thanh commune, Cat Trinh commune, Ngo May town and Cat Tien commune of Phu Cat district as shown in Figure 10.2. The outlet of the catchment is situated in the southeast of the Cat Tan commune.

10.1.2.5. Soil

According to the DONRE Binh Thuân province report, the La Vi catchment has five major soil groups: sandy clay loam, clay, silty loam, water and loamy sand, as shown in Figure 10.3 and Table 10.1. In particular, loamy sand accounts for the largest area.

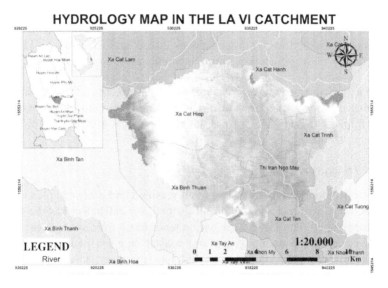

Figure 10.2. *Hydrology map in the La Vi catchment (source: DONRE, Binh Dinh province). For a color version of this figure, see www.iste.co.uk/laffly/torus3.zip*

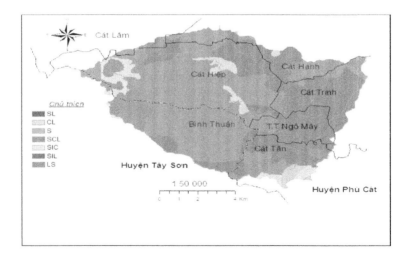

Figure 10.3. *Soil map in La Vi catchment (source: DONRE, Binh Dinh province). For a color version of this figure, see www.iste.co.uk/laffly/torus3.zip*

Object ID	Name	Area (ha)	Percent (%)
1	Sandy clay loam	372.861	3.72
2	Clay	112.684	1.13
3	Silty loam	708.679	7.08
4	Water	104.015	1.04
5	Loamy sand	8,713.561	87.03

Table 10.1. *Soil types in the La Vi catchment (source: DONRE, Binh Dinh province)*

10.1.3. *Land use/land cover*

According to the DONRE Binh Dinh province report, the La Vi catchment has 11 major land use groups: agricultural land, bareland, forest-evergreen, forest-mixed, industrial land, paddy field, residential, institutional, water body, transportation, residential-high density and residential-medium density, as shown in Figure 10.1 and Table 10.2. In particular, agricultural land-generic accounts for the largest area.

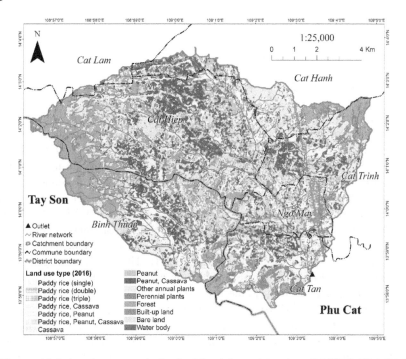

Figure 10.4. *Land use map in the La Vi catchment (source: DONRE, Binh Dinh province). For a color version of this figure, see www.iste.co.uk/laffly/torus3.zip*

Object ID	Code SWAT	Land use type	Area (ha)	Percent (%)
1	AGRC	Agricultural land-close-grown	3,964.597	39.64
2	BARR	Bareland	193.140	1.94
3	FRSE	Forest-evergreen	8.736	0.09
4	FRST	Forest-mixed	1,910.389	19.14
5	RICE	Paddy field	1,473.306	14.76
6	UIDU	Industrial	245.164	2.46
7	UINS	Institutional	563.848	5.65
8	URBN	Residential	164.441	1.65
9	URHD	Residential-high density	202.299	2.03
10	URMD	residential-medium density	1,062.662	10.65
11	UTRN	Transportation	63.780	0.64
12	WATR	Water body	126.425	1.27

Table 10.2. *Land use type in the La Vi catchment, Binh Dinh province (source: DONRE, Binh Dinh province)*

10.2. Materials and methodology

10.2.1. *Brief description of the SWAT model*

SWAT is a physically-based semi-distributed hydrological model with an ArcView GIS interface. It is developed by the Blackland Research and Extension Center and the United States Department of Agriculture – Agricultural Research Service (USDA – ARS). It can be applied at the river basin scale to simulate the impact of land management practices on water, sediment and agrochemical yields in large watersheds with varying soils, land use and agricultural conditions over extended periods of time (Arnold *et al.* 1998). The design of SWAT makes it useful in modeling ungauged watersheds and, more importantly, simulating the impact of alternative input data such as changes in land use, land management practices and climate (Neitsch *et al.* 2005; Arnold *et al.* 1998). The interface in geographical information system (GIS) is convenient for the definition of watershed hydrologic features and storage, as well as the organization and manipulation of the related spatial and tabular data (Luzio *et al.* 2002). While specialized processes can be simulated if sufficient input data are available, SWAT also runs with minimum data inputs, which is advantageous when working in areas with limited data. SWAT is computationally efficient and therefore able to run simulations of very large basins or management practices without consuming large amounts of time or computational resources. Lastly, SWAT is a continuous-time model able to simulate long-term impacts of land use, land management practices and buildup of pollutants (Neitsch *et al.* 2005).

SWAT delineates watersheds into sub-basins interconnected by a stream network. Each sub-basin is then further divided into hydrological response units (HRUs) based upon unique land cover, soil and slope and management characteristics. The HRUs represent percentages of the sub-basin area and are not identified spatially within a SWAT simulation. SWAT calculates the flow, sediment and nutrient loading from each sub-basin HRU, and the resulting loads are then routed through channels, ponds and reservoirs to the watershed outlet (Arnold *et al.* 2001).

The main driving force behind the SWAT is the hydrological component. Since the objective of this study was to examine the water discharge and sediment flux responses to land use and climate change, the surface runoff and sediment yield components of the SWAT, SWAT simulates the hydrology of the watershed in two phases: 1) the land phase, which controls the amount of water, sediment, nutrient and pesticide loadings to the main channel in each sub-basin, and 2) the water or routing phase, which controls the movement of water, sediment, nutrient and pesticide loadings through the channel network of the watershed into the outlet. In the land phase of the hydrological cycle, SWAT simulates the hydrological cycle based on the water balance equation as follows:

$$SW_t = SW_0 + \sum_{i=1}^{t} \left(R_{day} - Q_{surf} - E_a - w_{seep} - Q_{gw} \right) \qquad [10.1]$$

where SW_t is the final soil water content (mm); SW_0 is the initial soil water content on day i (mm); t is the time (days); R_{day} is the amount of precipitation on day i (mm); Q_{surf} is the amount of surface runoff on day i (mm); E_a is the amount of evapotranspiration on day i (mm); W_{seep} is the amount of water entering the vadose zone from the soil profile on day i (mm); and Q_{gw} is the amount of return flow on day i (mm)

SWAT provides several options when simulating hydrological processes, which can be chosen by users based on their data availability. For example, the surface runoff volume from HRUs can be simulated with the SCS (Soil Conservation Service) curve number method (USDA-SCS 1972) or the Green-Ampt infiltration method (Green and Ampt 1911). SWAT calculates the peak runoff rate with a modified rational method. The model offers three options for estimating potential evapotranspiration: Hargreaves (Hargreaves *et al.* 1985), Priestley–Taylor (Priestley and Taylor 1972) and Penman–Monteith (Monteith 1965) methods.

The SWAT model calculates the surface erosion within each HRU with the Modified Universal Soil Loss Equation (MUSCLE) (Williams 1975). The MUSCLE is:

$$sed = 11.8 \left(Q_{surf} . q_{peak} . area_{hru} \right)^{0.56} . K_{USLE} . C_{USLE} . P_{USLE} . LS_{USLE} . CFRG \quad [10.2]$$

where sed is the sediment yield on a given day (tons); Q_{surf} is the surface runoff volume (mm water/ha); q_{peak} is the peak runoff rate (m^3/s); $area_{hru}$ is the area of the HRU (ha); K_{USLE} is the USLE soil erodibility factor (0.013 metric ton m^{2}hr/(m^3.metric ton cm)); C_{USLE} is the USLE cover and management factor; P_{USLE} is the USLE support practice factor; and LS_{USLE} is the USLE topographic factor and CFRG is the coarse fragment factor.

Sediment transport in the channel network is a function of two processes, deposition and degradation, operating simultaneously in the reach. SWAT computes the maximum concentration of sediment in the reach at the beginning of the time step. Depending on the concentration of sediment in the reach and the transport capacity of the channel, deposition or degradation process will occur.

10.2.2. Materials

Database Server

WebGIS Server

PostgreSQL/PostGIS, Microsoft SQL Server

ArcGIS Desktop, ArcSWAT, VizSWAT, SWAT-CUP

In this study, two automatic hydro-meteorology stations have been installed in the La Vi catchment, Phu Cat district, Binh Dinh province.

10.2.3. Data collection

SWAT requires meteorological data such as daily precipitation, maximum and minimum air temperature relative humidity, wind speed and solar radiation. Furthermore, spatial datasets include digital elevation model (DEM), land use/land cover and soil maps, calibration and validation of water discharge simulation use and water discharge data. Table 10.3 shows the sources and types of data collected.

Data type	Sources
Topography map	Department of Natural Resources and Environment Binh Dinh province ASTER Global Digital Elevation Model (http://gdem.ersdac.jspacesystems.or.jp/)
Land use map	Department of Natural Resources and Environment Binh Dinh province Global Land Cover Characterization (http://www.globallandcover.com/GLC30Download/index.aspx)
Soil map	Department of Natural Resources and Environment Binh Dinh province Global soil data (http://www.fao.org/fileadmin/user_upload/soils)
Weather	The National Hydro-Meteorological Centre Climate Forecast System Reanalysis (http://globalweather.tamu.edu)
Water discharge	The National Hydro-Meteorological Centre

Table 10.3. *Sources and types of data collected for SWAT simulation*

10.2.3.1. *Assessing the impacts of land use change and climate variability*

The approach of one factor at a time is used to evaluate the effect of land use/land cover change and climate variability on hydrology (i.e. changing one factor at a time while holding others constant).

10.2.3.2. *Land use/land cover change data*

The categories of land use/land cover in 2010–2015 collected from the Department of Natural Resources and Environment (DONRE), Binh Dinh province are: (1) forest, (2) agriculture, (3) urban/settlement/industry, (4) bareland/open land and (5) special land. The definition and characteristics of each land cover type is described as follows:

– forest (P_1): the permanent natural forest and reforestation. The main natural forest is *evergreen forest* type;

– agriculture (P_2): the permanent or temporary agriculture area that mostly occurs in flat plain or lowland including active shifting cultivation on highland. The agriculture includes paddy field, field crop and cash crops;

– urban/settlement/industry (P_3): the built-up areas consisting of residential and industrial and commercial areas;

– bare land/open land (P_4): the new cleared area or prepared highland agriculture area and water bodies (the water bodies are the natural and artificial reservoirs);

– special land (P_5): the land used for military and cemetery purposes.

10.2.3.3. *Impact of climate change*

Based on downscaled general circulation models, regional projections of climate change, SEASTART-AR4 (2009), developed climate change scenarios such as the A1B and A2 emission scenarios for two future periods (2010–2039 and 2040–2069).

The A1B and A2 scenarios are selected in this study because they are simulated by most GCMs in SEASTART-AR4, and our study focuses on mid-century change, in which period A2 and A1B exhibit similar greenhouse gases (GHG) emission forcing. The A1B (medium emission) scenario projects a future where technology is shared between developed and developing nations in order to reduce regional economic disparities, while the A2 (high emission) scenario assumes global population growth peaks by mid-century and then declines, a rapid economic shift toward service and information economies and the introduction of clean and resource-efficient technologies (IPCC 2007).

GCMs accurately represent climate on a global scale. Using the delta change method (Diaz-Nieto and Wilby 2005) it can be used in order to apply GCMs on a regional scale and create future climate scenarios for local hydrological impact assessment. This method has been widely used in previous climate change studies. In essence, it modifies the observed historical time series by adding the difference between future and the baseline periods as simulated by a GCM. The monthly differences between future and reference periods are calculated using temperature (maximum and minimum) and precipitation over the region covering at least one grid point, depending on the resolution of each GCM. Regional differences obtained with more grid points give more physically representative results than a value calculated with just one grid point (Boyer *et al*. 2010). There are differences to add the observed daily maximum and minimum temperature during the baseline period while the ratio is applied to precipitation.

10.2.3.4. *Combined impacts of land use and climate changes*

In order to investigate the combined impacts of land use and climate changes, the water discharge under land use/land cover change from 2010 to 2015 and the A1B and A2 climate change scenarios for the two future periods (2020s and 2060s) are compared to the corresponding current conditions in the baseline period.

10.2.4. *Methodology*

The SWAT model approach in the La Vi catchment is described as shown in Figure 10.5.

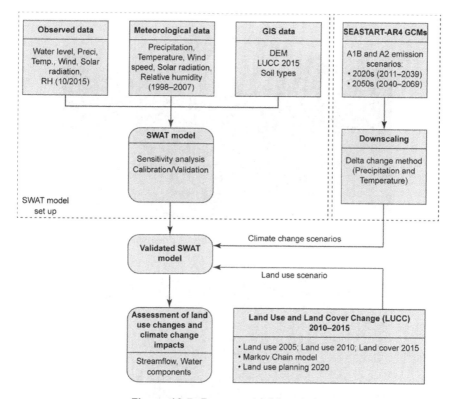

Figure 10.5. *Framework of the study*

10.3. Primary results

10.3.1. *The automatic hydro-meteorology*

In this study, we have already installed two automatic hydro-meteorology stations in the La Vi catchment, as shown in Figures 10.6 and 10.7. The automatic hydro-meteorology station was developed by Research Center for Climate Change (RCCC) – Nong Lam University, Ho Chi Minh City. The observed data include precipitation, temperature, wind speed, solar radiation, relative humidity and water level, which are transferred to the Nong Lam University web server at http://vgtb.hcmuaf.edu.vn/aup/, as shown in Figure 10.8.

Figure 10.6. *Automatic Hydrometeorology station 1 downstream the La Vi catchment*

Figure 10.7. *Automatic Hydro-meteorology
station 2 downstream the La Vi catchment*

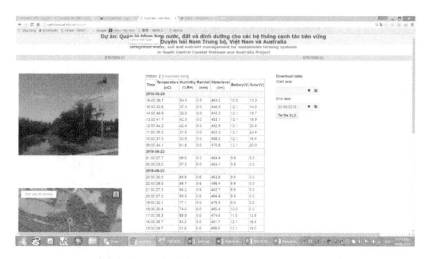

Figure 10.8. *Website for collecting observed data*

10.3.2. *Assessing water discharge in the La Vi catchment using the SWAT model*

The outlet of the two automatic hydro-meteorology stations was used to set up and run the SWAT model. The La Vi catchment has two seasons, a rainy and dry seasons. The rainy season is usually from late June to late December. The rainfall is one of the decisive factors to the hydrological regime of the catchment. The simulated water discharge in the La Vi catchment is shown in Figures 10.9 and 10.10. We also found that the water discharge in the La Vi catchment depends strongly on rainfall and the forest cover in the upstream part of the La Vi catchment.

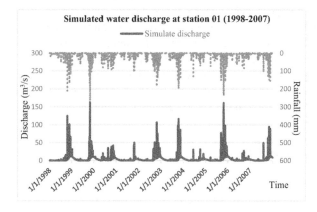

Figure 10.9. *Simulated water discharge at HM station 1 in the La Vi catchment. For a color version of this figure, see www.iste.co.uk/laffly/torus3.zip*

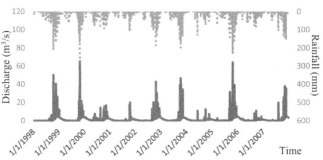

Figure 10.10. *Simulated water discharge at HM station 2 in the La Vi catchment. For a color version of this figure, see www.iste.co.uk/laffly/torus3.zip*

10.4. Conclusion

The SWAT model has been applied in the La Vi catchment to assess water discharge under land use change and climate change. In this study, we have done modeling of an ungauged basin so that no calibration or validation is possible. The water discharge under land use/land cover change 2010–2015, and the A1B and A2 climate change scenarios for the two future periods (2020s and 2060s) are compared to the corresponding current conditions in the baseline period on the catchment of La Vi, Binh Dinh province. Besides, we have already installed two automatic hydro-meteorology stations in the La Vi catchment, Phu Cat district, Binh Dinh province. The observed data include precipitation, temperature, wind speed, solar radiation, relative humidity and water level. The rainfall is one of the decisive factors to the hydrological regime of the catchment. We also found that the water discharge in the La Vi catchment strongly depends on rainfall and the forest cover in the upstream part of the La Vi catchment. The results of this research provided useful information that decision-makers need in order to promote soil and water resources planning efforts in the La Vi catchment, Binh Dinh province.

10.5. Acknowledgments

We acknowledge the Australian Center for International Agricultural Research (ACIAR) for funding this research. We would like to convey our special appreciation to our students in the Geographic Information System Laboratory, Research Center for Climate Change (RCCC), Nong Lam University (NLU), Ho Chi

Minh City, for their valuable contributions toward this study, whose jokes always brought some smiles during tough times.

10.6. References

Akiyuki, K., Masatsugu, T., Janet, H., Peter, R. and Srikantha, H. (2010). An integrated approach to evaluate potential impact of precipitation and land use change on streamflow in Srepok River Basin. *Theory and Applications of GIS*, 18(2), 9–20.

Allan, J.D. (2004). Influence of land use and landscape setting on the ecological status of rivers. *Limnetica*, 23(3–4), 187–198.

Arnold, J.G., Allen, P.M. and Bernhardt, G. (1993). A comprehensive surface-groundwater flow model. *Journal of Hydrology*, 142, 47–69.

Arnold, J.G., Allen, P.M. and Morgan, D.S. (2001). Hydrologic model for design and constructed wetlands. *Wetlands*, 21(2), 167–178.

Arnold, J.G., Srinivasan, R., Muttiah, R.S. and Williams, J.R. (1998). Large area hydrologic modeling and assessment. Part I. Model development. *Journal of the American Water Resources Association*, 34, 73–89. DOI:10.1111/j.1752-1688.1998.tb05961.x.

Bauwens, A., Sohier, C. and Degré, A. (2011). Hydrological response to climate change in the Lesse and the Vesdre catchments: Contribution of a physically based model (Wallonia Belgium). *Hydrology and Earth System Sciences*, 15, 1745–1756. DOI: 10.5194/hess-15-1745-2011.

Costa, M.H., Botta, A. and Cardille, J.A. (2003). Effects of large-scale changes in land cover on the discharge of the Tocantins River, Southeastern Amazonia. *Journal of Hydrology*, 283, 206–217.

Crooks, S. and Davies, H. (2001). Assessment of land use change in the Thames catchment and its effect on the flood regime of the river. *Physics and Chemistry of the Earth, Part B*, 26(7–8), 583–591.

De Roo, A., Odijk, M., Schmuck, G., Koster, E. and Lucieer, A. (2001). Assessing the effects of land use changes on floods in the Meuse and Oder catchment. *Physics and Chemistry of the Earth, Part B*, 26(7), 593–599.

Diaz-Nieto, J. and Wilby, R.L. (2005). A comparison of statistical downscaling and climate change factor methods: Impacts on low flows in the River Thames, United Kingdom. *Climatic Change*, 69, 245–268. DOI: 10.1007/s10584-005-1157-6.

Githui, F., Gitau, W., Mutua, F. and Bauwens, W. (2009). Climate change impact on SWAT simulated streamflow in western Kenya. *International Journal of Climatology*, 29, 1823–1834. DOI: 10.1002/joc.1828.

Green, W.H. and Ampt, G.A. (1911). Studies on soil physics 1: The flow of air and water through soils. *Journal of Agricultural Sciences*, 4, 11.

Ha, P.T. (2011). Srepok river basin council and IWRM in the Srepok basin. In *The International Conference on Watershed Management*, 10–11 March 2011, Chiang Mai, Thailand.

Hargreaves, G.L., Hargreaves, G.H. and Riley, J.P. (1985). Agricultural benefits for Senegal River Basin. *Journal of Irrigation and Drainage Engineering – ASCE*, 111, 113–124.

Hung, T.H., Giang, L.H. and Binh, N.D. (2010). Application of SWAT model to evaluate landuse change impact in Upper Ma River basin, Vietnam. In *The 2011 SEA-SWAT Conference*, Ho Chi Minh City, Vietnam, 6–7 January 2011.

IPCC (2007). The Physical Science Basin: Contribution of Working Group I to the Fourth Assessment Report of the Intergovernmental Panel on Climate Change. Cambridge University Press, Cambridge, UK and New York.

Kawasaki, A., Takamatsu, M., He, J., Rogers, P. and Herath, S. (2010). An integrated approach to evaluate potential impact of precipitation and land use change on streamflow in Srepok River Basin. *Theory and Application GIS*, 18(2), 9–20.

Khoi, D.N. and Tadashi, S. (2012). The responses of hydrological processes and sediment yield to land use and climate change in the Be River Catchment, Vietnam. *Hydrological Processes* 28(3), 640–652. DOI: 10.1002/hyp.9620.

Khoi, D.N. (2013). Impacts of climate change on hydrology in the Srepok watershed, Vietnam. *Climate and Land Surface Changes in Hydrology*, 111–117.

Kim, U. and Kaluarachchi, J.J. (2009). Climate change impacts on water resources in the upper Blue Nile river basin, Ethiopia. *Journal of the American Water Resources Association*, 45(6), 1361–1378. DOI: 10.1111/j.1752-1688.2009.00369.x.

Li, H., Zhang, Y., Vaze, J. and Wang, B. (2012). Separating effects of vegetation change and climate variability using hydrological modeling and sensitivity-based approaches. *Journal of Hydrology* 420–421, 403–418. DOI:10.1016/j.jhydrol.2011.12.033.

Li, Y., Chen, B.M., Wang, Z.G. and Peng, SL. (2011). Effects of temperature change on water discharge, and sediment and nutrient loading in the lower Pearl River basin based on SWAT modeling. *Hydrological Sciences Journal*, 56(1), 68–83. DOI: 10.1080/026266 67.2010.538396.

Li, Z., Liu, W.Z., Zhang, X.C. and Zheng, F.L. (2009). Impacts of land use change and climate variability on hydrology in an agricultural catchment on the Loess Plateau of China. *Journal of Hydrology*, 377, 35–42. DOI:10.1016/j.jhydrol.2009.08.007.

Lung, N.N. (1995). Research on scientific foundation of technical economic solutions for planning and designing watershed, upstream protective forests, and coastal mitigating storm forest. Report, National Project No. K03-09, Hanoi. (In Vietnamese).

Luzio, M.D., Srinivasan, R. and Arnold, J.G. (2002). Integration of watershed tools and the SWAT model into BASINS. *Journal of the American Water Resources Association*, 38(4), 1127–1141.

Ma, X., Xu, J., Luo, Y., Aggarwal, S.P. and Li, J. (2009). Response of hydrological processes to land-cover and climate changes in Kejie watershed, southwest China. *Hydrological Processes*, 23, 1179–1191. DOI:10.1002/hyp.7233.

Mango, L.M., Melesse, A.M., McClain, M.E., Gann, D. and Setegn, S.G. (2011). Landuse and climate change impacts on the hydrology of the upper Mara River Basin, Kenya: Results of a modeling study to support better resource management. *Hydrology and Earth System Sciences*, 15, 2245–2258. DOI: 10.5194/hess-15-2245-2011.

Mekong River Commission (2005). The MRC Basin Development Plan, Sub-area Report, Se San/Sre Pok/Se Kong Sub-area (SA 7V). BDP Library Volume 3-7V.

MONRE (Ministry of Natural Resources and Environment) (2009). Climate Change, Sea Level Rise Scenarios for Vietnam. Vietnam Ministry of Natural Resources and Environment, Hanoi.

MONRE (Ministry of Natural Resources and Environment) (2010). Vietnam Second National Communication: Under the United Nations Framework Convention on Climate Change. Vietnam Ministry of Natural Resources and Environment, Hanoi.

Monteith, J.L. (1965). Evaporation and the environment. In The State and Movement of Water in Living Organisms. *19th Symposia of the Society for Experimental Biology*, Cambridge University Press, London, United Kingdom.

Mueller, E.N., Francke, T., Batalla, R.J. and Bronstert, A. (2009). Modeling the effects of land use change on runoff and sediment yield for a mesoscale catchment in the Southern Pyrenees. *Catena*, 79, 288–296. DOI: 10.1016/j.catena.2009.06.007.

Neitsch, S.L., Arnold, J.G., Kiniry, J.R. and Williams, J.R. (2005). *Soil and Water Assessment Tool, Theoretical Documentation: Version 2005*. Agricultural Research Service and Texas A&M Blackland Research Center, Temple, USA.

Nie, W., Yuan, Y., Kepner, W., Nash, M.S., Jackson, M. and Erickson, C. (2011). Assessing impacts of land use and land-cover changes on hydrology for the upper San Pedro watershed. *Journal of Hydrology*, 407, 105–114. DOI: 10.1016/j.jhydrol.2011.07.012.

Priestley, C.H.B. and Taylor, R.J. (1972). On the assessment of surface heat flux and evaporation using large-scale parameters. *Monthly Weather Review*, 100, 81–92.

Prowse, T.D., Beltaos, S., Gardner, J.T., Gibson, J.J., Granger, R.J., Leconte, R., Peters, D.L., Pietroniro, A., Romolo, L.A. and Toth, B. (2006). Climate change, flow regulation and land use effects on the hydrology of the Peace-Athabasca-Slave system; findings from the northern rivers ecosystem initiative. *Environmental Monitoring and Assessment*, 113, 167–197.

The Government of Vietnam (2006). A Strategic Framework for Water Resource Management in the Sre Pok River Basin. [Online] Available at: http://mouthtosource.org/rivers/srepok/files/2010/09/Strategic-Framework-for-WRM-in-Sre-Pok.pdf. [Accessed 24 July 2013].

Tollan, A. (2002). Land use change and floods: What do we need most research or management? *Water Science and Technology*, 45, 183–190.

Tu, T. (2009). Combined impact of climate and land use changes on streamflow and water quality in eastern Massachusetts, USA. *Journal of Hydrology*, 379, 268–283. DOI: 10.1016/j.jhydrol. 2009.10.009.

Ty, T.V., Sunada, K., Ichikawa, Y. and Oishi, S. (2012). Scenario-based impact assessment of land use/cover and climate changes on water resources and demand: A case study in the Srepok River Basin, Vietnam – Cambodia. *Water Resources Management*, 26(5), 1387–1407.

USDA-SCS (1972). National Engineering Handbook, Section IV, Hydrology, USDA, USA.

Wang, G.X., Zhang, Y., Liu, G.M. and Chen, L. (2006). Impact of land use change on hydrological processes in the Maying River basin, China. *Science in China Series D: Earth Sciences*, 49(10), 1098–1110.

Wang, S., Kang, S., Zhang, L. and Li, F. (2008). Modeling hydrological response to different land use and climate change scenarios in the Zamu River Basin of northwest China. *Hydrological Processes*, 22, 2502–2510. DOI: 10.1002/hyp.6846.

Wang, W., Shao, Q., Yang, T., Peng, S., Xing, W., Sun, F. and Luo, Y. (2013). Quantitative assessment of the impact of climate variability and human activities on runoff changes: A case study in four catchments of Haihe River basin, China. *Hydrological Processes*, 27(8), 1158–1174. DOI: 10.1002/hyp.9299.

Williams, J.R. (1975). Sediment-yield prediction with universal equation using runoff energy factor, present and prospective technology for predicting sediment yield and sources. *Proceedings of the Sediment Yield Workshop*, USDA Sedimentation Lab., Oxford, Mississippi, 28–30 November 1972, *ARS-S-40*, 244–252.

Conclusion and Future Prospects

HAMLET: Do you see yonder cloud that's almost in shape of a camel?

LORD POLONIUS: By the mass, and 'tis like a camel, indeed.

HAMLET: Methinks it is like a weasel.

LORD POLONIUS: It is backed like a weasel.

HAMLET: Or like a whale?

LORD POLONIUS: Very like a whale.

(Shakespeare, Hamlet, III, 2)

The European Erasmus + capacity building program that financed TORUS made it possible to communicate for four years the sciences of information with some disciplines of the environmental sciences[1] confronted with the need to integrate the technologies of cloud computing to face the avalanche of data that overwhelms them – Big Data. This book is a summary of the main contributions made over the course of the seven workshops held in Toulouse (France), Hanoi (Vietnam), Ferrara (Italy), Pathum Thani (Thailand), Brussels (Belgium), Ho Chi Minh City (Vietnam), Nakhon Si Thamarrat (Thailand) and Pau (France). Two powerful computer equipments have also been installed at the Asian Institute of Technology (Pathum Thani) and the University of Engineering and Technology at Vietnam National

---

Chapter written by Dominique LAFFLY and Yannick LE NIR.
1 Recall that by environmental disciplines, we mean those that are not related to meteorology or petroleum geology with sufficient means to autonomously use HPC and cloud computing.

University in Hanoi. Finally, a common platform (PaaS) – HUPI – equips servers for the development of dedicated services (SaaS) while it is still possible to work at the level of infrastructure if necessary (IaaS). In fact, the common achievements are there, especially the research initiated during the four years of TORUS by more than five theses that were all funded by scholarships.

Aware of the challenge, Europe has supported TORUS by allowing us these four years of joint learning between disciplines. This book will be the common base of the teaching which will take body within the Master of the New Technologies Using Service (MONTUS), a new program Erasmus + capacity building (2019–2022) that comes following TORUS. We now intend to demonstrate that, having learned enough from each other, we can transmit this knowledge to younger generations of researchers and engineers in Asia while using the equipment in place. While three years ago in Hanoi, Quong Hung Bui and Dominique Laffly drew up on a whiteboard their crossed views on geographical information for a computer scientist and a geographer respectively (Figure C.1), today it is a common basis for the teaching of SDI (see Chapter 6 of this book) in the future master, MONTUS.

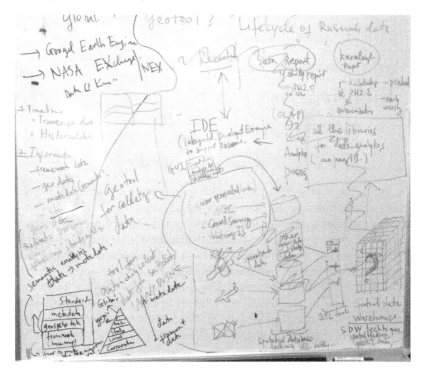

Figure C.1. *The whiteboard at the time of cloud computing. D. Laffly and Q.H. Bui believe that a geographer and a computer scientist can develop common approaches beyond technology for effective application in contemporary society (source: D. Laffly)*

This is because we have kept our word that Europe is supporting us once again. In this sense, one of the main objectives of TORUS is honored.

Despite this, we are perfectly aware that we are far, far from even having filled the deep void that separated the information sciences from those of the environmental disciplines that we mentioned at the origin of TORUS. Moreover, it is not because we have not tried in the last four years, but because the information sciences have continued their meteoric evolution: the platforms combining cloud computing and geographic information are now ubiquitous; in 2015, it was first Google Earth Engine and NASA Earth Exchange; the libraries available on Apache SPARK (https://spark.apache.org) are increasingly numerous for the greater good of the applications, and at the same time there is a greater difficulty to keep up to date with – in 2015, the binary images had to be converted into an ASCII array (which actually prohibited their use), but today they are directly integrated into the processing chain (see geotreillis.raster – https://geotrellis.readthedocs.io /en/latest/guide/core-concepts.html#raster-data); the parallelism proposed by Apache SPARK is ideal for the matrix calculus but is not adapted to the propagation of the information during the learning phase of the deep neural networks which give the best results in artificial intelligence at the moment. To do this, it is necessary to use the capabilities of graphics or GPU (Graphics Processing Unit) or TPU (Tensor Processing Unit – only in public cloud, Google technology) to fully exploit the unstructured data such as images and/or texts available at the time of Big Data. Finally, capacity building between the information sciences and geosciences remains a priority both by expanding to more thematic disciplines – urban planning, health and heritage... – and toward new partners in South East Asia (in this respect, MONTUS in addition to TORUS partners integrates Cambodia and disciplines of architecture/urbanism, archeology and cultural heritage).

Big Data, artificial intelligence, cloud computing and geoscience have to work together in transdisciplinary programs – it cannot be otherwise – such as those discussed here with TORUS and MONTUS. We hope that this will be a crucible of common intelligence, to offer our planet and the contemporary world effective responses to the great challenge that humanity urgently has to face: that of saving life on Earth.

List of Authors

Okke BATELAAN
Flinders University
Adelaïde
Australia

Quang Hung BUI
University of Engineering and
Technology
Vietnam National University
Hanoi
Vietnam

Sukhuma CHITAPORPAN
Walailak University
Nakhon Si Thammarat Province
Vietnam

Sathita FAKPRAPAI
Asian Institute of Technology
Pathum Thani
Thailand

Ngoc Thu Huong HUYNH
Nong Lam University
Ho Chi Minh City
Vietnam

Tan Loi HUYNH
Nong Lam University
Ho Chi Minh City
Vietnam

Thongchai KANABKAEW
Walailak University
Nakhon Si Thammarat Province
Vietnam

Dominique LAFFLY
University of Toulouse 2 – Jean Jaurès
France

Nguyen Huy LAI
Asian Institute of Technology
Pathum Thani
Thailand

Hoang Tu LE
Nong Lam University
Ho Chi Minh City
Vietnam

Quoc Tuan LE
Nong Lam University
Ho Chi Minh City
Vietnam

Truong Ngoc Han LE
Nong Lam University
Ho Chi Minh City
Vietnam

Van Phan LE
Nong Lam University
Ho Chi Minh City
Vietnam

Yannick LE NIR
EISTI (International School of
Information Processing Science)
Pau
France

Viet Hung LUU
University of Engineering and
Technology
Vietnam National University
Hanoi
Vietnam

Thi Kieu Diem NGO
Nong Lam University
Ho Chi Minh City
Vietnam

Duy Liem NGUYEN
Nong Lam University
Ho Chi Minh City
Vietnam

Duy Nang NGUYEN
Nong Lam University
Ho Chi Minh City
Vietnam

Huy Anh NGUYEN
Nong Lam University
Ho Chi Minh City
Vietnam

Kim Loi NGUYEN
Nong Lam University
Ho Chi Minh City
Vietnam

Le Tan Dat NGUYEN
Nong Lam University
Ho Chi Minh City
Vietnam

Minh Ky NGUYEN
Nong Lam University
Ho Chi Minh City
Vietnam

Nhat Ha Chi NGUYEN
Asian Institute of Technology
Pathum Thani
Thailand

Thi Hong NGUYEN
Nong Lam University
Ho Chi Minh City
Vietnam

Thi Kim Oanh NGUYEN
Asian Institute of Technology
Pathum Thani
Thailand

Thi Nhat Thanh NGUYEN
University of Engineering and
Technology
Vietnam National University
Hanoi
Vietnam

Thi Thanh Thuy NGUYEN
Nong Lam University
Ho Chi Minh City
Vietnam

Tri Quang Hung NGUYEN
Nong Lam University
Ho Chi Minh City
Vietnam

Trinh Minh Anh NGUYEN
Nong Lam University
Ho Chi Minh City
Vietnam

Didin Agustian PERMADI
Asian Institute of Technology
Pathum Thani
Thailand

Gia Diep PHAM
Nong Lam University
Ho Chi Minh City
Vietnam

Van Ha PHAM
University of Engineering and
Technlogy
Vietnam National University
Hanoi
Vietnam

Dang Nguyen Dong PHUONG
Nong Lam University
Ho Chi Minh City
Vietnam

Jantira RATTANARAT
Walailak University
Nakhon Si Thammarat Province
Thailand

Margaret SHANAFIELD
Flinders University
Adelaïde
Australia

Surasak SICHUM
Walailak University
Nakhon Si Thammarat Province
Thailand

Kok SOTHEA
Asian Institute of Technology
Pathum Thani
Thailand

Thong Nhat TRAN
University of Natural Resources
and Environment
Ho Chi Minh City
Vietnam

Ngoc Quynh Tram VO
Nong Lam University
Ho Chi Minh City
Vietnam

Imeshi WEERASINGHE
Vrjie University of Brussels
Belgium

Index

Summary of Volume 1

Chapter 9. Sensitivity Analysis

Astrid JOURDAN and Peio LOUBIÈRE

Chapter 10. Using R for Multivariate Analysis

Astrid JOURDAN

Chapter 14. Web-Oriented Architecture – How to design a RESTFull API

Florent DEVIN

Chapter 15. SCALA – Functional Programming

Florent DEVIN

Chapter 16. Spark and Machine Learning Library

Yannick LE NIR

Chapter 17. Database for Cloud Computing

Peio LOUBIÈRE

**Chapter 18. WRF Performance Analysis and Scalability
on Multicore High Performance Computing Systems**

Didin Agustian PERMADI, Sebastiano Fabio SCHIFANO, Thi Kim Oanh NGUYEN,
Nhat Ha Chi NGUYEN, Eleonora LUPPI and Luca TOMASSETTI

Summary of Volume 2

Chapter 3. Image Quality

Dominique LAFFLY

Chapter 4. Remote Sensing Products

Van Ha PHAM, Viet Hung LUU, Anh PHAN, Dominique LAFFLY,
Quang Hung BUI and Thi Nhat Thanh NGUYEN

Chapter 5. Image Processing in Spark

Yannick LE NIR, Florent DEVIN, Thomas BALDAQUIN, Pierre MESLER LAZENNEC, Ji Young JUNG, Se-Eun KIM, Hyeyoung KWOON, Lennart NILSEN, Yoo Kyung LEE and Dominique LAFFLY

Chapter 6. Satellite Image Processing using Spark on the HUPI Platform

Vincent MORENO and Minh Tu NGUYEN

Chapter 9. Spatial Data Infrastructure

Quang Hung BUI, Quang Thang LUU, Duc Van HA, Tuan Dung PHAM,
Sanya PRASEUTH and Dominique LAFFLY

Other titles from

in

Computer Engineering

2020

OULHADJ Hamouche, DAACHI Boubaker, MENASRI Riad
Metaheuristics for Robotics
(Optimization Heuristics Set – Volume 2)

SADIQUI Ali
Computer Network Security

2019

BESBES Walid, DHOUIB Diala, WASSAN Niaz, MARREKCHI Emna
Solving Transport Problems: Towards Green Logistics

CLERC Maurice
Iterative Optimizers: Difficulty Measures and Benchmarks

GHLALA Riadh
Analytic SQL in SQL Server 2014/2016

TOUNSI Wiem
Cyber-Vigilance and Digital Trust: Cyber Security in the Era of Cloud Computing and IoT

2018

ANDRO Mathieu
Digital Libraries and Crowdsourcing
(Digital Tools and Uses Set – Volume 5)

ARNALDI Bruno, GUITTON Pascal, MOREAU Guillaume
Virtual Reality and Augmented Reality: Myths and Realities

BERTHIER Thierry, TEBOUL Bruno
From Digital Traces to Algorithmic Projections

CARDON Alain
Beyond Artificial Intelligence: From Human Consciousness to Artificial Consciousness

HOMAYOUNI S. Mahdi, FONTES Dalila B.M.M.
Metaheuristics for Maritime Operations
(Optimization Heuristics Set – Volume 1)

JEANSOULIN Robert
JavaScript and Open Data

PIVERT Olivier
NoSQL Data Models: Trends and Challenges
(Databases and Big Data Set – Volume 1)

SEDKAOUI Soraya
Data Analytics and Big Data

SALEH Imad, AMMI Mehdi, SZONIECKY Samuel
Challenges of the Internet of Things: Technology, Use, Ethics
(Digital Tools and Uses Set – Volume 7)

SZONIECKY Samuel
Ecosystems Knowledge: Modeling and Analysis Method for Information and Communication
(Digital Tools and Uses Set – Volume 6)

2017

BENMAMMAR Badr
Concurrent, Real-Time and Distributed Programming in Java

HÉLIODORE Frédéric, NAKIB Amir, ISMAIL Boussaad, OUCHRAA Salma,
SCHMITT Laurent
Metaheuristics for Intelligent Electrical Networks
(Metaheuristics Set – Volume 10)

MA Haiping, SIMON Dan
Evolutionary Computation with Biogeography-based Optimization
(Metaheuristics Set – Volume 8)

PÉTROWSKI Alain, BEN-HAMIDA Sana
Evolutionary Algorithms
(Metaheuristics Set – Volume 9)

PAI G A Vijayalakshmi
Metaheuristics for Portfolio Optimization
(Metaheuristics Set – Volume 11)

2016

BLUM Christian, FESTA Paola
Metaheuristics for String Problems in Bio-informatics
(Metaheuristics Set – Volume 6)

DEROUSSI Laurent
Metaheuristics for Logistics
(Metaheuristics Set – Volume 4)

DHAENENS Clarisse and JOURDAN Laetitia
Metaheuristics for Big Data
(Metaheuristics Set – Volume 5)

LABADIE Nacima, PRINS Christian, PRODHON Caroline
Metaheuristics for Vehicle Routing Problems
(Metaheuristics Set – Volume 3)

LEROY Laure
Eyestrain Reduction in Stereoscopy

LUTTON Evelyne, PERROT Nathalie, TONDA Albert
*Evolutionary Algorithms for Food Science and Technology
(Metaheuristics Set – Volume 7)*

MAGOULÈS Frédéric, ZHAO Hai-Xiang
Data Mining and Machine Learning in Building Energy Analysis

RIGO Michel
Advanced Graph Theory and Combinatorics

2015

BARBIER Franck, RECOUSSINE Jean-Luc
*COBOL Software Modernization: From Principles to Implementation with
the BLU AGE® Method*

CHEN Ken
*Performance Evaluation by Simulation and Analysis with Applications to
Computer Networks*

CLERC Maurice
*Guided Randomness in Optimization
(Metaheuristics Set – Volume 1)*

DURAND Nicolas, GIANAZZA David, GOTTELAND Jean-Baptiste,
ALLIOT Jean-Marc
*Metaheuristics for Air Traffic Management
(Metaheuristics Set – Volume 2)*

MAGOULÈS Frédéric, ROUX François-Xavier, HOUZEAUX Guillaume
Parallel Scientific Computing

MUNEESAWANG Paisarn, YAMMEN Suchart
Visual Inspection Technology in the Hard Disk Drive Industry

2014

BOULANGER Jean-Louis
Formal Methods Applied to Industrial Complex Systems

BOULANGER Jean-Louis
Formal Methods Applied to Complex Systems:Implementation of the B Method

GARDI Frédéric, BENOIST Thierry, DARLAY Julien, ESTELLON Bertrand, MEGEL Romain
Mathematical Programming Solver based on Local Search

KRICHEN Saoussen, CHAOUACHI Jouhaina
Graph-related Optimization and Decision Support Systems

LARRIEU Nicolas, VARET Antoine
Rapid Prototyping of Software for Avionics Systems: Model-oriented Approaches for Complex Systems Certification

OUSSALAH Mourad Chabane
Software Architecture 1
Software Architecture 2

PASCHOS Vangelis Th
Combinatorial Optimization – 3-volume series, 2nd Edition
Concepts of Combinatorial Optimization – Volume 1, 2nd Edition
Problems and New Approaches – Volume 2, 2nd Edition
Applications of Combinatorial Optimization – Volume 3, 2nd Edition

QUESNEL Flavien
Scheduling of Large-scale Virtualized Infrastructures: Toward Cooperative Management

RIGO Michel
Formal Languages, Automata and Numeration Systems 1: Introduction to Combinatorics on Words
Formal Languages, Automata and Numeration Systems 2: Applications to Recognizability and Decidability

BOULANGER Jean-Louis
Industrial Use of Formal Methods: Formal Verification

BOULANGER Jean-Louis
Formal Method: Industrial Use from Model to the Code

CALVARY Gaëlle, DELOT Thierry, SÈDES Florence, TIGLI Jean-Yves
Computer Science and Ambient Intelligence

MAHOUT Vincent
Assembly Language Programming: ARM Cortex-M3 2.0: Organization, Innovation and Territory

MARLET Renaud
Program Specialization

SOTO Maria, SEVAUX Marc, ROSSI André, LAURENT Johann
Memory Allocation Problems in Embedded Systems: Optimization Methods

2011

BICHOT Charles-Edmond, SIARRY Patrick
Graph Partitioning

BOULANGER Jean-Louis
Static Analysis of Software: The Abstract Interpretation

CAFERRA Ricardo
Logic for Computer Science and Artificial Intelligence

HOMES Bernard
Fundamentals of Software Testing

KORDON Fabrice, HADDAD Serge, PAUTET Laurent, PETRUCCI Laure
Distributed Systems: Design and Algorithms

KORDON Fabrice, HADDAD Serge, PAUTET Laurent, PETRUCCI Laure
Models and Analysis in Distributed Systems

LORCA Xavier
Tree-based Graph Partitioning Constraint

TRUCHET Charlotte, ASSAYAG Gerard
Constraint Programming in Music

VICAT-BLANC PRIMET Pascale *et al.*
Computing Networks: From Cluster to Cloud Computing

2010

AUDIBERT Pierre
Mathematics for Informatics and Computer Science

BABAU Jean-Philippe *et al.*
Model Driven Engineering for Distributed Real-Time Embedded Systems

BOULANGER Jean-Louis
Safety of Computer Architectures

MONMARCHÉ Nicolas *et al.*
Artificial Ants

PANETTO Hervé, BOUDJLIDA Nacer
Interoperability for Enterprise Software and Applications 2010

SIGAUD Olivier *et al.*
Markov Decision Processes in Artificial Intelligence

SOLNON Christine
Ant Colony Optimization and Constraint Programming

AUBRUN Christophe, SIMON Daniel, SONG Ye-Qiong *et al.*
Co-design Approaches for Dependable Networked Control Systems

2009

FOURNIER Jean-Claude
Graph Theory and Applications

GUÉDON Jeanpierre
The Mojette Transform / Theory and Applications

JARD Claude, ROUX Olivier
Communicating Embedded Systems / Software and Design

2005

GÉRARD Sébastien *et al.*
Model Driven Engineering for Distributed Real Time Embedded Systems

PANETTO Hervé
Interoperability of Enterprise Software and Applications 2005

Printed and bound by CPI Group (UK) Ltd, Croydon, CR0 4YY